SUSAN SONTAG

S U S A N

THE
ELEGAIC
MODERNIST

S O H N Y A

ROUTLEDGE · New York and London

Published in 1990 by

Routledge
An imprint of Routledge, Chapman and Hall, Inc.
29 West 35th Street
New York, NY 10001

Published in Great Britain by

Routledge
11 New Fetter Lane
London EC4P 4EE

Library of Congress Cataloging in Publication Data

Sayres, Sohnya.
    Susan Sontag : the elegiac modernist / Sohnya Sayres.
      p.   cm.
    Includes index.
    ISBN 0-415-90030-1.—ISBN 0-415-90031-X (pbk.)
    1. Sontag, Susan, 1933–   —Criticism and interpretation.
    I. Title.
    PS3569.06547Z87   1989
    818'.5409—dc20   89-10087

British Library Cataloguing in Publication Data
Sayres, Sohnya, 1947–
    Susan Sontag: the elegiac modernist.
    1. English literature. criticism—critical studies
    I. Title
    820.9

    ISBN 0-415-90030-1
        0-415-90031-X (pb)

Contents

Contents

Introduction

By way of introduction, let me weave together Sontag's fiction and essays with an eye to the evidence Sontag provided in titling her book in 1969 "Styles of Radical Will." True, that title offers an oxymoron special to those times, true also that Sontag has been tagged to the 1960s in ways that misconstrue her work. A classicizing instinct directs her, a high modernism her first love. The life of the mind and the creation of art were always for her a matter of serious, willed heroics. That 1969 title is intriguing because it draws style from the deepest resources of being, the will. At the same time it elevates style to a practice, as if one could will a new understanding and act on it by means of having a style—style alone. The old modernist dream that art could oppose the determining power of history is updated by this true aesthete into a new axiom: the battle against the forces of anonymity would have to be won by style born from the radical will. Having several styles preserved the resilience of the self against mistaken judgment.

As I write now, the words "will" and "history" in their connection to one another have lightened so much they have to be held down. Almost twenty years have past since they were woven together by hope, activism, and outrage from some ideological loose ends. In the present mood, seemingly, we wait in glass slippers for the pumpkin, our millennium, to take its final shape. No slouching beast rises from within us, no David stands to slay him. Our architecture reaches into its bag of symbols for quotes, our writers skid around on the slickest surface literature has ever confronted, here in the instant world. The legitimation crisis that should have happened, has not yet, at least not for most. So many contemporary essayists have never been more comfortable in the West, Sontag among them. She has shifted the basis of her outrage to totalitarian states that punish their artistic-intellectual classes, and they are all elsewhere. In this, by the way, she is not back in anyone's fold. Neoconservatives have been vicious; the left wounded and quick to call her simpleminded.

It is too early to complete the curve of American left liberalism or to be certain whether Sontag, in the longish view, has not anticipated its trajectory. Some parts of this book do include thoughts on its history,

1

in the terms of how politics flushed out issues for the literary intellectuals to select among, and more importantly, how the shape of Sontag's
ideas predisposed her to a certain view. She is a controversial figure for
her politics, one could almost say because she has been political. Her
reputation in academic circles has been comparably quiet. Scholars so
far have withheld their interest. She rarely writes for them, nor has the
force of her ideas carried her to a larger synthesis of the kind they wait
upon. Rather she writes out of the tradition of the independent woman
of letters to a larger public, moralizing, admonishing, directing attention to what she wishes. Her art—her novels, short stories, and films—
have yet to find a welcoming reception, academic or otherwise. For
most critics they seem too Europeanizing, too cold, too laden with ideas
and given over to sadness. Even those literary, affectionate portraits of
Sontag, by Elizabeth Hardwick or Leon S. Roudiez, for example, lightened her, to borrow a phrase, unbearably.

At the approach of this millennium, Sontag still thinks that the
present ought to hold our attention as if it were the last stage of history.

> We may not be living in the final stage of enlightenment. However,
> from the point of view of the writer—and, for that matter, from the
> human point of view—its is always better to believe that we are living
> in the last stage of human history, if only because that attitude makes
> you scrutinize what's going on much harder, pay greater attention to
> every detail. Maybe the curtain won't fall tomorrow, but it's better
> to think that it may. Then we will take care of what's going on in
> front of us.[1]

These remarks were made at a conference in Toronto called "The
Writer and Human Rights," October, 1981, and rightfully they should
be compared to an answer she made in an interview with Roger Copeland in February of that year. To his question "Do you see any way off
the avant-garde escalator?" Sontag replied:

> Today, we are living out of the paradoxes of eschatological thinking.
> Actually, the various avant-garde "isms" were not supposed to replace
> one another. Each conceived of itself as the terminal "ism." But we
> have discovered that there is no terminal "ism"; the messiah doesn't
> come. History doesn't end although particular histories end.[2]

Both comments reveal her often shown need to balance and correct,
to search out the paradoxes of modernist ideas. They are consistent in
this: what can be found here is an attachment to the present as the
hard way. "The greatest achievements of 20th century art have been
hard, demanding a certain kind of commitment, piety, and investment

of attention," she told Copeland, when he asked whether people are not too eager to see the avant-garde phase of modernism dead and done with. "Absolutely," she replied. "And now one is obliged to start defending again the things that one had begun to take for granted" (Copeland 85).

She has never been far from expressing that obligation. What must be remembered most is that modernism—that difficult heritage of being too much in the avant-garde—emerges from the background of Sontag's concerns to latch onto whatever other sensibility she examines or whomever she addresses. Even when she tackles a subject that lives in the antipodes to the modernists' ideas, such as the Camp sensibility, she incises it out of a matrix of ideas that are modernist. Not everyone's modernism, of course. Specifically, her focus is on a late European aesthetic modernism, from the inter-war period to the 1950s, hyper-aware of its own history, and like many aesthetics late in their development, twisted into extremity.

She does not use the term 'late modernist,' I should add. She writes as if there were one ethos; she senses an overripeness, they are still fulminating ideas. She is not particularly attracted to decay; hers is not fundamentally a *ruiniste* sensibility. Or rather she holds off that melancholic, elegiac side of herself by probing the limits of the modernists' predicament. "Being" in their world queries its very source. "The artist is a consciousness trying to be," Sontag explains of her modernists. " 'I am who, in order to be, must whip his innateness'," she quotes Artaud as saying.

Pondering its darkness, elevating it to the most serious incorporation of the effects of 20th century history, she is drawn to this modernism by affinity, and interestingly, wariness. In her hands, it is no mere style, or manner, or period. It has the dimensions of an ethos, the bearing of an ideal carried on to a particular "enervation" and "morbidity." The fate of an ethos for her depends on the contradictions of living out its values, on the tests of its limits and its moral floundering. In that sense, it is eternal—the mark that best identifies the age. Decidedly, though, her modernism is fused from two cultures. The predominant one derives from the postwar years in France, the novels of Robbe-Grillet, Sarraute, Bataille, Leiris; the plays and films of Artaud, Ionesco, Genet, Bresson, Resnais, Godard; the philosophy and criticism of Sartre, Camus, Lukács, Lévi-Strauss, Barthes, Cioran, and Canetti.

The second culture too, interestingly, is not native to her. She tells us that as a young teenager in a California bookstore she discovered an article by Trilling and dreamt of coming to New York to write for the *Partisan Review*. Twelve years or so later she accomplishes that dream. What beckons her has been called America's first intelligentsia, the

quarrelsome, vigorous, politically committed, mostly Jewish writers of
New York—all those writers so much subject at the moment to book
length studies and to the crossed views of their own memoirs. They
have come around to taking an accounting of themselves, their enmity
not eclipsed by the respect that has fallen over them.

Since Sontag is often grouped with them (not usefully in my opinion),
the climate they created and into which she entered deserves outlining.
Despite all that vigorous finger pointing, to which they were prone
from the beginning, they were always loosely associated, those writers
of *Partisan Review, Commentary, Politics,* and *Dissent,* and they stay
ever more distanced from each other now. Many have veered hard to
the right, and the others who have held on to left-liberal or even
anarcho-liberal sympathies find themselves trying to make sense of
how the critique of American society slipped away from them, as a
group, just as America was attaining world ambitions. They had to
reorient themselves for the united war effort against fascism, certainly.
But then most were already staunch anti-Stalinists. More comfortable
in the postwar prosperity, the New York intelligentsia, writes Alan W.
Wald,

> came to embrace the very supraclass theories they had once rejected.
> They did so by reorganizing their thought around a cluster of key
> terms that began to appear increasingly in their writing: "modula-
> tion," "variousness," "skeptical realism," "moral realism," "imagi-
> nation of disaster," "the end of ideology," and in the arena of political
> polemic, "liberal anticommunism," and "anti-anticommunism."[3]

"Even their cultural interests became more American-centered,"
continues Wald,

> as Rahv, Trilling, and Dupee devoted themselves to promoting Henry
> James as a home-grown modernist, while Clement Greenberg and
> Harold Rosenberg secured their positions as the foremost defenders
> of the New York school of abstract expressionism. . . . In some in-
> stances the political pressures of the time brought peculiar results, as
> in the case of Philip Rahv, who abandoned his efforts to advance a
> Marxist aesthetic for a dubious attachment to high modernism as the
> salvation of the radical intellectual. (218)

Take up that sense of high modernism as the salvation of the *radical*
intellectual, put it on as rusting armor: one can see Sontag, standing
there, preparing to do battle with her times. That stance was her inheritance. A company of artistic and mental giants had passed this way;
their great experiments were being enshrined; they had defeated the

Philistines. The modernists' attack on the presuppositions of form may have worsened their relationships to "meaning." It was an old meaning, anyway, with which the world was shamming. Thus, whatever the costs had been to themselves, or however they lost their audience, whatever imperious, crude, or even regressive political vision they held, the modernists bore within them the radicalizing will. This was the essence Sontag squeezed out of the critical debates that were concurrent with her growing up, what she would formulate into her critical demeanor. The essence blended well with her own spirit; the demeanor would prove restrictive. In the 1960s, she found it a near impossible guide to political clarity. Yet, if the matter at hand was aesthetic, she usually would sound strident notes for the seriousness of modernist experimentation. In her own fiction, she would follow her own demands for the emphasis on minimalist effect, brilliance of design, and the isolation of the characters deep in pursuit of their detachment. Western culture had become a burden in itself to itself, she would declare, many times, and she would stare hard at this thing that had to be, yet could not be, "disburdened."

How different, though, was her understanding from what now sometimes passes for understanding of the moderns. Now it is the modernists who sustained the center. It was America, after all, middle class America, claim the neoconservatives, that welcomed these war exiles of the European artistic and intelligentsia avant-garde. And it was America which in turn was replenished by the spirit of abstraction it infused. It is too early to say if Sontag will fall into step with this yet another campaign to clean up and command the past. I do not think she will. Trilling may have been Sontag's introduction to the American intellectual climate, but her essays do him several times over. She set out to draw the contours of a sensibility that could neither be contained nor propagated—a modernism so intensely adversarial it needed nothing but itself to feed upon, so deeply conservative it could not be used to foster anyone's positive thinking.

One might ask what loyalty Sontag has ever felt to the American political-cultural milieu of the old New York intelligentsia. Though she may yet be tempted, in her own autobiographical efforts, to recast her career as part of theirs, the answer now must be: tenuous at most. She missed what bound many of the older New York writers to this country, watching America fight fascism. She missed too the immigrant experience, the working class identities, the struggle with Party affiliation. She was from Arizona and California, the University of Chicago and Harvard, coming of age in a decade Norman Mailer has said nearly killed him. And though it was not long after she arrived in New York at twenty-six, in 1959, before she was a writer among them, as a contributing editor at *Commentary,* and though her essays won her the honor of being selected as one of their new stars, it was not their theorizing but the art scene that was exhilarating then. She soon would become friends with John Cage, Jasper Johns, Merce Cunningham, and Marcel Duchamp. She set about apprehending them, to make their work her own. The 1960s spilled over and she never had to choose sides in the endless break up of the New York intellectuals. What she missed in these older New York writers' political education, she gained (for a while) in not having to explain quietism and accommodation.

She also soon cut the cords to the theoretical defense of the naturalism and impressionism that plays about in American art. The wearied-over contentions for social realism were simply not to be her fight. The American novel particularly made Sontag harsh:

> To narrate is palpably to employ one's intelligence; the unity of narration characteristic of European and Latin American fiction is the unity of the narrator's intelligence. But the writing of fiction common in America today has little use for this patient, dogged, unshowy use of intelligence. . . . Thus American writing is grossly rhetorical . . . in contrast to the classical mode of European writing, which achieves its effects with . . . a style that holds back, that aims ultimately at neutral transparency. (AI 51)

But then, the whole novel making enterprise, she writes in "Nathalie Sarraute and the Novel," has "sunk to a level of an art form deeply, if not irrevocably, comprised by Philistinism;" because it is so dependent on the 19th-century's "wholly mundane conception of reality." Sontag is herself a writer of novels of decided surface transparency, works that set out to evoke new pleasures, such as "the pleasure of solving a problem." Simply, by 1965, after the publication of her own puzzle novel, *The Benefactor,* she could assert:

> the novel as a form has nothing to lose, and everything to gain by joining the revolution that has already swept over most of the other arts. It is time that the novel become what it is not, in England and America, with rare and unrelated exceptions: a form of art which people with serious and sophisticated taste in the other arts can take seriously. (AI 118)

Another observation needs to be made about the muted climate of ideas that Sontag finds in the United States, and towards which she holds some contempt. The undercurrent of American thought still runs deep with pragmatism. Americans are inherently resistant to the dialectics of abstraction against abstraction, willfully deaf to the thunder and clash of parties warring in theoretical disputes. The existentialism that had been introduced in the mid-1940s by the likes of *Partisan Review*, for instance, was already a standard in the universities when Sontag was a student. There it was noticeably depoliticized by being an exercise in reflection rather than an attempt to conquer the demoralization rising out of the horrors of war. Freudianism had gone through several stages of incorporation and revision when Sontag helped her then husband Philip Rieff with *Freud, The Mind of the Moralist* (1959).

A good part of this critique of Freud is dedicated to stemming the "popular drift" of the psychoanalytic community which tries "to free the individual most of all from the burden of opposition." The neo-Freudians, Rieff explains, never shared the respect for the repressive function of culture that Freud did in working out (not successfully) his dialectic of repressions. In the therapist's firm hands, the neurotic must be made to understand that a freedom exists for him or her: they will have to " 'confess to the instincts that are at work in them, face the conflict, fight for what they want, or go without it'." "A more forthright assertion of the nature of freedom has never been made," asserts Rieff. "Freud did not glove the fist that symbolizes freedom, nor mistake it, as liberals often do, for the helping hand."[4]

Rieff's book ends with the resignation that humans, on their quest for a healing doctrine, have found in Freud yet a new illness. It is better to read Freud not as a psychologist of adjustment, but as a magnifier of our condition. Our hope depends on the struggle for honesty.

I find a number of arguments in this book congruent with Sontag's thinking and which may represent her contribution. There is a surprising support for the consolation of religion. Sontag majored in comparative religion. She could not have allowed Freud to get away with mistaking the "latent content of Christianity with the manifest content of Christiandom." There is also in this book a knowingness and warning about the omnipotence that accompanies a thought persisted in too long, a trap in which Freud himself may have fallen. There is a reminder (against Freud's meliorists) that reasonableness is one of the most "tenacious forms of resistance." Most of all, there is that exasperation with, if not dread of, the psychological man's faint character: out of the "emergent democracy of the sick," where the "hospital is succeeding the church and parliament as the archetypal institution of Western culture":

> We recognize in the case history of psychological man the nervous habits of his father, economic man: he is antiheroic, shrewd, carefully counting his satisfactions and dissatisfactions, studying unprofitable

commitments as the sins to be avoided. From this immediate ances-
tor, psychological man has constituted his own careful economy of
the inner life. (Rieff 391)

Psychological man can only justify his "science of self-concern" nega-
tively, having lost faith in the world and in himself. This "lonely ego"
makes the author regret the passing of the "rectitude and energetic
naiveté of the ideal type during the Protestant phase" of American
culture. So much in Sontag betrays that longing for rectitude and the
simple truth; we hear it in her essay on Vietnam, or in her short story
about traveling to China; it wafts through her portraits of intellectuals,
and sounds the bass note to her thoughts on photography. It is the
moralist in her speaking for the "ideal of right" over its demotion into
the "ideal of insight." Most of the characters in her fiction voice the
quandary of the psychological man. She shows them little kindness.
They must persist in the task of self-examination until, like the protagonists of her two novels, they make up their worlds which are also
the hospitals in which they are confined. Their reasonableness almost
tricks us. Ultimately, they must be resigned to repeating themselves.
   Between the American and European cultural climates, the European
holds Sontag more strongly. In explaining this to us, (emphasizing
between the lines what the distinction means to her) she recalls a visit
at age fourteen to Thomas Mann, then living in exile in the Pacific
Palisades. In a memoir entitled "Pilgrimage," she writes that she was
already "steeped in admiration and impatience for the reality to which
I would travel once released from that long prison sentence, my childhood."[5] Two years younger than her classmates, a "resident alien" in
her family, she had assigned herself a task: to ward off drivel. She had
found rapture in the books she collected, she knew her "destiny": the
University of Chicago. "O golden age! It not only was, I knew it was."
She wrote stories, journals, read herself "sore-eyed" every night, and to
her surprise, attracted two great friends, Peter and Merrill, mad like
herself to talk about books, socialism and Henry Wallace, but mostly
music:

> Towards John Cage's squawks and thumps we were deferential—we
> knew that we were supposed to appreciate ugly music, and we listened
> devotedly to the Toch, the Krenek, the Hindemith, the Webern, the
> Schoenberg, whatever (we had enormous appetites and strong stom-
> achs). But it was Stravinsky's music we sincerely loved. And since
> Stravinsky seemed grotesquely old . . . our fears for his life had given
> rise to a compelling fantasy à deux about dying for our idol. ("Pilgrim-
> age" 41)

From there on in this narrative of calling and escape, a little comedy ensues, almost unacknowledged. Sontag keeps busy "accumulating gods" while high school California pulses around her, with its wrinkled condoms on the lawns, drugs in the corners, and English teachers who pass out *Reader's Digest* from which the students are to summarize one article. She and Merrill park above the city to quiz each other on Kochel's listings, as the lights twinkle below and couples mate in cars beside them. "Reading and listening to music," were, she says, "the triumphs of being not myself. That nearly everything I admired was produced by people who were dead (or very old) or from elsewhere, ideally Europe, seemed inevitable to me" ("Pilgrimage" 41). Some of these are very close by, in the chrome-and-rush-to-suburbia of the 1940s Southern California; they—she names Stravinsky, Schoenberg, Mann, Brecht, Huxley, Isherwood—make the place "electric with celebrity." "The gods of high culture had disembarked from Europe, to dwell, almost incognito" among the wildly incongruous. To this young girl, theirs is "a world beyond childhood, a world of seriousness."

The date written into her copy allows her to recall the night she began *The Magic Mountain*: "All of Europe fell into my head—though on condition that I start mourning for it" ("Pilgrimage" 42). In the disease it told of, "the very epitome of pathetic and spiritual interest," she could delve into the pain left by her father's death from tuberculosis. And she could explore her own asthma that brought her mother to Tucson, the city of tuberculosis, to raise Susan and her sister. In the character of the "mild, good-natured, chaste Hans Castorp, Mann's orphaned protagonist," Sontag thinks she found her own "unprotected heart."

> What if Hans Castorp was a Goody Two-Shoes (appalling accusation my mother had once let fly at me)? That was what made him not like but unlike others. I recognized his vocation for piety; his portable solitude, lived politely among others; his life of onerous routines (that guardians deem good for you) interspersed with free, passionate, conversations—a glorious transposition of my own current agenda. ("Pilgrimage" 42)

Sontag still protests that she didn't want to meet Mann; it was Merrill's idea. Shamed by the intensity of her admiration, anguishing over what Mann understood and didn't understand about American teenagers, she remembers every detail of her awkwardness, and Mann's thinness. The great man served them tea and in his distracted, stiff way, offered a lesson in the "sententious formulas" writers are apt to deliver. The deep memory of it still embarrasses her; nonetheless, "admiration sets her free." That "zealot of seriousness," "already full-blown in the child," slams the door shut on childhood and goes off to college at fifteen.

This "Pilgrimage" to gods and revelations, in flight from stifling provincialism on the quest for the beautiful, is probably ironic in its mythic dimensions, while not in its portrayal of the cavernous sadness of Europe. Europe lies before her as that place from which the deep, the brilliant, the most powerful creative forces have been bred and yet have taken leave too—a hollow, poisoned, yet hallowed ground. After Sontag's many years in Europe, she'll retain the suspicion that Europe's culture produced the best there is, and, paradoxically, that which seeks to empty itself. She finds how to mourn in what Mann himself called (in "The Making of *The Magic Mountain*," *The Atlantic Monthly*, January 1953) "the strange mixture of death and lightheadedness, the conflict between bourgeois decorum and macabre adventure" that constitutes this work. Mann's gentle parody may have escaped this rapture-filled teen, herself shy and impatient. The pathos that bathes the mountain in magic recondenses in several of her stories, most notably in her film *Brother Carl*. A macabre adventure takes her two bourgeois characters, each in their separate novels, past the limits of the decorum inherited from their class and privately attenuated by them. Through her experience with her own cancer, and in defense of her father's tuberculosis, she will answer this use of illness as metaphor.

This "Pilgrimage" may prove the beginning of an autobiography. It has the makings of it. She is poised at its end for a rapid rise and early recognition. She has been honest; she found the adult in the child, though not, significantly, despite her statement at the conclusion of this piece, the child in the adult. One suspects that Sontag will never choose to write about childhood, those stories of coming of age, the unpeeling of layers of attachments sealed by over-long and keen family relationships. Sontag's stories will be about power and will, intense reflections of conscience, and about mourning.

One of my arguments is that the impact of a mourning Europe and the modernism it exported becomes for Sontag a megatheme in her fiction, just as the tracking down of a characterization of this ethos is the underlying purpose of her essays. Like the fates of her characters, her arguments doubles back on itself at the end of her pieces. One character begs to be Sisyphus in order to carry on the burden of despair. More often than not, the narrative juggles the protagonist back into cycles of repetition. One story, "The Dummy," even makes a parable out of this fix. A man decides to make a mechanical replica of himself because he is tired of being a person. The dummy takes his place as husband and breadwinner, but soon falls scandalously in love with the secretary and demands to be replaced in turn by his own dummy. "The problems of this world are only truly solved in two ways;" the man decides, "by extinction or by duplication" (*I,E* 88). Extinction, he believes, is not a modern option.

As representatives of this modern dilemma, Sontag's characters welcome their trials of renunciation. They begin in dessicated conditions and end falsely, no more fulsome than they began. They nonetheless often assume the air of outright satisfaction. Their complaints have been extended until they describe the corpus of their worlds. They exist in pockets of being that reflect themselves. Sontag almost never drives them out of their unhappiness: she drives them through it, and punishes them, seemingly, for their hubris of consciousness.

In this hubris they do replicate one of the paradoxes of the modernist ethic: its great freedom to negate the aesthetics of the past (the various ways art may reflect reality) turns into a confinement. The rule against reference in art swells the eye. Perception aestheticizes all that it recognizes. The artist's object becomes solely the object of art. This object is understood to be primal, a first and only creation, and it is understood to be sufficient, equal to its definition. What is art? cried the age. It is what the artist does, came the tautological answer. In making this inviolate object the artist becomes a figure *sui generis*. The modernist aesthetic turns idolatrous in its very efforts to be iconoclastic. It implants a mystique of invention over the object and the maker. The artist must suffer the anguish of deleting all that's tarbabied to the contingent, and live a "real" self equated only with consciousness.

In other words, modernism in Sontag's terms validates a heroism of self that does not get tested in any arena of "right." It raises the self up, but on a pair of stilts. Some gnostic quest might lurch this self forward; it might try to justify itself in some existentialist gratuitous act. Mostly, the modernist self dances in place while it gnaws on its sinews. Ultimately, it must become the tyrannical analyst of its own being, having repudiated connectedness. "Art becomes a statement of self-awareness—an awareness that presupposes a disharmony between the self of the artist and the community," writes Sontag. "Indeed, the artist's effort is measured by the size of its rupture with the collective voice (of 'reason')" (*USS* 16).

From her own commitments to reason and mortality, then, Sontag seeks the point at which the ethos of modernism can neither be defended nor abandoned, not as long, anyway, as she venerates it as the most powerful artistic force in the present. In other words, Sontag finds herself committed to an ethos she cannot wholly accept. She reveals her hesitancy in that strange reliance on the words *serious, will, hero*. When the other side of her comes back to demand an accounting in terms of collective purposes, she yields, notwithstanding the force of her intentions, to the intractability of her subject. Especially in her early essays, she is game enough to tell us that she writes as a way of "drawing the contours of a sensibility" in order to be "disburdened" of it. Finally, "disburdenment" becomes an act, a practice, a way of being modern in order to countermand, as it were, modernist contradictions.

When Sontag begins writing in the 1960s, she is looking back at this inheritance of modernism. As in her memoir of Thomas Mann, the modernists are the gods who descended, the heroes who set the terms of heroism in this age. Each of her essays expresses that tension between her exhilaration over and disappointment with, even warning away from, the figures she admires. And even though her fictional characters are not admirable in this way (they tend to be "poor slobs" or "despicable"), they are elevated figures nonetheless. They are that special case of the modernist dilemma working against the individual: they seek a deleted form of themselves. Similarly, as in her essay portraits, one has the sense that their author holds them up for argument.

If any one aspect of Sontag's work could be said to defuse over the whole, it is this push-pull grid of demanding the severe and the experimental in ways of being. She both asks for an accountability of art and intellect and at the same time refuses a theory of criticism that would go beyond the explanation of "that it is what it is."

So far I have been sketching out my understanding of the inner workings of Sontag's aesthetic. What she has contributed to contemporary letters, how she has been received, how she has managed being famous—these are all concerns I am tempted to say are mere externals to her work. Not so, of course, never perfectly so, anyway, for anyone, and especially not so for a writer/intellectual/filmmaker who has had such a spotlight shown on her which demands that she be current, bracing, politically on the right side of the most important issues, to be one of the few women—before the women's movement, before the great burst of women (in numbers) in the academy and professions—to be these things. She can never be less than knowledgeable, never less than intelligent. By her own terms, she cannot play to the crowds. Her speechifying has thrown her back on her weakest resources. Her so-called public can make her feel ridiculous. Seated next to potted plants signing her books, she is the very picture of harassment. But she often takes on that look on podiums and in seminars.

In crediting Sontag's accomplishments in fulfilling this role as public intellectual, it must be said that she's shown consistent prescience. She has been one to stride across boundaries, for instance, that lie between Europe and America, with the thought of introducing works that were hard to fit, or, worse, about to be lost to contemporary eclecticism. She has been especially gifted in this, not hesitating to shape her subject strongly by her own ideas. For years, her advice on what to read was unerring and well ahead of what was read generally. When given the task to analyze "what is happening" culturally, she sought her answers in the powers of the forms. Considering the fluffy excitement, patronizing, or sheer opinion mongering typical of writing on mass forms of art and entertainment, Sontag's carefulness became a model for many others to take seriously the imagination of mass culture. Theorists as distinct from her as Fredric Jameson have acknowledged her influence on them. And by the 1980s, of course, for all the har-rumphing dismay expressed by those who cling to the sacred font of the canon, the study of mass and popular culture has attracted the liveliest and most generous of the new critical generation.

To her credit, *Against Interpretation* is now a classic in American criticism. *On Photography* broke years of critical silence about that art form. *Illness as Metaphor* collected testimony from what might be genuinely called the reading public: simply, people were grateful. No doubt they are now grateful again for a recent short story "The Way We Live Now" about Max, dying of AIDS, told by who-said-what to-whom as his friends consider his fate. The commonplaces that fretfully circulate among these friends reveal the edges where Max's experience can-not be transposed to them. The silence of which Sontag has so often written, the hole that language makes around its object, does in this story what she says it does: it dignifies the pathos of the separateness of dying.

She has had a public that has stayed appreciative, overall, and she is still being discovered, as in Brazil where her work is now being trans-lated. Unfortunately for her, she fell out with powerful company. It was not advisable in the eyes of the New York intellectuals, with their stiffening resistance to the cultural climate of the 1960s, to catch any of the fervors of those times. Sontag was not only making a break from their high culture stance, she was taking up some of the issues of and writing in the journals of the New Left. She had crossed the line the generations had drawn around themselves. And perhaps she revealed to the high culture-liberal politics advocates that they mistook them-selves in their objections. Behind the justifiable dread of American know-nothingness, unfairly directed at the hard working thinkers/art-ists/activists of the 1960s, hung a greater dread that the new politics of culture would rattle the old bones of the debates from the thirties. Many on the re-emerging right had their own disavowals to preserve.

Another matter troubled many about Sontag, and that was her sense of society. As intellectuals drifted into and blended with the academic world, however much they might have imagined themselves rebels, however much they were still redbaited, basically they agreed to the rules. Few of them would be likely to appear in *Vogue*, as Sontag did, as *Vogue's* darling—America's own, glamorous, young woman intellectual. Some critics got nasty. "Miss Camp" she became dubbed, after her essay on the camp sensibility appeared in *Partisan Review*. (Later Sontag would write that it was a surprise to her how fast an essay in a relatively obscure journal would circulate as public coinage.) She has a genius, others snarled, but it's for publicity. What was she doing, a philosopher and a social theorist, in the slick magazines?

Or going to Cuba, China, and Vietnam, for that matter? Did she actually like the repoliticization of culture? Tall, commanding in voice and form, with a power in her body she rather displayed—in cowboy boots and long-limbs draped on jacket covers of her books. What was she doing calling for the erotics of criticism? Intellectuals were not supposed to be favorite figures that way, even if they had been young and could be forgiven modest, thwarted *enfant terrible* impulses.

She was making a place for the writer-intellectual in yet another gulf that has stayed mostly unbridged in America, the gulf between the small intellectual journals and the popular media. Unlike Europe no weekly glossy sought out a Marcuse or Sartre for comment on events; indeed *The New York Times* hardly gave them an obituary. Mary McCarthy was writing often in these years, on issues like Vietnam, but she was ignored. Who could weld the enclaves together—the wry, the satirists, the raconteurs of literary, and occasionally intellectual life, in *The New Yorker* perhaps? But what a frail vehicle, what a deflated message. It was a good thing for Sontag that the *New York Review of Books* and *Ramparts* were being born; arguably, it was an embarrassment that she published a short story, "Baby," in *Playboy* or filled the cover of *Vanity Fair*.

Even so, in the 1960s and well into the present, writers who are not commentators, not reviewers, not intellectual journalists, nor cultural historians, or Sunday observers, who work very close to their subjects to bring about an aesthetic, a mode of thinking into being, (as Roland Barthes did, for example) have little mass media ground to claim for themselves. The freedom to travel, lonely, and, for oneself, into forbidden territory, yet conscious of one's representative position, the right to rebuke smartly the imprecise, to cleave the half-truths into many parts; the right to shun television talk without inventing obscuring monisms of one's own; the right to feel like, pattern oneself after European *literati*—in that sense of having a publicly admired tradition; to be a handsome, near beautiful woman with a never spoken of, but never hidden bisexuality; to keep from being disliked as a woman for not lampooning one's own power: in the 1960s, few intellectuals had won these rights from the American media culture. The media's clamp on discourse has not loosened much. Sontag plays a strange game trying to win its respect; her manner is always at odds with its satiric or sensationalizing agendas. On the podium or over the air, she sounds too brittle, too quick to anger, too insistent on her erudition, contentious. She has a way of sending an airless lock over the shifts and slides of feeling, of the giving and taking in conversation. Listening to her, one cannot help but reflect on her fiction. The passion she offers there comes with a strained knowledge of the mechanics of conflict; typically, the lover is closed out of escape. The paradoxes are worked relentlessly to fix the grounds of unhappiness; loss has been anticipated.

But it's not the hauteur nor the melancholy that strides in with Sontag, in those occasions where she is being watched as the writer/ intellectual, that makes one think again. There is that unexpected generosity—her remarks are laced with references to the people she wants others to read. It is not uncommon for her to ask to be introduced to someone because she has been reading him or her and wishes to acknowledge her appreciation. She becomes disarmed, very quickly, by specific and thoughtful questions, not lecturing. Her large even features, with that great weight on black hair and its swath of grey (the favorite touch of caricaturists), survey the room quietly. When she speaks she rarely corrects herself; she sounds, indeed, very much like her prose.

Ellen Willis recalls a moment when she considered herself still a junior writer, a rock critic at *Rolling Stone*, when Sontag walked into a party and asked to meet her: "I was tongue-tied; she was approaching me, and now when I think back on it, how turned on I was. She was an exciting, sexy woman." I have heard men say that they were fascinated and put-off by women so aggressively smart and so, seemingly, confidently sexual. Germaine Greer had that effect in the early 1970s; it was fun watching her and Sontag move back and forth over gender and intellectual conventions. If there were women who stood for the arguments the early feminists were making for androgyny (the command men learn from being responsible for power, the grace woman learn from being power's observer), gender feelings so finely remade that there were few forbidden interests—then Greer filled the image, but Sontag almost overwhelmed it. The permission they gave women summarizes badly, but it can be said that women then, in greater numbers, more publicly, were beginning to look at each other admiringly, without wondering first if they were seeing what men admired. When the look was returned, equitable, it passed on the thrill of a new age. Sontag was someone men could not easily belittle, though that did not stop many from trying, and she had fended off the stale attacks that pass between academics and journalists (that journalists can't handle theory and poorly understand the history of their subjects, that academics can't write and lack the courage of their positions). She expanded the place for many who have to presume that they are being asked to think for their country, when their own nature is adverse to pontificating, when their politics tends to be self-invented, and when their willingness to come from behind their books is forced.

If something of our discomfort over the absurdity of stance and attention grabbing lingers on, it's anticipated by Sontag, agonized over, even, when what is at issue is more important than a *People* magazine layout. About Vietnam or China she would try to hold at bay that mixture of truths that brings a star to the front of the demonstration. She would never excuse herself, simply, by believing she was needed.

Those drawings and photo-portraits of Sontag, accumulating now over twenty years tell a tale of their own. When she was still in her thirties, *Esquire* published a sketch of her head by way of loving refinement. The lines moulded over her features, their outlines precise and flowing—she was given a lyrical moment of such regality one is tempted to say *Esquire* found its young Athena. Her look was clear, quiet and inward as a classic marble. It stood as a prototype for other photographs. A later image, on the back cover of *I, etcetera* has Sontag squared off in a window ledge like a pediment sculpture, somewhat too engaging for a timeless being, yet body-easy in a superior way. With her face all but filling the cover of *Vanity Fair* in 1984, the expression concentrated, more weighty, the photographer and cover designer seem at last comfortable with a stronger image of thoughtfulness, loveliness aside. It could be said she glared down the mockery attendant in the conventions of the cover person (-girl) as no other famous face on that magazine has yet been able to do.

In these matters of fame and presence, Sontag has had the honor of being mentioned four times by Russell Jacoby, in his *The Last Intellectuals: American Culture in the Age of Academe*—a book pretending admiration for those who escaped the compromising seduction of the universities. He recalls how Sontag was one of the top ten American intellectuals listed by Kadushin in 1970. "None," writes Jacoby, "could be considered young, with the possible exception of Susan Sontag, then 37."[6] She had been named as part of the "second generation" of New York intellectuals by Daniel Bell in 1976, to which there was added no younger names. In praising her independence, Jacoby does not mention the modest living she scratched for herself. He is more interested in reviving the often heard complaint that *The New York Review of Books* froze entry for new writers early in its history. He cites Kostelanetz's study for his evidence that "the New York brokers allowed no one younger than Susan Sontag and Philip Roth, both born in 1933, to enter the big time."[7]

"Big time" suggests the bluster and hypocrisy of the big shots, the jockeying, the exclusivity. It's a jealous word. To those who have their opinions about the big-timers, Sontag got tagged as someone who loved the limelight despite crudely concealed insecurities, who loved to pounce, for sport and territory, in face-to-face competition. When she taught, said the scuttlebutt, she confused teaching with lance throwing. Though she has had her protégés, Stephen Koch, for instance, she shows less and less interest in promoting young writers. Editors chafe that she reigns over a network of hidden influencers who see to it what authors, if not whole presses, get their books reviewed. They want to know what sways the big-timers, what their mood is, and to whom their favors go next. In the crass power plays that are New York's signature, Sontag, others are certain, must play her part. So far, none of this has been a matter of public record.

She has been close to her publisher Roger Straus, of Farrar, Straus & Giroux for many years. Now, as president of PEN she has been reinforcing its welcome of Eastern European writers. She can, when she wishes, write a piece for the *New York Review of Books*, the *London Review of Books, Salmagundi, Partisan Review*, and probably most other journals. She's the star guest at most of the conferences she is called to, and always a newspaper item. Considering the spectacle of PEN's latest appearance on the society page, dined by the fabulously rich, I suppose Sontag's brokerage could take on real clout. So far her direct hand in matters of privileged access has not included starting a journal of her own, the benchmark project of high stepping academics.

But, it is impossible not to feel that New York City has not had its influence in other ways. Deference strikes the wrong note there, humility is bizarre, the slow comeback is lost. Of course, the outsiders temper the city's conduct, and Sontag is an outsider, or was when she was young. They can also overcorrect themselves, find the city too much a study, bind themselves to its exaggerations, grow nasty. What has become even harder in New York since Sontag arrived is to carry off the writer's retreat. Cheap neighborhoods have not held the line at the perimeter and have almost disappeared in the center. Though she now lives in a comfortable neighborhood where the west Village melds with Soho, Sontag has been heard to worry whether she won't be forced to leave New York altogether. She has lived off her writing and lecturing. When she became ill with cancer, there were efforts to start funds for her to help pay for her medical treatments. If she is enjoying the attention of the rich, in her role at PEN, she has never enjoyed, even modestly, their sense of security. Whatever temptation their company may hold for her now, above the fascination they have often drawn from writers, remains to be seen. Her growing conservatism developed from its own roots.

Another dubious honor has come to Sontag, more surreptitiously in this case, yet in the same vein of setting her up as a grand dame. In this role she allows people to become wistful for some rarefied society not the equal of Sartre's and de Beauvoir's, perhaps, but ambitious and unfailingly brilliant, nonetheless. She is the subject of a novel. Out of the small pond of the New York Institute of Humanities, where she has been a senior fellow for many years, along with her son David, Edmund White fished his material for his novel *Caracole*. In it she and David appear as Mathilda and Daniel, the aging mother and queen of her city's cultural and intellectual life with her 30-ish son, a debauché, a snob, maybe and maybe not a *manque*, her "darling." Their portraits are not entirely vicious, actually, in that they are given lovers they both need, however absurdly mismatched, and they both lose, both suffer intensely. Their faults—drawn from life and ill-disguised—and their world betray them. This world, however, is fabulous, not New York. It has conquerors and collaborators, indigenous dark-skinned tribal people and old decayed mansion families set in a city of carnivals, canals, court life, revolution, and, of all things, seminars.

> To be sure, hers was a strangely solitary notion of writer, since her irritable honesty caused her to reject all groups as self-promoting, all public discourse as theatrical . . . numbing to skepticism. But if the moralist in her required gloomy solitude, the aesthete required company. . . .
>
> In actual groups Mathilda was bored when attention wavered away from her, offended when it returned to her, always dismayed by the vulgarity of the tone and the lassitude of the intellectual level. But at the prospect of a new "colloquium" or "seminar" she was gleeful, even though her fame and snobbism had made her so distrustful of outsiders and newcomers that she could only imagine forming such seminars out of the people she already knew, as though a capricious officer of an oasis garrison were to keep casting his handful of besotted soldiers into more sprightly roles in ever less likely operettas.[8]

This passage is followed by a crude scene of Mathilda being rebuffed by the enemy general, "when she had been ready to grace his viceregal court and steer his reign" (*Caracole* 272). That part and others in the story are not meant as shadowy references to actual episodes in Sontag's life, to be sure. The novel's bigger concern is the search for a beautiful cultured salon life to write about, to stir its young protagonist Gabriel through, from the murky barbarism of his country estate to the desig-

nated hero of the resistance. Gabriel has learned the "tricks" of educated conversation—the subject of White's surest satirical touch. Gabriel's second lesson, the seduction of the middle aged, and Mathilda's
crumbling defenses in the face of her love for him, are more kindly
explored. What the novel groans for is the tawdriness of it all, the
intellectuals and the effetes, their opposites, the aristocrats. The first's
sumptuous wit and ideas dissipate to nil; the other's glittering inconse-
quential talk, proves exhausting and dull. It is the society of an Albright
painting in which the young innocents are united without innocence
and without honor; the others are interesting only to the extent that
they have played up to this society and are about to be vanquished in
it—especially Mathilda.

Jacoby and White hardly occupy the same frame of reference, and
together they do not comprise a movement, but they do make a similar
complaint. There is an anger afoot in American cultural worlds that
Sontag has shared and expresses too. She sadly agreed when George
Steiner voiced it some years ago: the thought that America has essentially a "caretaker culture" to European intellectual and artistic life.
The Los Angeles curse, which Sontag fled as a child, seemingly floats
over the whole country. What an interesting fate that she herself has
been singled out as a cause of that failure. If there was to be a grand
dame, would not it have been her? Why did she not succeed in establish-
ing a second generation of New York intellectuals as rivals of the first?
And if she is the grand dame, she resides over a company anxious over
its second classdom, or so disparate it cannot gather a locus of force.

The real-life Sontag has always distinguished herself in attracting
more hostility than that usually given self-serious and abrupt women.
She has a way of speaking in imperious negations, refusing to be included in anyone else's enthusiasms. Before she is pegged she shifts
directions; she provokes her public, in a manner in which she is now
famous, by eminently quotable retorts. It was very much like her, on
a panel discussion in June 1985 with Polish writers, to congratulate the
one speaker who suggested that the Polish underground culture, which
is energetic and to which most were there to pay homage, has been
skewed by resentment and over-ridden by testimonials. And while the
audience murmured, she snapped at a young woman, who had risen to
make the point that we not forget the Polish artist's isolation, with: "I
think we Americans are isolated."

Admittedly, public forums in America are unsubtle places of knee-
jerk anticommunism and/or knee-jerk reactions to this anticommunism, especially now with the left quieter and the right flaunting prized
East European émigrés. They are not places for the clearing away of
presumptions and the sharpening of distinctions that constitute Son-

tag's métier, not even in the safer realm of the visual arts. For when she writes a book on photography, and does the curious thing of writing an ethics of photography, she finds herself in the same kind of match-wits with her audience, as she did in late 1970s discussing photography at the Corcoran Art Gallery. Does she have to explain, her manner indicated, why a critic makes judgments about the consciousness that an art form brings into being?

The air was stinging with attacks from the photographers who loathed the tread of reason into what they must preserve: inspiration and en-thrallment. Taste or the critic's snobbishness might be nettling, but these were distractions with which they were well familiar, comic distractions considering how little attention photography received. But Sontag brought Platonic notions of the illusionary and the treachery of the aesthetic to her discussion. To many there, she seemed antiphotog-raphy. These were not graduate students who might have known French discourse on the troubled eye; these questioners were practitioners, like the practitioners of cultural politics at the Poland forum. She evinced no patience with the discussion and no interest in mitigating the ill feeling.

Sontag has an argument with culture, so much so that I can think of only one occasion when she seems to be writing out of obligation: her essay on feminism. It functions as a distant, anatomist introduc-tion to feminists' positions, written on a body of ideas she advocates rather than one she has participated in developing. Having none of that turn toward modernist darkness that marks her true subject, the essay gives one the sense that she was never there when women were shaking each other free from victimization to empowerment, and thus, that she has no feel for the collective project. More typically, she writes about what she is attracted to but does not wish to be, because she is troubled by what it reveals about herself as well as her times. She squirms under the power of her own questions, even when the language is as shaped and spare as an epitaph, intended for distilled appreciation.

That hard work against herself confuses many; they are apt to reduce her ideas to confessions and retractions, and to suggest that, like an ideologue focused on set operations, she lacks taste. She is not a critic of that kind of taste, that is, of those works balanced and harmonious and refined to a lively ease, but of the source, the attack of a work, how much it closes its grip over its theme.

Early, she would be identified with the call for an "erotics of criti-cism." It was a phrase she tagged onto the "Against Interpretation" essay to punctuate it and to give the theme a manifesto ring which, in truth, it does not otherwise have. She never repeated the phrase. It was used against her in willful misreadings of her work. However, to the extent that it does stand for a kind of method, it means being first inside the force of a work of art, seduced by, allowing it its power. Then, in its sway, the critics explains "that it is what it is."

In becoming a figure for the larger community, she compares to only a few others in the American context, writers like Paul Goodman, of whom she writes a warm eulogy, and Norman Mailer. She would never get avuncular like Paul Goodman, holding up the word "human," "acceptance," himself like an orb. That gentle way of Goodman's, freeing children by calling them to his own fantasies, full-sexed and riding ponies into skies, that knowing way of his of entering his subject benignly in order to pull off the audience's style of radical will, with all that it meant for the radicals of the 1960s, would be the antithesis of what Sontag reveals as her style of radical will. She intimidates, complain many, deliberately. She would rather tower over than reach under for her audience's soft spots. Her style is more with the spirit of Marcuse's phrase, negating the negations.

Since *Advertisements for Myself* and with all those existential errands, Mailer, unarguably also positioned himself in the American mind as a *bona fide* radical stylist, so confrontational had been his own nature and so willing to peer into the guts of American social life. In the *March on the Pentagon* he let his language rise to the siren plains of messianic history, then let it fall back to the possibility of American self-understanding.

Sontag had then and has now very little invested in the American scene; to her, political understanding is not gained by collective show as much as insight by contrast with what remained alienated and unradical in the self. She would almost always pose those questions from the position of solitude of an outsider. In that odd essay on Vietnam, Sontag writes to herself to teach herself what is required to understand that place. She must have felt the loneliness of her circumstance, the near certain probability that her hosts would not appreciate her difficulty, nor radical audiences in the United States her interest in her difficulty. The essay radiates loneliness, as it does a self-rebuke.

In this book, I trace the structure of Sontag's ideas. Increasingly they make a pattern of which she is aware. That pattern forms a kind of practice, in the old distinction between theory and practice. This is how Sontag sets about making the issues she writes about matter. In the newer sense, in the distinction between discourse and practice, this is how Sontag reproduces her habits of selection, this is how she works with the contradictions internal to her ideas, and this is how she responds to the times and the force of politics. Chapter I offers some chronological notes on Sontag's activities. Chapter II discusses the terms supporting Sontag's approach to the contemporary sensibility, its arts and its people she writes about. Chapter III looks at both novels as continuing, in their own fashion and relative to one another, the project of investigating a "dramaturgy" of this later modernism. Chapter IV opens up her aesthetic to a more general critique, following her ideas from *Against Interpretation* to *On Photography*. Chapter V asks what her portraits and auto-portraits of intellectuals mean to our understanding of that kind of life. The Conclusion returns to Sontag as the public person, back on the podium, in the defense of a cause. It asks, from that pattern of thinking and writing and being a public person that is special to her, what kind of politics she practices. The Conclusion ends with some thoughts on the recent debate over her book *AIDS and Its Metaphors*.

1

Biographical Notes

The "besotted aesthete," "obsessed moralist," and "zealot of serious-ness," as Sontag thinks of herself, was conceived in China where her mother and father negotiated in the trade of animal skins in Tien-tsin (Tianjin). She carries images of them in her mind as the glittering and least concerned of foreigners, "playing Gatsby and Daisy at the British Concession." Her grandparents' house was filled with the Chinese jades and porcelains of the kind "colonialists collect." Her mother returned to New York City to deliver Sontag, January 16, 1933, and then went back to China leaving the baby behind in the grandparents' care. (She was raised "mostly by aunts.") Whether these were her maternal or paternal grandparents Sontag has not yet revealed. Nor has she ever given her mother's maiden name or her father's name, though one or the other is probably Jacobson. *People* magazine published a photograph of Sontag and her younger sister Judith standing on either side of grand-father Charles Jacobson. Sontag was her stepfather's name.

The child may have liked the specialness in all this, the glamorous, absent parents; the marvelous, obscure Orient that held her parents and filled her house with treasures. One of the first lies Sontag remem-bers telling is bragging to her classmates that she was born in China. She was so convincing in that guise that even her parents' Chinese friends would tell her that she looked Chinese. She does not, of course, not a trace. But then, her household seemed to compound the effect of a deracinated, wandering identity. Sontag told Geoffrey Movius in 1975:

> If immigrants retained a tie with their country or culture of origin, it was very selective. The main impulse was to forget. I once asked my father's mother, who died when I was seven, where she came from. She said, "Europe." Even at six I knew that wasn't a very good answer. I said, "But where, Grandma?" She repeated testily, "Europe." And so to this day, I don't know from what country my paternal grandparents came. But I have photographs of them, which I cherish, which are like the mysterious tokens of all that I don't know about them. (Movius 13)

Sontag's sister Judith was born in New York in 1936, and again their mother returned to China to help with the export business. At this age

23

Sontag was already beginning to read independently and, she believes, thinking about "moral" things. She has not mentioned if anyone noticed or encouraged her. She leaves us with the impression, rather, that her inner life formed under the pressure of self-defense and that it sprang entirely from her. ("I think of myself as self-created—that's my working illusion" [Cott 53]). One wonders what was happening in that first household, if, for instance, the Depression or a prescience of the coming world calamities ever filtered in under the door. She does hint that the family moved around a lot and that until she was an adolescent she shared a room with her sister. Perhaps the shock of her father's death in 1938 overrode those memories. He died of tuberculosis in China; Sontag is not sure where he is buried.

"I still weep in any movie with a scene in which a father returns home after a long, desperate absence, at the moment when he hugs his child. Or children," she writes in "Project for a Trip to China," a short story that is set on the eve of her departure to China as an official visitor. Her oldest wounds open on the page as she considers how she understands things Chinese and what she expects from this trip. Mother merges into "M." in the short story, and we hear how M. had waited several months before she had told Sontag her father was not coming back. She was brief, writes Sontag. "Dearest M. I cannot telephone. I am six years old. My grief falls like snowflakes on the warm soil of your indifference. You are inhaling your own pain."

Sontag confesses that she has been bitter, that she is not sure she has forgiven her mother, if one can forgive. But that thought rests in her knowledge that there has been continuity and repetition in grief between the generations. M.'s own mother died in Los Angeles when she was only fourteen; the grandmother had been born in Bialystok. Sontag recalls M. telling her of how, on her way to New York to visit her daughters, she was not allowed to leave the sealed cars that foreigners rode in on the Trans-Siberian Railroad. When the train stopped in Bialystok, she wept. "She wanted to feel the ground of her mother's faraway birthplace under her feet. Just once. . . . She didn't tell me she wept, but I know she did. I see her."

The other possibility is that M. had already learned how to immunize herself in the face of departures. Perhaps she had not wept, perhaps she imparted to her daughter an "Oriental detachment." What Sontag is more sure of, which she has mentioned in several places, is that childhood was a prison for her, a kind of sentencing against which she used all the force of her will and intellect to escape.

That escape did not take very long. Sontag showed asthmatic symptoms in 1939 and her mother decided to take her and Judith to Tucson, Arizona, to live in a modest stucco bungalow on a dirt road at the outskirts of town. They had an Irish nanny, who was "notionally sala-ried" and with whom Sontag went to Catholic services on Sunday. About her religious upbringing she has said, "My family, which was Jewish, did not practice. The first time I was in a synagogue I was twenty-four years old. I was visiting Florence, when I passed for the first time in front a synagogue that had a plaque with the names of the Jews of Florence who had been deported to Auschwitz, and I entered" (Costa 187).

Her mother took a job teaching school. In that feminine world, the tall child accelerated. "Childhood was a terrible waste of time," she told the *People* magazine interviewer, Barbara Rowes. "I was put in 1A on Monday when I was 6 years old. Then 1B on Tuesday, 2A on Wednesday, 2B on Thursday, and by the end of the week they had skipped me to third grade because I could do the work" (Rowes 79). She never got less than an "A" grade after that.

Recently, when asked the beginning of her interest in the moral, Sontag remarked:

> I believe that it began when I was three years old. In other aspects, I am not very clear about when I was young, which is a source of strength and a problem at the same time. I remember that I would think much on the things that I think about now before I was ten years old. If I were able to begin again, I would give myself a greater capacity to enjoy my childhood. (Costa 187)

To have gained a beautiful, young, sorrowing mother at the cost of a father barely met; to have been taken from her grandparents and sent to live, on account of her own inexplicable weakness, so much like her father's, in the American desert; to soon lose her paternal grandmother, that woman of vague places—what a hard mixture of mourning and guilt and dislocation the child must have borne. She may have also sensed a strange empowerment—to be now at the center of concern and quite likely the center of delight for the newly constituted house-hold. She had inward gifts, already exceptional and outward energies for which no father was around to mold or to dampen. She had discovered writing, all kinds, at age six or seven. Soon, she would ride about the neighborhood on her bicycle selling for 5 cents a four-page journal of articles and stories she had created and run off on an old hectograph machine. She wrote plays and poems and short stories. Into her adoles-cence she wanted to be a chemist (she set up a chemistry lab in a garage), then a doctor, but always a writer, too. In fact, she says, she thought seriously again, in her twenties, about becoming a physician, and even now sometimes muses that she is sorry she never studied medicine.

But she does study pain and disease, in several short stories and in the famous essays on illnesses and metaphors, as perhaps she has always been studying them, intimately and with the certainty, that for one to be free, disease must be stripped of its unscientific, "controlling metaphors."

Her lungs got stronger in the desert. Apparently the asthma does not now trouble her or, at least it did not force her to stop smoking until 1987 (after "being a constant victim of the terrorism" of the anti-smoking campaign). She grew tall and slender; at eleven she is taller than her grandfather in the photograph and looking older, more confident by many years, than her actual age. She was already pushing herself when the second blow fell, a determining blow. For when she was twelve, her mother remarried, to a "handsome, bemedalled, and beshrapnelled Army Airforce Ace who'd been sent to the healing desert to cap a year-long hospitalization" ("Pilgrimage" 38). Captain Sontag soon took his new family to Canoga Park, a suburb of Los Angeles, to a "cozy shuttered cottage with rosebush hedges and three birch trees at the entrance to the San Fernando Valley." Here the "resident alien," "pretending to sit still for a facsimile of family life and the remainder of the unconvincing childhood," was, in fact, "already gone."

> On weekends my out-of-uniform but still militarily perky stepfather marshalled sirloins and butter-brushed corn tightly wrapped in tinfoil on the patio barbecue; I ate and ate—how could I not, as I watched my morose, bony mother fiddling with her food. His animation was as threatening as her apathy. They couldn't start playing family now—too late! I was off and running . . . . ("Pilgrimage" 38)

"The end was almost in sight." She would finish high school while still fifteen and be off to college. If she never moped or sulked (the "truth was, I dreaded conflict"), she had the arrogance of adolescence to protect her: "What other people thought of me remained a dim consideration, since other people seemed to me astonishingly unseeing and uncurious, while I longed to learn everything": and she had the special privilege of having it never occur to her "that I could be stopped." There was also a "flip side" to her discontent. In California she had a room of her own, literally, for the first time. "The demon reader in her" ("to read was to drive a knife into their lives") experienced "near nightly bouts of jubilation." She became a different "Lone Ranger" than she had been in Arizona; instead of snakes and arrowheads, she tracked down real bookstores, international bookstands, record shops, and, with her friends, the artists that war-protected and postwar-exuberant Los Angeles had harbored. She writes about this rapture over art in "Pilgrimage"; it is in many ways a very believable portrait of her hurried-up, urgent youth, rescued at the tenderest points and in the earliest stages by an enthralldom to art and ideas. In another interview, she reminisces:

> [when] I was a fifteen-year-old kid at North Hollywood High School, I discovered a newsstand on the corner of Hollywood and Highland that carried literary magazines. I'd never seen a literary magazine before; certainly I'd never seen anybody read one. I picked up *Partisan Review* and started to read "Art and Fortune" by Lionel Trilling; and I just began to tremble with excitement. And from then on, my dream was to grow up, move to New York and write for the *Partisan Review*. Then within a year, I'd read all the New Critics and had become a great fan of Kenneth Burke. The following year I went to the University of Chicago where I became a student of Kenneth Burke's. Nobody knows that I was a student of Burke's. (Copeland 87)

She stayed at the University of California at Berkeley for only a year, and then transferred to her first choice, the University of Chicago. As the story goes, she decided one winter morning in 1950 to audit a course on Freud taught by an interesting young lecturer, Philip Rieff. She had to walk to the back of the room for the last empty seat, and when the lecture was over, she was the last to leave. "He was standing at the door and he grabbed my arm and asked my name. I apologized and told him I had only come to audit. 'No, what's your name?' he persisted. 'Will you have lunch with me?' " (Rowes 79). They were married ten days later: Sontag was 17 and Rieff 28.

What did this abruptness solve? It is hard to say. Sexuality, of course, but also, surely, a way to carry her excitement through and onto a plain of company—the graduate students, the young professors—already working on what she had been thinking about. Philip Rieff would go on to be an important sociologist, nearly himself a household name. He could sweep her up, help her leap past the tedium and "drivel" she had sworn to ward off, into a place where politics, ideas, questions of morality, were actually written about.

One can only guess from this story what Sontag thought of her exceptional looks. Men usually do not grab the arm of merely brilliant women. She never wears make-up, and until chemotherapy, had no cause to treat her lustrous black hair. When asked about her cerebralness, she is quick to describe herself as a lively, curious, sensuous person. She did write a piece when she turned forty called "The Double Standard of Aging" which by inference suggests her consciousness of facing a changing set of relationships. However, the essay includes only one direct reference to herself, and that was when she was sixteen. She recalls being mystified by her friend's fear of turning twenty-one. "I didn't understand at all what could be demoralizing about turning twenty-one. To me it meant only something good: being in charge of oneself, being free. At sixteen, I was too young to have noticed and become confused by, the peculiarly loose, ambivalent way in which this society demands that one stop thinking of oneself as a girl and start thinking of oneself as a woman" ("The Double Standard . . ." 33). In marrying Rieff, she helped others, perhaps helped herself, think of her as a woman.

In 1951 Sontag completed her B.A. at Chicago and then she and Rieff moved to Boston where he taught at Brandeis. She must have kept her habit of auditing classes. Irving Howe remembers her in the back of his lectures at Brandeis in these years, as a woman of radiating beauty and intelligence. The next year she enrolled at Harvard, graduating with an M.A. in English (1954) and an M.A. in philosophy (1955). In the meantime, two weeks after she had enrolled as a Ph.D. candidate in philosophy at Harvard, she gave birth to her first and only child, David (September 28, 1952). "I named him David after the Michelangelo sculpture" (Rowes 79).

David would be her nearly constant companion in the following years. He was the big, dark-eyed boy in the background of the few interviews she granted in the 1960s. Once he remarked about his grammar school life, "Susan was not the type to go to PTA meetings." She responded, "I have nothing against the PTA. I'm just allergic to institutions" (Rowes 80). At thirteen, James Toback describes him as having "slipped into conversations on Reichian analysis and the philosophy of history with the self-assurance of a Harvard graduate student" (Toback 60). In contradiction to Sontag's swift movement through school, David took his time completing a degree at Princeton, a matter she sometimes teased him about. But still in his twenties he joined her as a fellow at the New York Institute of the Humanities, and along with her became an editor at Farrar, Straus, and Giroux. "My first editor," Sontag tells Charles Ruas, "was the late Cecil Hemley, then Robert Giroux, and starting with 'Under the Sign of Saturn,' my editor has been David Rieff, who also happens to be my son. Someone said to David, 'Don't you think you're mixing church and state?' But I am very pleased with the arrangement. I have great confidence in Mr. Rieff's judgement" (Ruas 39). She has hinted that before David's position as her editor was acknowledged he was the first and usually the only person to see her pieces before they were sent out. About this arrangement she has said, "But I really shouldn't [do this] because it is probably a great burden to him. I just can't resist the feeling that it [a piece of writing] exists first for just one other person, before it goes to the editor" (Brennan 102). David Sontag Rieff has recently published a book on Miami.[1]

When David was a newborn, Sontag commuted to the University of Storrs, Connecticut, to lecture in English. From 1966–7 she was a teaching fellow in philosophy at Harvard while working on her doctorate. In 1957 both Sontag and her husband Philip Rieff won scholarships to study abroad. "At the last minute," she has explained, "he decided that he didn't want to do it. So I went anyway." Sontag went to St. Anne's College, Oxford.

A lightly sketched, female-ironic portrait of Sontag's brief stay at Oxford is worked into Judith Grossman's autobiographical novel *Her Own Terms*. The protagonist is struggling against the snobbishness of Oxford and against the manipulativeness and superciliousness of the men who have recruited her into their poets circle. One of the men is speaking:

> "Had to have dinner with Scofield, y'know, then stopped at Randolph on the way up. This woman, there! American! Brightest woman ever met, drank me under the table. Eleven Scotches, I gave up. No wonder they killed Dylan Thomas. Heads like iron pots. . . ."
>
> "Think she's layable?" Roger asked. . . . "Come on, Sean! Roger held out a mug of beer to him. "We're all friends here, so what's her name? Let's have a little verification— . . . "
>
> "Coming to that. Calls herself Sontag."
>
> "*What* Sontag. Or Sontag what."
>
> "That's all; that's it." . . .
>
> "What does she look like?"
>
> "Tall. Taller than you, Rog. Dark, darker than Sarah. Very dark. Dresses like a guerilla, only all these thick scarves."[2]

As it turns out, Sontag never makes her appearance among them.

> " . . . what happened to Sontag? You promised she'd come."
>
> "Ah, yes. Well, it didn't as they say work out. She seems to have got browned off with Oxford—last time I saw her she was planning to go off to Paris."
>
> "What for, the art and so on?"
>
> "No—according to her, the philosophy."
>
> "In *France!*"
>
> "Well, that was my reaction. If you went anywhere in Europe, it'd probably be Germany. What is there in Paris? So far as I know, only the French. And they haven't had an idea since Sartre."
>
> Sean leaned forward to me. "Did you know there was a husband *and* child, in the States?"
>
> "No, I didn't. Interesting—I'd wish I'd met her—I'm furious."

"Not so much interesting as appalling, I should say. You don't just
leave, in those circumstances."
  "How do we know?"
  "Well, we wouldn't *imagine* doing something like that." I said
nothing: it occurred to me that we weren't very strong on imagination,
'round here (Grossman 232).

A few lines later, the protagonist muses: "So she turned him down—
turned them all down, no doubt, and it was not unpleasing to know
that."

Sontag indeed went to Paris, to the University of Paris (1957–58);
and, certainly, the French were there, along with some friends, notably
Annette Michelson. It was a time of extraordinary cross-pressures. In
response, one group or journal after another found themselves contest-
ing, or splintering off from, revising, rejecting something of their own
intellectual and artistic past. The ground had begun to shift in the mid
1950s. The Cold War was passing its peak, the divisions on the Left
which it had forged were melting. Prosperity was returning to France,
softening the critique of the economy and heightening the critique
of personal liberty and autonomy. But to this springtime of personal
concerns came France's external defeats. Its empire was faltering. The
government was in the process of extracting itself from Vietnam after
Dienbienphu; it has just been trumped at Suez and was shamefully
embroiled in the Algerian war. The Left was readying itself for another
round on the questions of capitalism and empire, nationhood and identity, when, almost simultaneously, it received two blows: Krushchev's
revelations about Stalin, and the invasion of Hungary. It went reeling,
and those who had been trying to wrest Marx from communism, and
the dialectic from materialism, or dismiss "diamat" altogether, seized
the moment.

Sartre and Merleau-Ponty had already squared off following Merleau-
Ponty's *The Adventures of the Dialectic*. The dialectic had become an
empty category, claimed Merleau-Ponty, leading to voluntarism and
ultimately the cult of personality. Merleau-Ponty's phenomenology,
countered the neo-Marxists, was relativistic and could only end in
solipsism or theology. Into this debate, Lefebvre had introduced Lukács.
While Althusser was beginning to write his essays on how Marx had
seen through Hegel's idealist model, that Marx had not just "inverted"
it, Jean Hippolyte was carrying on the tradition of Kojève's Hegelian
seminars of the decade before. Marxism went wandering off—into lin-
guistics, anthropology, psychology, far from the Party's control. This
was the time of the minor revolution produced by Lévi-Strauss, Barthes,
Lacan, and the beginning of the New Left.

In more strictly literary matters, Leiris was continuing his autobiographical works in the vein of his earlier *Manhood*. Bataille was still alive; Klossowski active, all representing the wonderful, late surrealist, College of Sociology of twenty years before. Cioran had published *The Temptation to Exist* in 1956; Butor's novel *La Modification* received the Prix Renaudot in 1957. Robbe-Grillet had finished *The Erasers, The Voyeur, Jealousy* and had begun writing his essays on the new novel. Sarraute was discussed, Genet.

In film, Bresson was already well known; Resnais, Truffaut, Godard part of the renaissance. At twenty-five Sontag was exceptionally prepared to absorb all this; one only has to note how many of the above persons she would write on in the next five years. Since her adolescence she had been following the Left's inner convulsions; at Harvard, she had considered writing on the clash between phenomenology and existentialism. She already knew she could shift between the literary and analytical side of herself—her double degrees in English and Philosophy, for example. In France, that identity was confirmed; philosophers regularly wrote fiction. Besides, the French were so much more passionate about matters of aesthetics in the way she had always felt passionate—by hyperbole, exaltation in art. By contrast, in America, self-assurance had mixed badly with McCarthy-era fears. It was a time of consolidation. In France, one enacted style, and style directly conceived a moral and political point of view. Style was not interpreted; one argued about its way of being, the way it moved to encompass, about its erotic revealings. This understanding is fundamental to Sontag's first period of writing and stays with her all along.

During her stay in Paris (only a year, of course, supported by a grant from the American Academy of University Women), Sontag may have been busy polishing the manuscript *Freud, the Mind of the Moralist* (she had been collaborating with Rieff on it before she left, and presumably it was in its final stages). She would have been ready to explain, very articulately about American use of Freud.

She had not yet published anything of her own. Perhaps that fact handicapped her entree into French literary society; if it did, she may have been all the more ready to make up for it, and lose at last the "promising" younger member status she must have for years endured in the company surrounding her marriage. Paris, of course, for a whole half century had been a home to inspired and restless Americans; little more needs to be said.

When Sontag returned to New York she asked Rieff for a divorce. "It was in many ways a very good marriage. But I didn't want to go back to that. I thought there were other lives to live," she explained (Rowes 80). Some years later she was a little more expansive on the subject:

> I did have the idea that I'd like to have several lives, and it's very hard
> to have several lives and then have a husband—at least the kind of
> marriage that I had, which was incredibly intense; we were together
> all the time. And you can't live with someone on a twenty-four hour
> basis, never separated for years and years and have the same freedom
> to grow and change and fly off to Hong Kong if you feel like it . . . it's
> irresponsible. That's why I say that somewhere along the line, one
> has to choose between the Life and the Project. (Cott 52)

They were divorced that year. By mutual agreement, Rieff took sole
credit for *Freud, the Mind of the Moralist*. Sontag was impatient to
forge ahead with her project by becoming a freelance writer in New
York, with all "the insecurities and unpleasantness and anxiety and
frustration." Feminism had not motivated her:

> I didn't even know I was a feminist, so unfashionable was that point
> of view at the time, when I married at the age of seventeen and kept
> my own name; it seemed to me an equally "personal" act of principle
> on my part, when I divorced my husband seven years later, to have
> indignantly rejected my lawyer's automatic bid for alimony, even
> though I was broke, homeless, and jobless at that moment and I had
> a six-year-old child to support. ("The Third World of Women" 205)

With six-year old David in tow, two suitcases and $30, Sontag arrived
in New York "very much in the spirit of Misha getting to Moscow."
This was in January 1959. She found a job as an editor at *Commentary*
(for less than a year) and lecturer positions at Sarah Lawrence College
and the City College of New York.

An important chapter had closed, another begun just as the 1950s
were over. Though she continued to teach, she must have been shaking
loose from the hold that dissertation writing can have—the overly
careful, slightly toadying language; the endless putting off of other
projects. She may have her regrets that she did not finish a dissertation:
most do; that's the insidious aspect of having begun one. She told a
student interviewer: "I have often been asked to give commencement
addresses, but I'm always offered at the same time an honorary doctorate. I don't believe in honorary doctorates—I have too much respect for
the real ones. Wellesley is the first college that asked me to give a
commencement address without offering the honorary doctorate. That
amused me so much I felt I thought I must accept."[3]

It is not likely she suffered very much, for basically she was fulfilling
a dream to become the kind of writer that the New York intellectuals
had been—decidedly unacademic. And as Ph.D.-ism grew stronger in

this country, she had those writers (at *Commentary* and *Partisan Review*, for instance) as well as the model of the French to help her resist.

This was also the time when Sontag was exploring her differences with those models. She had another side to herself, which they did not understand. She actually liked some American popular culture. "You know," she told *Rolling Stone* in 1979:

> I think rock & roll was the reason I got divorced. I think it was Bill Haley and the Comets and Chuck Berry [*laughing*] that made me decide to get a divorce and leave the academic world.
>
> At that time, the late Fifties, I lived in a totally intellectual world. I didn't know one single person I could share this with. I didn't talk about it. People say a lot of stupid things about the Fifties, but it is true that there was a total separation between the people who were tuned into popular culture and those who were involved in high culture. There was nobody I ever met who was interested in both, and I always was. (Cott 49)

While she did not write specifically on rock, she poured out essay after essay in the next few years, book reviews, theater reviews, film reviews that took in a wider culture as a natural whole. (She published 26 essays between 1962 and 1965). She did this while she was an instructor in the department of religion at Columbia (1960–4), and while publishing her first novel, *The Benefactor* (1963).

The novel writing was a revelation. She wrote the first draft in a few months, "as if it had been dictated." Hereafter, that is, at the age of 28 and onward, she would identify herself as a fiction writer.

The Benefactor's narrator tells of his experiment of allowing his dreams to dictate his life. That life, such that it is, is conducted between the wars in France in a salon society of artists and intellectuals. His forays into his dreams become twisted into a bizarre caricature of the aesthetic and political debates of that period. Sontag has been careful to remind us that the narrator's stiff, brutal amoralism is as far removed from her own character as she could make it. When asked about how she discovered that voice, she told a story about herself and a woman friend having just sat down in the Cafe Figaro in Greenwich Village. She was complaining about how she could only write short stories, how she wanted to do something larger, with more energy. "Good," said the friend. "Begin right now." "Yes, I am going to do it," answered Sontag. But her friend insisted, "No, I said right now."

> Suddenly something passed through me. I said, "I agree, pay for the coffees." They hadn't even arrived yet. . . . I grabbed a taxi, went to my house, sat down and wrote the first phrase. I was there a couple

of hours, I wrote some three pages, and these were the first three pages of the novel. Of course, the first phrase is a kind of fanfare: "If only I could explain to you how changed I am since those days!" This type of phrase is like a white ticket, as are the two that follow. But then I began to see a person (Costa 186).

Sontag explains in this interview that in her fiction she begins by imagining her characters through language, with a phrase that identified their voice. That phrase would haunt her. "Nothing, nothing could pull me from this rock. Then I would think: 'Who speaks like this?' When you ask this question, you open up the element of your own landscape. There was someone stoic, and this was his or her manner of speaking about grief" (Costa 185).

This technique fixed her characters, often without bodies, sometimes even without gender, into the first person. It is a technique that frustrates many when they read her fiction; they wonder if she intends to get outside of her head. Her characters rarely escape the fate of being inside their own heads, or at the very most, their success is ambiguous. She has also said recently that beginning with language is the way she composes her essays. After the first draft it is then not untypical for her to rewrite as many as twenty times. In fiction, however, "I'm almost there on the first draft."

Following the publication of *The Benefactor*, she was writer-in-residence at Rutgers University, New Brunswick. She won the George Polk Memorial Award for her critical work in 1964; she was given a grant by the Rockefeller Foundation in 1965, and was a Guggenheim fellow in 1966.

For the most part, *the Benefactor* was received politely, respectfully. It sold 4,000 copies, slightly better than average for a first novel. It was her 1964 essay "Notes on Camp" that drew fire. She had dragged lowbrow culture into the halls where being able to distinguish between high and low and defend the former was the mark of a critic. *Partisan Review* had paid her $75 for it, but it interested *Esquire* enough to have them offer her a steady job as a movie critic. She turned *Esquire* down. She did not want to be that kind of writer. That essay, and some nasty epithets (such as being "Miss Camp") followed her for some time. In complaining about reviewers and how tired she was of being misquoted, she said in 1968:

The most obvious example is the essay on Camp which many people seem to think is all I've done. But it's only one of about forty essays, and even by itself it's been misrepresented. People are always using terms like 'high camp' and 'low camp' in reference to it, and in fact

I never mentioned either one. I don't know what they mean. I guess
I shouldn't complain. The audience I'm really concerned about is
small—my close friends and the writers I respect. I don't even read
most of the stuff that is written about me. (Toback 59)

She had to show this temper, probably, because her derring-do in
crossing cultural boundaries typically had been received with statements like Alicia Ostriker's review of *Against Interpretation*. Sontag's
call for a "sensuous modern criticism gives minor artists too much
credit." Ostriker continues:

> Many of the styles and authors that Sontag admires, like Surrealism,
> Pop, Happenings, Genet, Peter Weiss in *Marat/Sade,* can be classified
> as representing what Coleridge called Secondary Imagination, or
> Fancy, as opposed to Primary Imagination. That is, they are works of
> combinations and juxtapositions, not synthesis. In dripping watches
> in the desert, in Campbell's soup cans in the Modern Museum, in
> baby dolls glued to machine parts, in black people playing white
> people, in "discussing the deepest issues of contemporary morality
> and history" used as "decor, props, sensuous material," we see artists
> having ironic fun, fooling around with things. There is nothing wrong
> with this, until fooling around tries to impose itself on all other
> possibilities.[4]

As her fame grew, so did the attempt to diminish her accomplishment. Recently, Norman Podhoretz repeated an often heard, mean-
spirited idea that the young Sontag had a place made for her by friends,
and, with the absence of Mary McCarthy from the scene, had been
selected to fill a slot as the next "dark lady" of letters. Richard Bernstein
asked Sontag about this view of her in 1989:

> Ms. Sontag bristles at that idea, even though she doesn't reject it
> altogether. She remembers once, some 20 years ago, meeting the
> novelist Mary McCarthy, a combatant in many literary controversies
> who was often identified as her predecessor in the "dark lady" role.
> Ms. McCarthy told Ms. Sontag, "Oh, you're the imitation me."
> "She said it to embarrass me, I suppose," Ms. Sontag said, going on
> to denounce as misogynous any effort to give her or any another [sic]
> woman a preordained role. (Bernstein C17)

Her fame was becoming intrusive; she was becoming something of
a legend, and a "legend is like a tail," she said back in 1968, "it follows
you around mercilessly—awkward, useless, essentially unrelated to
you" (Toback 115). The few interviews she gave in this period were
directed at fending off the image of her as yet another "personality" of

the youth movement. She had to insist on her privacy, and nurse the impression of her seriousness, and endlessly explain why she combined her tastes. Her loves where Beckett and Kafka, Wittgenstein, the opera—especially Wagner—and yes, the Supremes and Patti Smith. Had she experimented with drugs? Yes, for a while she smoked grass, and the memory of the relaxation she felt under its influence is enough now to help her relax. "I didn't know you were *supposed* to relax or that any good could come out of it [*laughing*]" (Cott 50).

She has also been described as exploiting coffee and taking speed. Her picture of her working habits seems speed driven. "I don't eat, or I eat very irregularly and badly and skip meals; and I try to sleep as little as possible. My back hurts, my fingers hurt. I get headaches. And it even cuts sexual desire. . . . I'm totally undisciplined, and I just do it in long, obsessional stretches" (Cott 50). However, most of all, she wanted her readers to know her stand on the current variety of dangerous drugs. Why do it, she asks, after telling a horror story of a good friend in Paris, a writer of twenty, who went through a sequence of hallucinations and had to be treated with longterm chemical antidotes. "I want to be wide-awake and lucid, not deaden myself into stupor or agitate myself into frenzy." Of Leary she said: "He's unspeakably vulgar. Even when drugs are a mistake, the error is lessened if the intention is serious. But the kind of blatant exploitation and intellectual sham that Leary represents and promotes can only be destructive" (Cott 114–5). Now (in 1979) she does not even drink. *Time* magazine ignored these remarks and titled its piece on her "The Dark-Lady of Turn-On."

With that kind of sorry media attention, Sontag would never shake off the detractors, from the ones who insisted that she had her opportunities made for her, to those who said she had just enough sense to follow the trends. As late as 1982, Stanley Aronowitz in reviewing *The Susan Sontag Reader,* called her "the major American example of the Critic as Star," the "idol" of the New Left and the feminist movement and a "guru." He makes this remark: "As with many gurus, Sontag followed her followers for a while; she wrote polemics against the Vietnam war, temporarily leaving behind her searing renunciation of social reality as a object of critical exploration."[5] Aronowitz parallels Sontag to Mailer, as one of those writers "engaged in perennial advertisements for themselves."

Aronowitz wrote the above for *The Village Voice,* a journal that especially likes to place itself squarely in the midst of its own legend-making powers. Little in Sontag's language suggests the iconographic self-painting of the idol-to-be; what she has written about soul-questing and human-potential movements would paralyze with confusion any tribe who sought her spiritual guidance. She just could not use her persona the way Goodman did or Mailer did, she said back in the 1960s, and so far she has not. The other matter, whether she has worn her fame well or used it for the good, the answer is, probably. Fame is a dragon's tail.

Her politics were never "instantaneous," as others have accused. "Whatever challenges this [American existential] chauvinism, which is the basis of American consensus on foreign policy, is good—however simplified and unelaborated," Sontag wrote in 1965 in her chance to respond to a *Partisan Review* statement on Vietnam and the Dominican Republic ("On Vietnam" 656). It is not a position she has retreated from, even now. Then it marked her first step into American politics on the side of the New Left and away from the liberal "appeasement" of Cold War ideas she had too often found among the other signers. She had gone over to the other side, with Rahv and Mailer. For this, she had to part company. To the older New York Intellectuals she had joined what Howe said, what most of his generation would end up saying, was the "crude, fashion-driven, smugly moralistic" politics of "posture, gesture, and *frisson*."

Sontag went to Hanoi and wrote about it, to Cuba in 1969 and wrote about it for the left journal *Ramparts*. Again for *Ramparts*, she wrote about Sweden after having lived there for seven months while working on her film *Duet for Cannibals*. Around this time she developed her habit of staying half the year in Paris. For all Paris's attractions, perhaps one included being away from the U. S. at a time when her conscience was torn. In 1969 she explained:

> I feel more like the people who left—or wanted to leave—Nazi Germany in the Thirties. The internal situation in America today may be better than it was in Germany then, but I don't see any differences at all in the foreign policy . . . I guess what keeps me going is a sense of responsibility. I have no illusions about my power, but even if I affect only a handful of people, I feel obliged to stay here and speak. (Toback 60)

Overall, the 1960s were an immensely productive time for Sontag. She published *Against Interpretation* in 1966, *Death Kit* (a novel) in 1967, *Trip to Hanoi* in 1968, *Styles of Radical Will* in 1969. *Duet for Cannibals* was shown at the 1969 New York Film Festival.

Sontag's third medium, film, absorbed the next four years. As in conceiving, writing, directing, controlling the appetite of the camera, building on the artistry of others, can absorb. She got her chance back in 1967 when her reputation as a critic won her a place on the jury of both the Venice Film Festival and the New York Film Festival. Shortly thereafter, Goran Lindgren, president of Sandrew Film and Theater AB, invited Sontag to make a film in Sweden. Sharon Smith reports her as saying: "I would have taken any offer, just to show I could do it. I would gave gone to Afghanistan."[6]

In July 1968, after seeing a screening of *Duet for Cannibals* seated alone, Lindgren came out to tell Sontag that she was "welcome" to try another. "So accustomed was I by then to the laconic, shy, spectacularly honest Swedes that it never occurred to me to wonder if I needed a contract or a letter to be sure that Sandrew really meant to produce my second film. And, of course, I didn't," she writes in her introduction to that second film, *Brother Carl*. At the end of the screening for the second film, unfortunately, Lindgren shook her hand and said nothing. If she was disappointed, she was also, she reports, relieved. "I find that I am relieved not to be asked back. That particular, intense, "Swedish" trip inside my head is over. I can start making films elsewhere" (BC vii–viii). That "elsewhere" became Israel after the Yom Kippur War of 1973, and to the battle sites strewn with wreckage. She had intended to make a feature film, but "reality was something you didn't invent," she explained to Smith. The result is an 87-minute documentary of desert and death called *Promised Lands*. David Rieff is credited as an assistant director.

Promised Lands, a tormented response to the dry land that so many centuries of fighting has littered with the dead, is yet a study in her themes. It takes no position; instead like her other films and novels, it roams in a desert where emotions had run high and what has been lost is a postulate for the other questions. Her most recent film, *Unguided Tour* (1983), tells of the end of romance of two lovers who are touring the decaying monuments of Italy. It too is another walk through a cemetery.

The early 1970s called forth a shift in self-awareness in Sontag, as it did for many women. The feminist movement was demanding a raised consciousness. "I was conscious of being an exception," she writes in 1972, in response to a general questionnaire sent to her and five other women by *Libre*, a Spanish language, left-wing quarterly edited in Paris:

> but it hadn't ever seemed hard to be an exception; and I accepted the advantages I enjoyed as my right. I know better now.
> My case is not uncommon . . . Granted a good dose of talent and a certain cheerful or merely dogged lack of self-consciousness, one can even escape (as I did) the initial obstacles and derision that are likely to afflict a woman who insists on autonomy. . . . Every liberal grouping (whether political, professional or artistic) needs a token woman.
> . . . My good fortune is really beside the point. What does it prove? Nothing.

Any already liberated woman who complacently accepts her privileged situation participates in the oppression of other women. . . .

The first responsibility of a "liberated" woman is to lead the fullest, freest, and most imaginative life she can. The second responsibility is her solidarity with other women. She may live and work and make love with men. But she has no right to represent her situation as simpler, or less suspect, or less full of compromises than it really is. . . . . ("The Third World of Women" 206)

1975 brought a terrible shock. While she was finishing her book on photography, during a routine check-up, breast cancer was discovered. Her doctors were pessimistic; they thought she had only a ten percent chance of living for two more years. She faced five operations, including mastectomy, and several years of chemotherapy.

In the beginning, "besides feeling the physical pain, I was terribly frightened. I was experiencing the most acute kind of animal panic. But I also experienced moments of elation. A tremendous intensity. I felt as if I had embarked on a great adventure. It was the adventure of being ill and dying" (Cott 48). It wasn't long, "two weeks" before she "cleaned out" those ideas about the stimulus of deprivation and about having caused her disease. "The first thing I thought: What did I do to deserve this? I've led the wrong life. I've been too repressed. Yes, I suffered a great grief five years ago [possibly the drowning-suicide of her friend Susan Taubes] and this must be the result of that intense depression" (Cott 48). When she asked her doctor about these fears, he so quickly dismissed them that "I began to think about TB; the argument of the thing fell into place. . . . Tuberculosis is particularly interesting because its cause was discovered in 1882, but the cure only in 1944. The myths and fantasies about TB—*The Magic Mountain*'s it's-just-love-deferred, or Kafka's it's-really-my-mental-illness-connecting-itself-into-a physical-thing—started to vanish when almost no one died of TB anymore. And if the people discover the causes of cancer but don't find a cure for it, then the myths about cancer will go on" (Cott 48).

For the first six months she could not write. She was drugged with sedatives. When the idea for *Illness as Metaphor* came to her, she wanted to start right away, but felt she had to finish the last two essays of *On Photography* (the first six had already been published in *The New York Review of Books*). Then she wrote *Illness* in a month and a half, the fastest she had ever written; it was "cathartic." She knew that it was going to be important for many people, and it was. She received many letters telling her how the book saved their life or how it encouraged them to go to a doctor or to change doctors.

Since her brush with death ("nothing would be the same again"), contact with people has become much more important to her. "Now I debate with myself about the intensity of solitude that is required in order to write and the necessity for me to be with people. What saved my life, beside the extraordinary chemotherapy, was the effect of having received, not only from persons close to me, but also acquaintances and strangers who appeared suddenly, the sympathy they showed in such a marvelous way" (Costa 189). To help pay her medical bills, friends raised several thousand dollars.

On Photography (1977) won her The National Book Critics Circle Award and a $50,000 advance for the paperback rights. In 1978 both *Illness as Metaphor* and her collection of short stories, *I, Etcetera*, appeared. During the 1970s she received another Rockefeller grant (1974); a second Guggenheim (1975); an Ingram Merrill Foundation award (1976); an Arts and Letters award from the American Academy of Arts and Letters (1976) and was made a member of that Academy. In 1978 Sontag joined New York University Institute for the Humanities as a founding fellow. This is an unfunded position.

In 1980 Sontag published her third collection of essays, *Under the Sign of Saturn*, and in 1982 was honored with *A Susan Sontag Reader* (though she says she feels only "a little past the starting point") which begins with an appreciation by Elizabeth Hardwick. She was also asked to stage the Pirandello play *As You Desire Me* for the Teatro Stabile di Tormo, Italy, for the 1980–81 season. Again, she is comfortable in using the opportunity to examine her own themes:

> What fascinates me about the Pirandello play is the theme of psycho-logical cannibalism. So I moved the character played by Greta Garbo in the film version to the center of my production as a sort of queen bee who entraps the other characters, but ultimately she is their victim. Of course, to do this, I had to leave a great deal out. But I think in some ways I made it a better play than it is. By defining something that is also part of my repository of fantasy . . . [like her essay on Canetti] [it is] filtered through my temperament. (Copeland 87)

In 1983 she finished directing and editing her fourth film, *Unguided Tour*, with help from the Italian government. She was next asked by Harvard's American Repertory Theatre to direct the premiere produc-tion of Milan Kundera's play *Jacques and His Master* (January, 1985; Music by Elizabeth Swados).

Sontag has her enthusiasts for her film work and theater work, but American reviewers at least seem of one mind: one way or the other they say that she substitutes intellectualized concepts for dramatic sense. They have said the same about her fiction. On her side, her models have been Godard, Bresson, Bergman; Kafka, Beckett. She is apt to recall the early influence of Paul Goodman's *Johnson* stories and Laura Riding's *Progress of Stories*, and lately the beautifully wrought imaginative pieces of J. G. Ballard.

Sontag is the voice of Sarah Bernhardt in the documentary film *Sarah*, which premiered at the New York Film Festival in September 1988. She has been publishing throughout this time short essays on dance, Dutch painting, Fassbinder, Mapplethorpe, Wagner, and has nearly completed her third novel *The Western Half* about Polish and Soviet émigrés in Paris, New York, and Midwestern academe. No doubt, the novel draws from her friendship with Czeslaw Milosz and Joseph Brodsky.

She is now in her fifties, and she senses her seniority. Often, lately, she has been called upon to speak on the condition of writers. She could hardly not do so, since the 1980s seem to be a time of the international conference. What have been the motives for writers to respond? Conservatism at home, terrorism and censorship abroad, the end of militarist regimes and amnesty, the rise of religious totalitarianism, apartheid; for Sontag, especially, there is the paradox of ameliorations between East and West in a tide of refreshed concerns about the abuses of communism. There are many reasons why this somewhat fluid body of writers has been called to the podium. A "superpopulation," Sontag has grumbled.

The podium turns out to be an uncanny place. Sontag is still defensive about her now infamous Town Hall Speech (New York City: February 6, 1982). A rally had been called to demonstrate for the Polish Solidarity Movement and to deny, according to its organizers, "the Cold Warriors the support of a workers' mass movement in Poland which they would be first to suppress in the United States, just as their clients were doing in Turkey and El Salvador." There were to be twenty speakers.

Sontag has said that she wanted to say something a "little different, to make a little trouble." What she did was to make her audience out to be unwitting dupes of Marxist "angelic" language, discounting what the émigrés from the Soviet block were saying, trying to shore up communism by making equivocating distinctions between the bad old Stalinist regimes and the fledgling socialist ones. "Communism is fascism with a human face," she stated to a round of boos and hisses. *The Soho News* printed her speech without permission, and then gathered and printed dozens of replies; the debate raged on in *The Village Voice* and *The Nation*; within weeks, enough of the campaigners from the Old Left and New Right, or New Left and New Post-Marxists, had made such "violent, sneering, vituperative" statements that Sontag could justifiably feel stunned. She sued *The Soho News* (it folded for other reasons), but that act only added fuel to the fire.

Several years later, writing as one of the organizers of the upcoming 48th Congress of PEN International (New York City, January 1986, over 600 writers with their guest in attendance, a spectacular event, a fuming cauldron of dissent beginning with Norman Mailer's selection of Secretary of State George Schultz as keynote speaker) she shared some more thoughts on that speech. First, she considers generally the irony of the writer "starting out as the sole devotee, as well as deity, in a sect of one," who is "eventually convened to take part, as an elder, in the Church of Writers" ("When Writers Talk Among Themselves" 22). More and more she has become one of the "reliables" at such affairs, part of the "fellow graying and gray eminences who I know will likely be future co-invitees."

She then shifts to her own political views by dating the "current character" of international writers' gatherings from an ambitious congress on dissidence organized under the aegis of the Venice Biennale in December 1977 where the only Italian writer present was Alberto Moravia. "Hard as it is to believe now, in 1977 it still felt premature for *bien-pensant* Italian writers to be anti-Communist in this blunt fashion." Finally, she slips in her Town Hall speech of four years before. It was a matter of the wrong context. She had not been speaking to a defined audience. "One reason for cherishing the writers' congress is that it may be one of the last places in our current cultural life where the closed session still has some viability" ("When Writers Talk Among Themselves" 23). She explained to Bernstein, "I have a lot of anxiety about being understood."

In 1987, Sontag became president of PEN, following Mailer's confounded leadership and the fiasco at the 48th Congress. Among other things, he had refused to apologize to the women who had protested the poor representation of women. Mentioning Sontag by name, he declared: "there are not many women, like Susan Sontag, who are intellectuals first, poets and novelists second." Sontag reputedly called Mailer a "mean-spirited dog." Sontag's job as President has taken her to Seoul for 52nd International PEN Congress where she participated in the general protest and embarrassment tactics against the South Korean government on behalf of jailed writers and publishers. Most recently she has been a chief spokesperson for writers in defense of Salman Rushdie. The New York PEN chapter organized a public reading and protest over Khomeini's death sentence.

In 1989, Sontag published further thoughts on metaphor and illness, *AIDS and Its Metaphors.* She had been weeks at the deathbed of a friend, out of which came a short story "The Way We Live Now." The story dispassionately recounts what people say under such circumstances, as a study in the swirl of voices about a center. It is moving. The book, however, landed in the middle of issues where words count in the millions of dollars of potential funding and in the comfort of the dying. So far, it has had a rough time.

She has plans to write an essay on intellectuals and Communism, beginning with the example of André Gide's disillusioning trip to the Soviet Union in 1936. She has said she is also thinking about an essay on Japan.

2

Key Terms

Most of Sontag's fictional characters are neither heroes nor anti-heroes as we have come to understand these figures. They lack the appeal of having mirrored our condition, satirically or otherwise. They live too separately; they are too much governed by dreams. In a sense, her fiction itself displays what the characters suffer from—excessive control: enigmas tend to reverberate interiorly. Dilemmas and glimpses of the other, non-self-referential world are replaced too often by closed possibilities and imposed wisdoms. Into these hermetically sealed lives come these intrusions, these truncated, pithy, antithetical statements seemingly in the mouth of her characters yet distinctly like Sontag in her other aspects. They are one of her most recognizable devices.

In her essays, she includes so many of these kinds of statements that the logic of her arguments jigsaw. One comes to understand that sharpness and objection matter more than development and substantiation. She cannot be much of a theorist then, some complain. Her interest in the individual work is too slight. Her statements have a melodramatic cast, her thoughts are merely compiled in that moralizing, French epigrammatic way. Then too, occasionally, in the midst of her "reason-dictates" tone, she tosses hand grenades.

How striking is the difference between her voice in her first volume of essays and Trilling's graceful, methodological circumventions of virtually the same years—in *Beyond Culture*, 1965. What Sontag has to say is held in tension, the terms of her questions are more directed, as if she were prompted by a determination to enter the arena, during that lull in the critical controversies, more ready to fight. She writes as if she is taking up a gauntlet, however gingerly it had been laid down before her.

That was a time when criticism was smothering modernism in its welcome, a welcome so reasonable that Trilling could write in "The Fate of Pleasure" (1963):

> The energy, the consciousness, and the wit of modern literature derive its violence against the specious good. We instinctively resent questions which suggest that there is fault to be found with the one saving force in our moral situation—that extruded "high" segment of our

general culture which, with its exigent, violently subversive spirituality, has the power of arming us against, and setting us apart from, all
in the general culture that we hate and fear.[1]

Obscured in Trilling's impenetrable "we" lies a challenge: "whether
the perverse and morbid idealism of modern literature is not to be
thought of as being precisely political, whether it does not express a
demand which in its own way is rational and positive and which may
be taken into account by a rational and positive politics" (73). What
Trilling means by this is a general permission, given in other times to
heroes, saints, martyrs, and in these times to artists, to lead exemplary
subversive lives or to create exemplary subversive works.

Sontag recently told an interviewer that she remembers being moved
by Trilling's essay. While that remark is an offhanded hint only to the
origins of her own search for a method, her essays are full of queries
into the exemplariness of this age's spiritual project, full of discussions
with herself about what this politics might be like. She is spying into
tenets of modernism as if it were a practice, as if it could be put to the
test of a politics.

In 1963 Sontag had just published a novel in which she examines
that inheritance of the "perverse and morbid" in literature, especially
as it might have been reinterpreted by the younger writers in France in
the 1950s from the generation that had preceded them. When Trilling
makes his call for "a novelist we do not yet have but must surely have
one day, who will take into serious and comic account the actualities
of the spiritual life of our time" (71), she had just finished being that
kind of novelist. To Trilling's thought that the "life of competition for
spiritual status is not without its own peculiar sordidness and absurdity," she could have pointed to the whole character of her protagonist
and episode after episode in his story.

Sontag had acceded to a time in America's critical life when the
residues of left puritanism were blowing away, when the hard work to
drum out the 1930s' broad realist aesthetic (of sentiment, type, and
brotherhood of victims and the folk) was finished. What was still being
done were efforts to accommodate that "extruded 'high'" art into
American ideals. That became Sontag's stepping off place, almost certain as she was from the beginning that this was an aesthetic that forbad
accommodation. Trilling, on his side, could end his essay with the
reassurances that:

> before we conclude that the tendencies in our literature which we
> have remarked on are nothing but perverse and morbid, let us recall
> that although Freud did indeed say that 'the aim of all life is death,'

> the course of his argument leads him to the statement that 'the organism wishes to die only in its own fashion,' only through the complex fullness of its appropriate life. (76)

To Sontag, the impact of those lines might have come too close to the other forms of pious "fellow-traveling" Americans are all too prone to. For what was this complex fullness of a life in such extreme negation? Sontag would write with a sure and quick defense for artworks that shared next to nothing with this imperious aesthetic, such as Jack Smith's *Flaming Creatures* or Camp. But that question kept returning to her, sending her to Europe to become a critic of all manner of Europe's coming to grips with its recent past. She would skirt the revivals of left Hegelianism, left Freudianism, left Nietzscheanism, left existentialism and left structuralism, listening and thinking about them, but not captured. What captures her is the attempt to "name the contours of the sensibility" Trilling felt came after pleasure as a motive in art and life.

The following is a discussion of the terms of her discourse. I have emphasized features that filtered out over time and give some thoughts to their individual troubles. This is not offered as an anatomy of a system—Sontag has avoided systems—rather as a spotlight on certain repetitive elements that lead her through her questions, while revealing her instincts, which begin to have a dialogue with another. These terms form part of her practice (for want of a better word) as a writer and critic.

Epigrammatical Mode

Sontag's writing is epigrammatical, though this is no special observation about her unless one keeps in mind that the epigram, unlike its close cousins the aphorism and the apothegm, embraces a sense of inversion. The contradictory inspires a writer given to writing in epigrams, as a mode of thought in itself. The epigram rests on its turn of thought away from sense, as in C. L. Kline's "the sacred duty of lawlessness." The epigram may be sage and witty but it rarely assumes the burden, in good faith, of addressing the principle of the thing it observes—that's the aphorism's function. Mouthed often, epigrams instead profess, as one character in Sontag's fiction explains, a "line of gnomic crap."

The epigrammatical mode can be recognized, overall, by the penchant of the writer to make these quizzical statements as little or as large as his or her subject warrants (the set piece for the whole plot, perhaps) and then confound them. The point of the statement seems to be its pointedness, the encapsulation of what is experienced as a paradox—the interminable way in which meanings turn in on themselves, values reverse, and the only worthy gestures are the disruptive ones. The modern epigrammatist writes wisdoms, but not for the sake of enlightenment. They are instead intended as didacticisms of the perverse—truths that hold true because of their power to evoke the negation of what seems. Or truths neatly conceived yet so bland they blow away under the force of the contrary evidence of the story. Combine the hyper-reflexivity of modern writing with the later focus on the independence of writing, reading, and interpretation, and the effect is to move the writer towards a voiceless speech that comes from nowhere. In Sontag's fiction, for example, even though the fate of her characters tends to belie what they offer as rationalizations, their voices carry their neutralized assertions out of the story. That is, Sontag's characters are often shown to be quite mistaken about what they think they are doing, yet their formulations, suddenly in heaps, are not really to be disregarded. The vacuity of their experience is already presumed. They have explored nether values and the diminution of things, and in that realm their observations hold.

Yet Sontag aches for simpler truths, for aphoristic writing, perhaps the homiletic. Proverbs and folk sayings, everyone's favorite mottoes lay strewn about on placards in the charnel house of the last pages of *Death Kit*. The dead there have marched to their graves carrying their little judgments. The next reader finds these doomed, happier assurances in splinters.

As for irony—the epigrammatist works inside the strictures of an elaborate awareness of forms; to that extent she or he participates in the spirit of modernist gamesmanship. But the game takes on an edge when the language approaches the discursive wisdom of the epigram. Because the epigram is about reality and its negation, it may be the joke of jokes. Few writers find it a whimsical matter.

As for suffering—the epigram bears the writer away from suffering, being abstract and not dependent on things of the senses. In fact, a text composed of epigrams is tighter than one in which the eye passes over detail. One feels the precision which the writer's intelligence (Sontag's revered adjective) confers on the world as a triumph for the speaker, against some lesser successes such as the connoisseur enjoys. "Intelligence" finds these other modes a little lugubrious, a little obsequious, a little rhetorical.

This mode attracts the philosophical writer strongly given to thoughts about the enlightenment's demise, who, nonetheless, takes no delight in the irrational, rather discounts metaphorical vehicles, and distrusts nothing as much as the springs of feeling. The thrilling possibilities of living in mediavision, a melee of fired perceptions, which so excites some recent writers barely touches the epigrammatist. Sometimes, she may feel left out of the party, and tries to get into the swing of things, high on analytical wit. But she dances in weighted shoes.

On Silences

I have emphasized the efficacy of the mode of writing in epigrams, when of course epigrams give pleasure. They let the space around them grow rich, like the grass around tombstones, on what is buried. To the very extent they are pointed, precise, they outline the silence of what they do not speak. The pleasure is in the poise won. All around the silences reverberate anew. This is the kind of pleasure that entices the writer who sits reflecting before a commitment or a journey. Afterward the experience may want telling for its own sake. So she stops in unfinished propositions, readying herself against surprises, content to explore some of the contradictions before meeting them. She means to undermine the fallible, or to pay homage to mortality before disappearing beneath.

This mode fits Sontag's purpose well, for example, in her short story "Project for a Trip to China." We are invited to sit with Sontag as she considers what it means to her to go to China after so many years thinking about it as the place of her father's death and of herself as a political figure. She works downward just as she tells about how, when she was ten years old (her father had died a few years before):

> ... I dug a hole in the back yard. I stopped when it got to be six feet by six feet by six feet. "What are you trying to do?" said the maid. "Dig all the way to China?"
>
> No. I just wanted a place to sit it in. ... The ivory and quartz elephants had been auctioned.
>
>
>
> —my refuge
> —my cell
> —my study
> —my grave
> (I,E 8)
>
>

In this story Sontag creates that epigrammatical feel—that uncertainty structured into the assertions—by the interlocking of thought and objects rather than by letting the statement brush up against its foil. What she evokes is a lattice work of spaces in which she can place the accounts of what she will see. In this spareness, we do find an orient of the heart, a porcelain beauty, a world dignified by silences. She prefers not to write about what is consecrated by history. In this hesitation, we recognize a tribute to enormity.

The end story in *I, etcetera* "Unguided Tour" (made into a film by Sontag) pulls her themes of repetitions, pain, language and literature along on another journey. The woman speaker confesses to her weariness with travel, to the predictability of thought and feeling. She knows before she begins, "all the possibilities of travel," "all the words I am going to utter again." Wherever she travels, "it's to say goodbye." Yet she continues to wander insatiably; some wound compels her. And only the wound is sufficient to give "lyricism" to the going which words would otherwise make redundant.

Silence restrains that self, protects it from contact, from being measured by life. This aspect of the "aesthetics of silence" goes unexamined in Sontag's longish study. There's hardly any mention of a personal or historical correlative to the artist's use of silence, as if it were so ubiquitous a choice in the twentieth century, the century itself has borne it.

What Sontag intends for us to understand, though I always suspect she is thinking of the European epoch after the war, is that sensibility which had been nurtured by Gide, Artaud, Genet—composite figures in her fiction—and which came up in the silences of Blanchot or Duras. They walked about as emotional skeletons, these postwar survivors. If they chose life it was from some incomprehensible, innate desire, of the kind Frau Anders displays in Sontag's *The Benefactor*. The seeming amorality of Genet, the murderers and criminals he came to love, was an image through which they came closer to their own manipulativeness and arrogance as ideologues who were as likely to kick as save those cowering in the Nazis' shadows.

After the war the cruelty in themselves damned them to equations: "I am like them," writes Duras in *The Lover*. "Collaborators, the Fernandezes were. And I, two years after the war, I was a member of the French Communist Party. The parallel is complete and absolute. The two things are the same, the same pity, the same call for help, the same lack of judgment, the same superstition if you like, that consists in believing in a political solution to a personal problem." Survivors by accident, they link themselves to survivors by cowardice and betrayal, and conclude: "It's in the silence that the war is still here." Toward the cool, distant silences, or above the feverish one, their language strikes poses. It is that kind of voice which plagues Sontag, so close in tone and purpose to Blanchot's narrator in *Death Sentence* of 1948: "The unfortunate thing is that after having waited for so many years, during which silence, immobility, and patience carried to the point of inertia did not for one single day stop deceiving me, I had to open my eyes all at once and allow myself to be tempted by a splendid thought, which I am trying in vain to bring to its knees. Perhaps these precautions will not be precautions".[2]

Lately Sontag is more prone to wandering in the halls of old cathedrals via their paintings, musing on the melancholy of the body as it is transformed by paint and camera. Even so, her language strains for the epigrammatical effect embedded in the silences of those experiences.

Spirit of Negation

One cannot be a modern epigrammatist without the spirit of negation running through one's head. The "no" advanced the project of the Enlightenment in its strike at authority; the "no" sends one's defiance out against destiny. The "no" outlines the self from all that would incorporate it. The "no" is the moveable force of the dialectic, and as such it thus affirms what it negates. Negation's spirit is vigorous, astute, independent. It does not, however, lighten one's way. It sees the world in terms of powerful, weighty oppositions. In the sway of that spirit one is apt to give oneself moral dignity, so strong is the sense that what one is battling against is the necessary enemy.

In 1967, Sontag writes in "The Aesthetics of Silence" that the modern artist is "committed to the idea that the power of art is located in its power to negate." From the comfort of that widely held assumption, Sontag can enter the silence that beckons her with a brisk, objective mind. Silence can then exist "as a *decision*—in the exemplary suicide of the artist", and it can also exist "as a *punishment*—self-punishment, in the exemplary madness of artists" (*AI* 9). She continues to feel along the walls for the limits of the artistic uses of silence, "boundary notions," not to be understood without the dialectic.

The dialectic calls up the "leading terms of a particular spiritual and cultural rhetoric" (*AI* 11). From the earliest past of this century, the dialectic of negation of contemporary values upheld the widest promise of experiencing a whole set of new relations. In art, negation was that tenet of modernism which called upon creation at the moment of destruction of older artistic forms. In the realm of the spirit, for the sake of the autonomy of the spirit, negation was to be exercised in all spheres. In Sontag's carefully retired language of "that particular rhetoric" one can hear that she senses, concurs in the idea, that by the middle of the century that credo was slipping away.

Curiously, when one considers how she was identified with 1960s radicalism, her phrase was deaf to or cynical about the re-enlistment of the ethos of negation in the political upswing of those times. The

Frankfurt School had taught that negative dialectics had the power to break through those dementing forces of modern life—its monolithic structures, its paradoxical tolerances, the looney ways it fed consumerism and anaesthetized with media. Perhaps Sontag sensed that despite its apocalyptic moods, the age's allegiance to negation was thin. There were too many benefits in living in a very rich, compulsively expansive society. (Or, as Sontag puts it: "in the post-political, electronically connected cosmopolis in which all serious modern artists have taken out premature citizenship" [AI 34].) The age's feeling for negation, at least as evidenced in its art, was growing more attenuated and mannered. In her words, the aesthetics of negation was living off of myths.

"In my opinion," she writes, "the myths of silence and emptiness are about as nourishing and viable as might be devised in an 'unwholesome' time—which is, of necessity, a time in which 'unwholesome' psychic states furnish the energies for most superior work in the arts. Yet one can't deny the pathos of these myths" (AI 11).

Pathos of Heroes

That "pathos" cues Sontag's readers that an iconic evaluation is going on. Her moderns possess pathos, as some gift they have for endurance. Pathos keeps futility at bay, when it fixes on that subject with all of its attention. Then the two emotions lock in a kind of tug of war. This is the struggle of tragic heros, and it is tragedy that brightens the star of pathos in the pantheon of sentiments. In any other sense of the word, we tend to be less sure of its virtues.

Sontag has spoken of the pathos of children, by which she invokes our more commonplace appreciation of their fragility and their neediness. A touch of these qualities can be felt in that intimate and bonded way of hers of addressing the *hauteur* of the modernist aesthetic (but only a touch—the hopefulness of the childhood of an aesthetic). Mostly, it is her modern's steadfastness in suffering that raises them to heroic stature. She admires the inexorability of their ideals, which drive them step by step to self-dissolve, or should they be heroes of the mind, their inexorable pursuit of self-confrontation. They have claims to some of tragedy's merits, if only in their pathos. She would be the first to acknowledge that they would not themselves believe that they are worthy of tragedy's impulses or even believe in its forms.

Of course this pathos is the opposite of the quality of voice and approach to ideas the young Sontag liked to make, that is, those epigrammatical incursions. To steal a phrase from Sontag's essay on Sartre, where she describes his solution "to his disgust," the epigrammatical mode is "impertinent" (*AI* 98). Only later, into the 1970s, does the other side of herself yearn towards the fullness of pathos.

By then, she has had more time to wrestle with several sides of herself and more time to test the climate in which her respectful, ambivalent looking back at the ethos of modernism is being received. Our sympathy with the pathos of heroes includes the luxury of afterthought. Their stories tend to be conclusive. The pathos we carry away becomes a lovely haze in which we recall the world of their struggles, a far slighter thing than if we thought we were subject to the same purposes. Sontag, having directed her critical energies to the new temperament, has to sense what double or triple ironic release survives in her italicized references to the "heroic age" of modernism and the "pathos" of its myths. Or rather, her statements are an attempt at a release, because to her all serious art, such as the impassioned minimalism of that period, called forth and relied upon these, modernist "unwholesome" tenets.

Ethics

There is much at stake in this clash of formal temperaments, that is, between what might be called the classical or "heroic" modernism and its later variety (the literature and arts of the 40s and 50s and, arguably, modernism's roll-over into the postmodernism of the later 1960s and on). Two kinds of nourishments of consciousness are at stake, and thus, for Sontag, two kinds of ethical groundings.

Maire Jaanus Kurrik formulates the matter thus: classical [modern] novels *negate*, modernist [or, in my terms, late modernist] novels *delete*.[3] Admittedly, this is a gross oversimplification, a conceit. However, by taking a sight along this single line of inquiry, how negation metamorphoses, Kurrik can say things like this: later modernist novels make us uncomfortable not for what the books attack, but for what they override. The old humanist complaints against modernism—that modernism is nihilistic, tradition-destroying, the lamentable outcome of the excesses of Romantic mystification—can be countered with the argument that modernists say no to the power of God, destiny, authority, because the power of these things is mighty. The newer novelists are far less ambivalent: seemingly they can give up, erase, elide in a dispersed totality. The feel of deletion as it acts, then, is one of lessening, while the feel of negation is making something serious, complex, noble and ignoble.

One of the problems with deletion, as Kurrik writes, is that while "it may bypass the corruption of our yesses and no's" (236), "its own violence displaces the violence of negation" (232). It is left with a state of "nolition"—an inability to wish or want anything. Negativity turns to negativism, and from there a person descends to a deracinated, dematerialized, "gutted," and "drained" state.

Sontag's characters in her fiction play these scenarios out, literally perform these operations on themselves. Hippolyte sets out to "delete" himself; Diddy to die while his stomach is being pumped. Their stories are exercises in the farcical underside of the pathos of modernism's myths. They are meant to be "despised": that is, they are meant to be analyzed with wonder and indignation, sympathy and revulsion in a paradigmatically ambivalent fashion. They are antithetical portraits of a sensibility towards which Sontag has tried to establish a position that neither judges nor interprets.

But Sontag is motivated by a larger set of values. The ethics of negation can lift the spirit to the mountain top of mystical oneness; here the ethical secularist in Sontag is wary. The ethos of nolition of the new novel, on the other hand, cannot be abided with either, not directly, not by a moralist. It challenges Sontag to investigate Nietzsche's thought that art is a "complex kind of willing" set alongside of this world, a way of nourishing through its graces our capacity for willing. We are fed by the artist's autonomous spirit, we are provoked to will. But if that spirit claims no autonomy, if it likens the world to a rush of reception—then the challenge moves to the reader, to that artist inside the critic. It forces her to save the seriousness of the modernist project by herself working through it, until she has "exhausted it," silenced it imaginatively, or in that cryptic word of hers, "disburdened" herself of it. In Sontag's practice, modernism's turn towards deletion begins to dress itself in the vestments of an allegorical struggle.

The Authentic Moral Spirit

If all this battling with the paradoxes of deletion only mires one more in the paradoxical, it has to be thus. Paradox is a way of construing how it is to live in a time dominated by metacritical concerns, a time, as Sontag describes, that patronizes itself infinitely. One has to learn to live with that sense of being watched too closely, at every level too aware of historical indebtedness, structural imperatives or deceptive motives about one's own behavior and ideas. Looking back on the modernist flight from bad faith (the failed, incomplete project of negation), into nothingness, one realizes that the moment of pure freedom and creativity—the "present" of modernism—can never be achieved. One is hopelessly bound by the self thinking about the self striving for authentic life. One longs to be disburdened.

The authentic moral spirit, however, does not compromise with the world, and disburdenment can seem a compromise. So a kind of deal is struck: specifically, in the modernist scheme, one achieves authenticity by negating the authorities and conventions generating from one's own work. The self that is then transcended is not suspected of being the originator of sin, error, pollution, or arrogance (the mystic's demons); rather it is seen as an agent imposing false constraints. This self is both imperious and alienated from its own liberation. It can be won back to itself only by a downward slide to the very edge of existence.

Lionel Trilling finds in this ideal something he dislikes. In 1970, he writes in *Sincerity and Authenticity* (his way of retreating from that call for a positive politics of 1963) that it is indicative of our times that our intellectuals advocate the overcoming of alienation by completing it.[4] What bothers Trilling, what he distrusts in all that negating business of the rule of authenticity, is that the advocacy of completing alienation "involves no actual credence." To which argument, Sontag, in effect, replies: no actual credence, to be sure for no artist or intellectual can completely silence his or her own speech, adopt madness over sanity, destroy the creation upon which he or she experiences being an artist or intellectual without ceasing to be one. Short of that final, actual negation—utter silence, complete madness, successful suicide—there is that promise of acting out, and thereby learning from, the paradoxes of one's own positions.

Perhaps another explanation for the modernist phenomenon Trilling dislikes so much—the advocacy of overcoming alienation by completing it—is that advocacy play-acts the brave stance of negation while fulfilling a more primitive desire: self-consistency. In a state of total alienation a person finds a certainty of his or her own making. The insane person wills chaos and thereby escapes the disorientation of the sane person who merely suffers it. So does the artist of the aesthetic of silence. The sad realization comes upon the modernist, though, (perhaps then covering her with the honor of pathos) that in the self-made world of the alienated there can be a sense of being justified, but there is no justice; of being truthful to oneself, but of sharing no truth. There can only be an affirmation of a negative state in which we find others who are lost.

In Sontag's fiction and in a strain of her criticism—on Artaud, Cioran, Benjamin, for example—there is an advocacy, (sharply curtailed, argued with) for the allegorized world in which the artist pursues the negative state in order to know self-completion. And she is quick to point out that that state is morbid, like death if not a death itself. What surprises her is her own indelible "fascination with morbidity." Her frequent references to the need to "disburden" the self, to call modern thinking "disembowelment"—seemingly she regrets these capitulations to the reigning ideal. The political side of Sontag, the side that cares for moral action, repudiates both this apocalyptic sense of negation and its encroachment on well being. She is always buttressing the citadels of modernism to keep them from leaking into the present, spilling out their creeds into our lives.

Politics

History, though, has to offer at least a vision of that future where solitude is overcome and action is meaningful in order for it to sustain hope. In the 1960s there was a near devotional enthusiasm for pageantry, as if making a scene could reinforce the dream that progressive forces were alive. Sontag's politics had little interest in such events; she was more interested in having vision reflect on the categorical struggles within herself. Perhaps this is the one reason why "Trip to Hanoi" appeared to some as a romance. North Vietnam in the midst of its war with America provided a place to witness the instance of the opposite, a place making an "ethical fairytale." It offered her the chance to compare the spirit of positive action against the passivity of Western intellectualism, with that particular Western concern for individual style. In North Vietnam Sontag thought she found a unity of commitment, a simplicity of purposes and values. To her it was a place of unashamed moralism and nonironical values. It was a place, moreover, where there was no *avant-garde.* She believed North Vietnam challenged the premise she had helped establish—that the power of art was located in its power to negate; North Vietnam refuted her prescription for intelligence—there excessive self-consciousness did not even have an audience.

That she writes of her impression of the North Vietnamese with nothing less than the full presence of her complicating, modernist consciousness should not arouse the reader's cynicism. Sontag never intends to complete the transformation of herself into her negated self, since that transformation is an allegory. It suggests only that the self has to look to defeat its own material, intellectual, historical recalcitrance. Sontag's work is an exploration of the desire to negate, of the will to do it, not of the extent. The extent always troubles her.

What she would rather have us contemplate are the styles of this radical willing. She addresses these various styles in her first two collections of essays. By the time she writes of photography in the mid-1970s, she has come around again to adopt the position of some of the "left-humanist" critics before her. The modernist era has accomplished what she fears is a terrifying distortion of perception. Modernism, while negating itself as art, turns the world into art. It "aestheticizes" life. Modernism has made antiform, disaster, horror as much subject for aesthetic pleasure as beauty; it forces pleasurable regard beyond all boundaries until it becomes a wholly inadequate response. Experience and imagination can be both treated as spectacle. All that is needed is a very minimal integrity of elements.

Readiness, style, demonstration, action: these are the critical terms for the 1960s; Sontag's title "Styles of Radical Will" captures the essence of that preparedness, that nourishing of contemplation that provokes the will. Still consciously or not, the paradox of modernist action is already built into the phrase: having a style of radical will stands for the ultimate expression of the aestheticization of life, just as it stands for a complete response to the conditions of alienation.

One can live with contradictions as long as a greater cause by which one justifies oneself remains irrefutable. It is only later, under the sense that something has gone wrong, that paradoxical intentions are examined for what they are. After the radical culture faded in influence, it was not difficult to point out that its impact was weakened by its emphasis on modes or styles of being. Sontag was caught up in the same kinds of corrections, not repudiations, as were many others. In fact, Sontag soon distrusted the politics of style shortly after (see her essay on Cuba, 1969) and perhaps even while she was writing about it. The arguments for such a politics come too close to paralleling arguments for modernist art. In practice, this politics took too much from the ideals of freedom, and had too much the sense of individual volition, or rather, it dematerialized its sense of opposition, was too trusting of style, and too dependent on notions of the will.

But it has to be said, that in reading Sontag's "Trip to Hanoi" and the later "Project for a Trip to China," one realizes that Sontag cannot give up the essential esteem she has for both trips as trips and both places as opposites to her sensibilities. Rather than her attitude being romantic, or pastoral, or orientalist, her attitude reflects that tendency in her towards abstraction, a certain mechanical sense of negation—the very one that has been her target all along. She may "despise" her protagonists, she may be exasperated with the trajectory of modernist thinking—she spotted and roundly criticized this problem as early as her 1963 essay on Lévi-Strauss. She knows its power, nonetheless.

Melancholic Allegorist

In *Under the Sign of Saturn*, which is her sign as well as Walter Benjamin's (and by implication that of the others in this volume), melancholics seek to be contented with the ironies of mortality. But it seems that life is always outpacing them. Nervously, melancholics have a determination to sequester loss. They descend down the path to the contemplation of death and vileness and there, at that base, they find they are thinking in allegories. Faithless, they have been given a vehicle of redemption.

Benjamin writes:

> Ultimately in the death signs of the baroque the direction of allegorical reflection is reversed; on the second part of its wide arc it returns, to redeem. . . . And this is the essence of the melancholy immersion: that its ultimate objects, in which it believes it can most fully secure for itself that which is vile, turn into allegories, and that these allegories fill out and deny the void in which they are represented, just as, ultimately, the intention does not faithfully rest in the contemplation of bones, but faithlessly leaps forward to the ideal of redemption.[5]

Part of what Benjamin means by redemption is that which is gathered up into the idea, into a process which has its own essences but which at the same time bespeaks the totality. "That is its Platonic 'redemption' " (46). The melancholic here, in the German baroque drama, awaits a transfiguration that would bring him or her back into the eddies of becoming an authentic idea, presumably a tragic hero, or perhaps even a lesser being who is about to experience the satisfaction of self discovery. Otherwise, the melancholic's "wisdom is subject to the nether world," as a contemplation of dead things.

How strange that Sontag and others should take up as part of the idea of consciousness of our times this obscure artform, the German *Trauerspiel*, the emblem-ridden, allegorically coded, ceremony of sorrow, which the seventeenth century fetishized as melancholic contemplation. Perhaps some of that presumed affinity comes from the desire to write like Benjamin; another cause is that which Benjamin himself characterizes as the "fatal, pathological suggestibility" that is "characteristic of our age" (53). "Like expressionism," he continues, "the baroque is not so much an age of genuine artistic achievement as an age possessed of an unremitting artistic will . . . To this should be added the desire for a vigorous style of language, which would make it seem equal to the violence of world-events" (54–5).

It was an art of epigones, given to exaggeration, the "spectacle of spiritual contradiction," and the antithetical; its common practice is to "pile up fragments ceaselessly, without any strict idea of a goal, and, in the unrelenting expectation of a miracle, to take the repetition of a stereotype for the process of intensification" (178). The melancholic hero of the allegories adopts the world in ruins as his or her natural place, a place beyond beauty and without revelation, where the "events of history shrivel up and become absorbed in the setting" (179).

"To be exploited as muted cultural commentary does not exhaust the eloquence of ruins. As an allegory of personal as well as historical loss which cannot be repaired, they are an old figure in the aesthetic of melancholy," Sontag writes in 1986 in her introduction to *Veruschka: Transfigurations*. "What characterizes the aesthetic of melancholy is that there is no witness, only a single, unmoving protagonist—one who does not witness desolation but *is* desolation—and whose complete identification with the desolate scene precludes feeling (its exemplary forms: tears), whose gaze is unresponsive, withdrawn" (12).

In Sontag's rendering of the sensibility of our age, she begins to tire of finding "the politics of the perverse and the morbid" that Trilling had called for with a half-raised flag. Instead, she is beckoned by the melancholic allegorist. To her, late modernism passes into the shadows, becomes a shade of contemplation of the infernal; to her, the allegorical dimension of thinking sanctions the emptying out of colossal events and turns them into plays of the disembodied that await their and our "faithless leaps." The principle, as she says in her essay on Cioran, is that one save oneself.

In the baroque world of the seventeenth century, emblems, mottoes, and allegorical narrative were used unmistakenly to promote obeisance to the court, church, or some other ideal of incorporated glory. If allegory has returned as a favored explanation of our art and sensibility, it augurs this felicity: allegory is inaccessible to ironic deflation. The nearly dogmatic commitment to self-traducing—to Sontag, modernism's gnostic complaint—in allegory is relieved of its ironic trivializing. Something is believed in allegory, something stands behind and supports the whole apparatus. There is no meaning immanent in the ruins. But the alienation that exposed rituals—our more common modern experience—turns to the pathos of admiring what is lost. What could that be now but the energy and confidence of heroic modernism, now sheltered by its monumentality in a landscape of horrors.

On those topics she likes, Sontag writes very slowly. In that pace comes the melancholic attachment which sets out to devolve its reasons for empathy. From these dead objects and fallen virtues she discovers and forges a dramaturgy of relinquishment. Inside the writer of the "new" was the writer searching to name the contours of the modern sensibility in the already just past.

In her work to date, Sontag is never far from this strange allegory of disburdenment. Her fiction is a tale told from these ending processes; in her essay she puts herself to the task: she exacts from herself the charge of exhausting the Westernizing, metacritical, self-patronizing consciousness, that "digests" and "cannibalizes" itself, in order to re-cover a longed for . . . lighter state. In describing Sontag's choice, I have tried to take her advice and consider "that it is what it is." That the allegory of disburdenment has crystallized in her work, with its special, inner constitution and outward predilections, it has given her work a center and personality. It has become her way of "soliciting self-knowledge" as Cary Nelson has put it, a way of doing criticism as a "zone of permission, a special site on which self-extinction can be desired and verbally pursued."[6]

Sontag told an interviewer in May 1988, while in Lisbon on an inter-national conference of writers, that she does not "write about things, period. Everything that I write is fiction even when I write an essay. When I write an essay it is a type of fiction." She starts, in the morning at her desk, with language, "and then I go on an adventure for the next sentence. I try to follow ideas of seriousness and good use in language."[7] She wishes to present herself thus, as a formalist and artist. This essay takes her at her word, for the sake of what she is after.

3

The Two Novels:
The Benefactor and
Death Kit

Hippolyte goes to his daily bed committed to falling into the jeopardy that Baudelaire, for one, declares we are too cowardly to acknowledge. He is to himself, above all, a dreaming man. And he would assure us he has plunged into this experiment of pursuing his dreams with the contentment offered by the full weight of his singular character. Unlike other modernist figures wearied by the distance from their own feelings and standing restlessly at the worn edge, Hippolyte is smug. He writes that he has turned his preoccupation into a dictum—step by step he reveals how much of his life has become the responsibility of his dreams. Now, as he reflects on his life story, either for the repose he claims he has won, or because his character forbids him to be surprised, even by the thought that he might be insane, he is imperturbable. For all that he has risked, for all that befalls him in his life-dreams, Hippolyte writes without a note of regret. Like Magritte's *Man with a Hat* or the Escher print *A Hand with a Reflecting Globe* which covers the paperbound edition, he would portray himself as the very image of meditative absence, with possibly, just possibly, an apple in his mouth. Those quotes from Baudelaire and De Quincey with which Sontag prefaces *The Benefactor* are a tease, like so many other hints to this rarefied and arch book. We are to read it with the subtlest kinds of inverting skills.

The protagonist of Sontag's second novel, Diddy, is not a man who has ever enjoyed himself. It would not be a picture of himself, arrogantly posed, that he offers the world. He struggles against the humiliation his own honesty pours over him. But since he wins his death and the struggle takes place while he is comatose, he too presents a picture of absence, a voluntary departure. Neither man goes about in a world we inhabit mutually, only a world we separately could confront if we chose.

To be in their world we would have to choose to vacate our lives. We would first need to sweep everything tainted with our conscious being in this world and concentrate on the two gifts of nature: our dreams and our death. Our delight would be to do the unconscious's bidding impulsively, taking care to snub reason's curiosity in anything but ourselves. What are the dream figures, these novels question, but the unconscious thrilling at its chance to reconstruct the tale? What is our dying but a journey through the stations of our lives as we watch the loss of separate vitalities? In the end, we might discover the joy of completion that comes from a final emptying out, as these characters do—a vindictive, spite-filled, pathos-ridden joy of the self trumped.

I call these two stories allegories of deletion. They suggest an allegory on the mere principle that they seem like studies that beg their own purpose: they invite us to read them from the outside. Some code distinct from the narrative directs our appreciation. They are not, for instance, satires. *The Benefactor* may feel like a satire, in part. By the end of the novel Hippolyte's protestations have been undermined, whatever his aplomb. We can read him with the same fun we have with Italo Svevo's Zeno. He is certainly allowed the error of his ways—sadism, abusing a wealthy mistress, flirting with a perversion of religion and mysticism, dallying in films, marrying conventionally to indulge convention, being insensitive to the Jewish plight during the Second World War, and ugly about Arabs. Sometimes this demanding man, this impresario of the conscienceless motives, finds himself irked and on the run. Nonetheless, the sense never congeals that this is an ironic frolic into that late European sensibility. For one thing the tone isn't right. The wanness of Hippolyte's style, which might be parody, never trivializes. He is funny and absurd, a "comic fragment" his friend Jean-Jacques calls him. But his meditations have the authority of an original mind bent on subjects Sontag elsewhere has treated with her careful, even obsessive attention. He has, furthermore, her epigrammatical intelligence.

Sontag said of *Death Kit* that it could have been called *Why Are We in Vietnam?*[1] She sees it as speaking against the American sensibility. And Diddy is an American dupe. A bored minor executive, an ad man for a New York microscope firm, he's no intellectual and no aesthete. He kills to find his erotic potential and kills again to revive it. Only his story, unlike Mailer's DJ's, doesn't reach out to any landscape. Diddy's completely cut off on his trip to Buffalo. Though he brings to his death his own kit, the terms of his life, the terms submerge beneath the modern man's suicide: he must, he demands, be seen. He must peer through, penetrate into the blindnesses of his once-owned world; his is forever staring at lists of perceptual categories, linguistic oddities, fragmented homilies, or, more dimly, his nauseating condition. As a statement about American self-destructiveness, Diddy's story hooks into little that is more specific than American, deadening banality. Internally, it rides on the moral correlatives for the surges and ebbs of the body's strengths as it resists consciousness. The drama is the body's own, finally, trying for, and then letting go of, exoneration.

By bringing *The Benefactor* and *Death Kit* together here inevitably I overemphasize their contiguities (they read in altogether different narrative voices). But I wish to encourage a reconsideration of their importance in Sontag's overriding project. They have been much neglected, no doubt because of the "pain and effort of the Negative" (Richard Howard's phrase, in a review of *The Benefactor*),[2] with which they must be read, no doubt because of the main characters' "minor, even despised" (Sontag's description) ethic, their "morbidity." They resist approach, more so in some ways than the alienated, affectless, aimless characters found in so many late modernist fiction. These men are entirely given over to completing their deletion as humans. As Sontag warns us of Diddy's state: "One can redeem skeletons and abandoned cities as human. But not a lost, dehumanized nature. Having been freed for so long from human regard, from the scrutiny and aspirations of people, the barren mountains of Tyrrhenia cannot resemble any known mountains on the planet. How they would shudder and sweat in the unsubstantial air" (DK 3).

Lost then, to us, behind a complex of deflecting literary devices, truly buried, they do not tempt us to wish for their redemption, even though we may have warmed to Hippolyte's genius for epigrams, or Diddy's certain ironic grace, and have noted their suffering. These are closed-off novels, works of exacting refinement, meant to reproduce the consciousness of men who have locked themselves up with their natures (also to be read as having been locked up with their natures). We are to hold them up as objects; we are to feel the highly polished, sometimes lyrical, deliberated study their author has given her protagonists—for their own sake, first. Secondly, when dropped back into Sontag's larger work, we find a purpose to which they both speak. Hippolyte and Diddy exercise on themselves the experiential anguish of modernist art recognized above all by its solipsistic rendering of the world and a digestion of its own forms.

Once we grasp that they are allegorical figures, of a most modern kind, i.e. "uncontaminated by ethical virtues," the interlocking distancing devices of the novels can be seen as ways of intensifying their roles. Allegorical figures must stand from afar, completed, unidimensional. Their stories—their attempt to use up their characters—play out the fate of the "literature of exhaustion," the phrase John Barth coined in that period and has since somewhat regretted. In other words, the very difficulties these novels present to the reader, no less than real life modernists who shadow Hippolyte's world, comment on why these characters relentlessly seek completion through dissolution. What traps these men inside their consciousness, and then inverts what they then believe about themselves, tells the story of the modernist quest, its emptying out of itself.

At the end of *Death Kit*, allegorically, modernism dies and postmodernism lives on in the posthumous state Hippolyte made mere teasing reference to. The point of closure in the second novel has Diddy, lightened, at ease, having broken through the barrier to the charnel house of his own death, standing among the dusty coffins of past lives and the scraps of their mottoes. He "walks on, looking for his death." The novel ends with how he "has perceived the inventory of the world" (*DK* 312). The world as an inventory of things infuses much of what has become known as the postmodern aesthetic. It is the postmodernist's tendency to equalize rather than discriminate, to incorporate, ironically, rather than to delete and narrow, to be fascinated with show rather than causes, to tolerate the flippant and the slick for the sake of what all have accepted as the hollowness beneath. Bemused by artifacts, asking more questions about structure than purpose, delighting in the incongruous rather than in discovery, the postmodernist sees the world, above all, as an inventory of objects and broken ideas. What the postmodernist hopes to do is to neatly step out of what has been accepted as the defining paradox of modernism: that modernism transforms the negating power of consciousness into the deleting power of form. Objection and defiance, modernist negation, called for a stripping away operation—a jubilant process for some; for others, a dark paring down until the last knot of flesh is cut, the gut exposed. It is this second operation that Sontag's two protagonists start out to perform, so that these books may be read as an embodiment of the crisis of form, the modernist experiment rung out on two dubious beings. The contrivances that keep us suspended outside these novels, their odd, erudite tone and complexities are the ways Sontag contains the argument—more than just ambivalences—she feels towards that side of herself and of art that gets "regularly choked off by seizures of morbidity."[3]

The Benefactor

"Instead of accumulating ideas, we might be better occupied with dissolving them" (16), Hippolyte remembers thinking as a young man, and concludes his tale with the conviction that: "The advent of anything brings with it mainly the problem of its disburdenment, its dissolution. The only thing remarkable about me is that I approached this task more comprehensibly than most people do. . . . For me, the very advent of myself suggested the problem of my own dissolution" (223).[4]

By the end of the novel, we have almost been seduced by that kind of aplomb. Repose, after a neat stepping through nihilistic and gnostic thorny issues, has a sophisticate's appeal. Hippolyte triumphs in the goal of his beloved inconsequence. The troublesome manuscripts that challenge the legitimacy of his story, and his sanity—the events of his narration are the work of his dreams—the two in fact might be, if not interchangeable, about a third form, the novel he is writing about his own life—aren't sufficiently powerful enough to dislodge him from his success in becoming emptied.

With all this dream-life-novel-sanity mix-up, we may decide that Sontag is having us traverse surrealist grounds. If so, we are moving in reverse, by some opposing force, erasing the accumulation of juxtapositions. The impetus to explore joyously—what Sontag has described as quintessential to the surrealists—in Hippolyte rises to little more than the "driving, empty elation" on waking. " 'I am looking for silence, I am exploring the various styles of silence, and I wish to be answered by silence. You might say,' " I concluded gaily, " 'that I am disemboweling myself' " (36).

It is typical of Hippolyte to compare himself to the cruelest images with an impassive tone. This narrowing of his life, the drama of giving over to the commands of the dreams until he finds himself their puppet, titillates his fainting eros, an eros succumbing to the will-lessness of death. "I have been more lucky than most," he writes in his final pages. "I have had both my life and after-life: this posthumous existence of mine prolongs itself in meditation and a well-cleared landscape. . . . You may imagine me in a bare room, my feet near the stove, . . . enjoying the waning tribulations of subjectivity and the repose of privacy that is genuine" (224).

We would perhaps grant him that posture of delectation—it's so luxurious—except that we can read backwards and connect the hints buried in the dream symbolizing. The pieces of his narrative which he would blandly invert—so that this becomes real, that one a dream—are supported by a sound track. A silent scream. The dreams, and the reality-fantasy in which they are interwoven, are Hippolyte's efforts to denature the brutal therapy of an insane asylum. He may hold that the letter he has discovered, pleading for a re-examination of his case, is another invention of autobiography. We hear the rationalizations of a post-electric shock patient. The almost beguiling portrait of himself as a man who has completed the experiment of "choosing himself" collapses for us into a view of a man who has indeed been finished off, from something more palpable than dreams.

There can be detected a judgment on Sontag's part toward Hippolyte and his adventures, but it is a complex one. Sontag tells us, in a much later interview, that she wrote *The Benefactor* to "explore the contours of a sensibility" and that she chose among them one that was exotic, uncontaminated by ethical virtues, "in obvious ways minor, even despised."[5] She flinched hard when she was asked if Hippolyte in any way reflected her: "I am *nothing* like Hippolyte: at least I certainly *hope* I'm not. He fascinates me, but I dislike him intensely. He's purposeless, and wasteful and evil."[6] For such a protracted, intense study in a youthful, first novel that disclaimer calls attention to itself.

She must retreat from this novel, just as she keeps pulling the reader back because morally both the sensibility—this "morbidity"—and the man offend her. Yet the writers of morbidity number in her essays like a role call of heroes—Artaud, Gide, Pavese, Leiris, Cioran: their "uninhibited display of egotism devolves into the heroic quest for the cancellation of self" (*AI* 43). Indeed, in a case like Leiris' *Manhood*—from which Sontag used chapter titles, personages, narrative personality for *The Benefactor*—she finds Leiris "training to extinguish himself . . . [H]e wishes to prove, not that he is heroic, but that he is at all" (*AI* 65). In Sontag's delicate maneuvering around that "minor sensibility," she may be hiding from a complex set of feelings. The gutting of the self, the paring down into nothingness, the heave towards a final disburdenment: these are terms of the agon of the eviscerated sublime. At the end, in rushes power, or sainthood. Hippolyte is one of the first to stand in the box for an extended trial between two parts of Sontag: that which is guided by the ethical claims of this world and that which sees all about her the mystical absolute in a particularly ugly stage in history.

Hippolyte stands accused, of course, before a court mostly empty of personages. It's the references to Artaud's tragic experience—the scream silenced in the dream work—that crack the luminous surface of Hippolyte's posturing. In his new personality, he is indeed the man without qualities, or rather the man from whom qualities have been erased, one by one in the accumulated sequences in the asylum.

Not that Sontag has not made Hippolyte worthy of her fascination. His experiment is true to himself, heuristic and rigorous. He writes with no moral purpose. He seeks a truth, but not the truth of "arousing, convincing, changing another"; if he is admonitory, he means to admonish only himself. His sensibility, he would claim, is pure, without a second purpose. Moreover, Hippolyte believes himself to be a true revolutionary. Revolutions are only revolutions of the self, and in the future, he muses, perhaps all revolutions will be "of single persons, exemplifying not the cult of reason, but the cult of privacy whose worship is personified by a puppet" (109).

If we suspect that Hippolyte might be speaking for Sontag, he overrides or deletes our insights by sophistries we only later see as the craving kind. Nothing he says achieves the impact of the author's unambiguous defense. We have been warned by Sontag that "it is possible to elude the interpreters . . . by making works of art whose surface is so unified and clean, . . . that the work can be . . . just what it is (*AI* 21). From this impressively smooth surface, we have been given some hints. This is a *roman à clef*. As much as we can trust Hippolyte's facts, he's the double of a man very much like Artaud; Jean-Jacques, his friend, Genet. Their *pas de deux*, inside the shadow of their others, makes a play out of their—Artaud's and Genet's—respective ideas about drama. It must be remembered, though, that these are shadows upon shadows, since Hippolyte and his friend Jean-Jacques spend much time in the novel transformed into dream figures. And since his dreams can be read as his distorted understanding of his cure, we come back to the impression that I have stated before: we are to think of Artaud and Genet as composite (or allegorical) figures of the modernism Sontag had encountered in France in the 1960s—after it had been silenced.

In other words, Hippolyte stands in for the real-life writer as a double of the opposite orientation, like a shell of the same species found in an opposing hemisphere. He speaks from the end of his journey through the madhouse; he believes himself to have completed his project, the uncompromising "crawling through the tunnel of himself" (36). He has taught himself to be adept at stepping through the portals of the seeming. Artaud, after his treatments, still suffered terrors at the edge of his vision.

Hippolyte begins his book at sixty-one, looking back on a life he tells us was not a journey but a block of marble. Without ambitions, without opinions, amenable, he comes as a young man to the capital he refuses to name, though it can be no other than Paris, to pursue his studies. There he studies "avariciously" for three years, at the end of which he publishes a precocious article "in which I propose important ideas on a topic of no great importance" (13). For this he is given an invitation from the sensuous middle-aged Frau Anders to join her salon. Quickly at home in that place of display, he stops attending the university, stops writing, stops reading. We learn soon enough that whatever he is hewing away at makes this "stopping" a practice of keeping faith with himself.

His faith sinks its observances in him; each step in his "enlightenment" recapitulates an act of relinquishment. So as, perhaps, not to wish him ill, sometimes we are shown cool miracles of his progress. Later in his story, after the war, living alone (possibly) in his spacious, expensively refashioned home, he finds a robber has entered. "I told him that he could have anything in the house which he put a bullet through, on the first try, at a distance of twenty paces. . . . At the end of the tour I complimented him on his marksmanship. . . . 'Don't regret what you have done,' I said. 'You've relieved yourself of a great burden.

You have learned about disinterested violence, and I the secret of disinterested surrender' " (204).

One can't be sure what to make of that *sang-froid* in the grip of irony, especially when we think how, having abandoned his studies, he assigns himself the freedom to commit his "first immoderate act"—the first dream he can recall in its entirety. "This dream and its successors were indelible. They were written, as it were, by a firmer hand and in a different script" (27). This new hand signals a change in Hippolyte's life to which he gives himself over. The hand is a metaphor for his novel, his script. It is also a reference for the benefactor he comes to believe himself to be, and it is a symbol for the figure of authority who rules his dreams. The subsequent changes in Hippolyte are compelled by the force of the intricately woven symbols of the over-determined dream work. The bather of the dreams, for example, is a substitute for Hippolyte's friend and confidant, the boxer, writer, male prostitute Jean-Jacques, and the woman is Frau Anders. They have varying careers throughout the dreams, but they rarely fail to appear.

To these waking friends, Hippolyte is argumentative, insulting or murderous, as he understands himself provoked by his dreams. On awakening from his second dream, for example, he believes that he has been directed to make Frau Anders his mistress and does so. Unfortunately, Hippolyte's passion depends on his ability to "refresh his fantasies," and Frau Anders and Hippolyte's erotic life together becomes "a dream rehearsal rather than a dream reprise" (71). Eventually on their fanciful tour planned to stimulate the ever-jaded Frau Anders, Hippolyte grows bored with her easy compliance and posturing as a sexual adventuress, and sells her (she desires to be surprised) to an Arab merchant. Her fault was that "she no longer knew how to patronize" him.

We are given more to muse on in this camped version of male privilege. This indestructible, benighted woman will have her triumph, in becoming worldly-wise in her own terms. The dreams in the meantime are darkening, from threatening to punishing. He descends further into the contest of wills his "crafty humility and desire to placate" establishes between himself and the authority figures he seeks out. He repeatedly consults father-figures, shocking them with his obstinate self-destructiveness, complying with them in their dream transfiguration. With their foil or their whip, the dreams progress to the goal Hippolyte always imagines himself heading toward: to the puppet bear who mistakenly tears apart a child with whom he has been ordered to dance. That cosmic cruelty is what is squeezed out of the "devil's asshole," as he calls his experience; his march, he would have it, to his reward, his kind of will-lessness. In the torture of the devil's bowels he must be pressed through, in a place we are beginning to understand better.

The authorities first seduce by beauty or argument, by the pacifying, or admonishing hand they extend to Hippolyte; he knows them through obeisance, confinement, mortification, by that knowingness of the unconscious. It is that, he suspects, they wish to purify in him. If those dreams live on without him, hasn't he utterly won? Who would want the unconscious for a servant? The unconscious serves, by way of its fantastic distortions, only itself.

Hippolyte plays the fool to the "lavish, indiscreet, dishonest" Jean-Jacques throughout his story, to tempt that man out of his disguise and into the cruel Bather he knows him as. Hippolyte accompanies Jean-Jacques on his nightly homosexual encounters, finding in that world the unreality of dreams. To Jean-Jacques, these encounters are theater. "But you are not like them," Hippolyte says to him, referring to the transvestites. "You choose. They are obsessed." "So much the worse for me," replies Jean-Jacques.

> 'No,' he continued, 'to pretend one thing is only not to pretend something else. But to be obsessed is not to pretend at all. The sun does not play at rising every morning. Do you know why? Because the sun is obsessed with its tasks. All that we admire in nature under the name of order, and the basis of the confidence we repose in her regular movements, is obsession.'
>
> The idea struck me as true. 'Then obsession, not virtue, is the only sensible ground for trust.'
>
> 'Right,' he said. 'Which is why I trust you.'
>
> Then, I thought, that is why I cannot trust you, Jean-Jacques. But this I did not say. (57)

Poor, self-made *objet-trouvé*, as Jean-Jacques calls him, a character without a story—perhaps we have been willing to grant him sincerity in his efforts to achieve authenticity via the negative. Do we need the tragicomic inversion of his story, however neat the trick played on both of us, in its dovetailing of events/dreams and proselytizing/pleas? He discovers by means of an acquaintance that he might have been insane and hospitalized for the six years he occupied that house. Moreover, other evidence surprises him. Frau Anders appears, bejeweled, middle-aged, content, and full of marvelous tales of herself as a queen in the desert. She comes, she tells Hippolyte, to claim the home he intended for her and to evict him as he once abandoned her, for his own good.

> 'I have learned to love myself, Hippolyte ... I love my powdery smooth wrinkled flesh, my sagging breasts, my veined feet, and the smell of my armpits. Every time I look into the mirror, I can't tell

you how delighted I am that someone looks back, smiling, and that,
that someone is me. . . .'
  'You won't live forever,' I muttered.
  'Wait,' she said. 'Who can tell? I feel younger than ever. I shall die
a baby which is no death at all.'
  This was not the self-love as I had understood it. (211)

It could be said that Sontag had to extend to her character and her
naming of this sensibility all the possibilities, including self-deception.
Otherwise, the perverse logic of Hippolyte's experiment would be incomplete. Fulfillment is accomplished when all the possibilities have
come full circle, when they have viewed and encompassed their negation. Hippolyte can then nullify his most lucid pretensions with a
careless disregard. At no other point in the text is Hippolyte's posturing
more persuasive. That "true test of fulfillment" has reached an inviola-
ble stage: "I have had both my life and my after-life: this posthumous
existence of mine prolongs itself in meditation" (224).

One cannot argue with the perspective of the other side, except that
it is not hard to see that the element lacking in Hippolyte's self-regard
is the sense of his theater. In the end he can accept that his life may be
a novel, but he never knowingly plays it out. He substitutes a posture
for a performance; he succeeds, whether "intentionally" or not, in being
utterly styleless. It is clear to the reader of *The Benefactor*, though never
acknowledged by Hippolyte, that between Jean-Jacques and Hippolyte
there occurs a struggle in dialogue and dream whose substance is this
debate between authentic life choices, performance and postures. The
two men, in the symbology of the novel, dance a slave-master routine.
Jean-Jacques, the Bather, Jean-Jacques, the writer-friend (whom Hippolyte nearly murders as he dances about his ill wife's bed), Jean-Jacques,
who now still begs money from Hippolyte has been secretly bestowed
an inheritance on him; Jean-Jacques, the now famous author forgiven
for his affection for Nazi officers. Hasn't he grown a puppet to the
crowd? Hippolyte taunts.

> His acts have been transformed into postures, but not of his own will
> and in the privacy of his intimate life . . . For I have changed no less
> than he. But I and I alone have worked these changes in myself, a
> deeper change than any possible through the mere attainment of
> own's ambitions. (213)

This tiring man's "contracting of ambitions" by the end of the novel
have grown tiring; that we discover his story to have been a delusion
offers only partial relief. It's the growing sense that Sontag has a larger

scheme—the uses to which she puts Artaud—that keep our attention. Artaud and Hippolyte arrive in Paris about the same time. Both get drawn into avant-garde circles and the cinema in the 20s. It is probably Artaud's *The Seashell and The Clergyman* that is lurking behind Hippolyte's play about nuns, and, in the most straightforward hint, Artaud's performance as the confessor in Carl Dreyer's *La passion de Jeanne d' Arc* (1928). But the torment of Artaud, about to overspill into hysteria, into brilliance and madness, is buried in Hippolyte's voice under layers of his pontificating. When, for instance, Artaud becomes engaged to the modest, middle class Belgian Cécile Schramme, the double of Hippolyte's wife, he torments her with questions of sexuality and purity. Hippolyte "respects" the virginity of his young convent educated wife, only masturbating in her presence. "When I reached the climax of my meditation," he writes, "my wife came and dried me with a towel" (168). Artaud's marriage engagement was said to have been broken off when, according to one source, Artaud in lecturing in Brussels on his Mexican experiences, announced, "Since I've lost my notes, I am going to speak about the effect of masturbation on the Jesuit fathers." Another version has it that as he gave his lecture, he grew ever more heated until he was screaming "In revealing all that to you, I may have killed myself."[7]

Artaud thinks, like Hippolyte, that revolutions of his time are revolutions in sensibility. And this difficult, lonely man too embarks on fanatical self-absorption. When Artaud goes mad and enters an asylum during the Occupation (the time Hippolyte enters his house-asylum), he too writes letters to his doctors, like Hippolyte accusing them of punishing him for his fantasies. Photographs of Artaud after his release show a stilled man. Here, pointedly, the analogy weakens. Artaud's post-asylum writings remain angry, violent, fragmented, deeply embittered toward those "erotomaniacal" doctors. Artaud never gives up his consciousness, for all the electroshock treatments, never adopts a "styleless" literary voice: certainly he never calls the pain of his consciousness "mere tribulations."

One reading of Artaud's persona in this novel must include Sontag's turning the hourglass upside-down on Artaud's psychic life, letting it drain out. Genet is mentally fused to the persona because, on the other end of the pole of radical theater, Genet was the ironic groundling who pulled down the cruel cosmic-metaphysic of Artaud's vision. "Where is he?," Hippolyte questions Jean-Jacques' new fame, "the great bully, the charming liar, the inconstant friend, the unprincipled coquette who amused and taunted me in my younger days, the frivolous Virgil who watched me descend into the inferno of my dreams. He is gone: aged, transfixed by the great stare of the public eye, frozen" (213). Jean-

Jacques too gets "stopped"; his "agile transformations" transformed into an attitude, the only kind of transformation Hippolyte acknowledges, the only kind that justifies him.

Sontag needed a character who was capable of writing a whole book—Artaud never was. Hippolyte speaks in what one reviewer called the tone of "literary translation."[8] That tone would have haunted Artaud as his undead enemy. The fact that Hippolyte can write such a book, whichever book, testifies to his recovery. The malaise of the author he has worked through his own bowels. If Artaud had been "cured," he might have written such a book. Instead Artaud resisted: he remained anguished, paranoid, maddened. Perhaps this is why Sontag "despises" Hippolyte. Without pain or will, he can no longer be a "heroic" modernist. He has taken the reader through the steps of modernist anguish, through ritual, through repetition, through the paths of mysticism, without a poetics—because, and this is the chief point, he no longer suffers. He does not pose the no; he does not struggle against affirmation. Rather he feels affirmed, or almost. He has stepped through life into the lightness and peace of the posthumous state. Sontag is interested in Hippolyte because he recapitulates the process of modernism at its close—he shows us how one disestablishes oneself with a postmodern sensibility.

In her second novel, standing between the two books of essays, we see Sontag still indulging in a fascination in order to work it through, to "finish" it. *Death Kit* completes its own disburdenment as an art form yearning for self-annihilation. Unfortunately, Diddy is even less an artist than Hippolyte in that he is no composite of a famous artistic struggle. In his case, we can be less troubled about the parallels between his project and the modernists. Only Sontag's indebtedness to morbidity—to death and the yearning for deletion—comes through clearly. It is her fascination that lifts the whole narrative back into the modernist structure of thinking. Inside the work, she focuses Diddy's view down the tunnel to the charnel house; she gives him his best moments there. Diddy *actually* negates himself, past the posture of silence, into posthumous bliss. The novel resists political terms; disburdenment is literally completed.

In "Approaching Artaud" Sontag critiques the modernist project as "notably vulnerable"; "it is inevitably robbed of its adversary power" (*USS* 50). "Only a few situations," she writes, "in modern secular society seem sufficiently extreme and uncommunicative to have a chance to evade cooptation" (*USS* 50): "madness," "suffering that surpasses the imagination," and "silence." And, of course, suicide. These are the kits or schemes of limits the modernist carries into art; it is his or her "death kit."

Death Kit: In Morbidity's Dominion

Though a distance separates the European Hippolyte and his absurd-ist homilies on self-love from the American Diddy and his unremitting self-disparagement, the two books are sequential. The gathering mo-mentum of the lie in Hippolyte's rhetoric is taken up in successive stages of dying in Diddy's life. The death obsession in the dream-life of Hippolyte, with its images of dismemberment and draining away is the beginning, the point of departure, for Diddy. Even the confusion of Diddy's narrative is of another order. The "over-work" that is his dying must be interpreted with his body's truths. While one man can pose the languid, gentle lie of a posthumous existence, the other must taste blood.

In *Death Kit* Sontag releases her protagonist for that final venturing, already lightened, already sucked up into his death. Hippolyte had to crawl through the tunnel of himself; Diddy is driven through on a fateful train. The locomotion of the story is supplied by the inevitability and the imminence of Diddy's end. The train that carries him to murder, and then to return to remurder the incarnation of the dead man, conveys the energy and then the failing energy of Diddy's comatose path through the barrier and into the charnel house. He needs no principle, no experi-ment, no dialogue with the phantoms of modernism, no cruel psycho-therapy. Sontag loosened herself to explore the sensibility of morbidity literally, phenomenologically, as the life lived in the moribund state. We will miss Hippolyte's erudite formulations, the multitextual, multi-referential complexity of *The Benefactor*, its setting, its pace, its deli-cate poise between the funny and the horrible. But Diddy's quest for certainty—Did-he?—is all the more unified because it will not be inter-rupted from outside.

These mechanics of flitting consciousness and the remains of bodily needs are what Diddy brings to his death, but in contrast to his dreary life (at least as we understand it), death plays out a deal. It seeks to restore purpose, to heal schisms, to liberate him from judgment. Not that his death is noble; it is ignoble, it demands vindication of Diddy's follies while it promises redemption, it confuses him with its simula-tions of life. Death waits in a landscape, not Hippolyte's "well-cleared" one, but one fantastic and irresolute, fleeting, in fact, like the train he is on that's rushing to leave his body. Diddy views himself and this place in the way Hippolyte describes a state of absolute attention, where there "is silence and sometimes murder." What's striking is that it is otherwise utterly unlike Hippolyte's description of that state, for here there is indeed need for persuasion.

Diddy's drama is signalled by crudely imagined placards announcing and enumerating the forms of his self contempt. Or it appears in the stops, in the story, not in the argument, of word-catalogues around the central metaphor. Whatever Diddy "stops" to consider—tunnels, shells, domes, eyes, microscopes—pitches him into a fantasy spiraling downward where meaning flounders on symbolic overload. Diddy too dreams; in fact, he takes up a "residence" in his dreams. Diddy too "writes a novel" by reinventing a childhood text of a nurturing/dependence relationship he replays upon Hester. And Diddy, too, finally experiences release. But Diddy makes the gesture that is hard to discredit; he has taken his own life.

The second book answers the first: thinking self-deletion does not purge one of oneself. The self is tenacious; it is also dumb and quick to smash skulls. Sontag has been accused of writing a formulaic novel, an "idea kit" of contemporary thinking in which her voice oddly jars with that of her protagonists.[9] Those catalogues, parenthetical "nows" and shifts in person have been taken as her intrusion into the story in order to make her own phenomenological trips into the matter of seeing, or in the ordering of things. Indeed, Diddy seems a poor vehicle for these metareflections, rarely rising above his displays of self-pity. If he lived in that dense fluid of unseeing, how can he "(now)" speak with such clarity about his own condition? The living man wouldn't, unless Sontag would have us consider that the posthumous state lifts the cloud and the "fetid underlife" assumes an intelligence of its own. This intelligence would not be, of course, that of a "vivid" consciousness. These "philosophical" intrusions compete with the rhythm of the body's dying. They act as scene props, they anchor Diddy's imaginative drift, and they sometimes reinvest reality with the power of an outsider's view—sometimes lucid, sometimes grasping, sometimes deceitful. "We" find with Diddy on this trip that this other kind of consciousness is both self-serving and lashing.

Even the homilies in *Death Kit* are consistent with despairing nature, supporting itself with an American penchant for commonplaces. The "haze of abstractions" of which critics such as Benjamin Demott complain constitutes no epistemological adventurism in Diddy.[10] Typical examples include such judgments as:

He who despises himself esteems himself as a self-despiser. (8)[11]

No one should be burdened with inventing his own nature from scratch. No one should be asked to decide whether he's good or bad. (262)

To love one's work is a way of loving oneself. And that leaves one freer to love other people. (149)

> Love is beautiful and strong. So are the trees. And so is food. (235)

> Words cannot compel the unconditional movements of the heart. (227)

Compared to the convoluted inspirations of Hippolyte:

> War does not fail. But love always does. (*TB* 166)

> One becomes free precisely through those acts which have an inescapable end. (*TB* 85)

> True vigor results only from the knowledge of separateness. (*TB* 203)

> Dreams are the poetry, disease the prose of the imagination. (*TB* 170)

> There are two paths leading to two different goals. One is from event to knowledge; the celebrated path of wisdom. Another from knowledge to event; the much advertised path to action. . . . Are these all? Isn't there a third: from non-knowledge to non-event? And a fourth? From non-event to non-knowledge? (*TB* 197)

> At first my activities exceeded my knowledge. Then, as I came to know less, I gave up action. (*TB* 197)

Hippolyte incorporates the world only as a premise for his innumerable epigrammatical presumptions. Diddy is not idea-ridden; his thoughts "bully" him. His capacity to suffer depends upon "a kind of superior stupidity" in which he works for his death in a world of American television and Vietnam, business, working-class men and women, bad food, decaying cities. Diddy's "knowledge" gets tangled trying to forge through the last of consciousness as it divides everything around the question of nightmare: "The nightmare that there are *two* worlds. The nightmare that there is only *one* world. This one" (310). The search for the equation to pull him back into life or to pull him forward turns his story into dualisms: two worlds, two truths, two kinds of blindness, and into couples: himself and Hester, the Wolf-Boy and himself, the Wolf-Boy and Incardona, man-animals capable of inspiring love-sex; Joe and Charlie Incardona, two brothers who reincarnate the unresolved tension between Diddy and his brother Paul. Then there are Mary and Myra, Diddy's nurse and the dead man's wife, interpolated visions of seduction, guilt, and low-life feculence. The parallels, however, disclose only the clumsiness of his thinking. At the end, in the charnel house, like a merchant, he takes stock of the world as a clutter of dishonor about which is thrown the wreckage of favorite advice.

Sontag in this book almost makes time stand still. Diddy wants "motionless memory" to slow down the inevitable, to delay his death.

The very first line hints at the collapsed frame of action of the book: "Diddy the Good was taking a business trip"—a sentence that will be repeated. One cannot say that Diddy ever speaks for himself, nor can one say the opposite. The self no longer has a person, or rather what comes after the self is staging his life for a brief review, or better yet, a mean summary: "Diddy, not really alive, had a life. . . . Some people are their lives, others merely inhabit their lives. . . . Eventually, for such a person, everything is bound to run down" (2).

"Endowed with vast amounts of irony applied at his own expense," (now) thirty-three, handsome, genteel, expensively educated and a trifle sententious, "the sort of man who is hard to dislike," Diddy the Done vows to go on after an apparent suicide. But otherwise, he has been, is (now), an "insecure tenant" of a life whose "generator's amok" from which a "befouling protective fluid" evaporates revealing an "uncensored, fetid, appalling underlife" (3). He comes up only to be swallowed again by the nausea which is the condition of his existence (now). The vomit that partially rescues him, waves through him, and something like it reeks from all around. He, too, is emptying himself, with stomach pumps and murder, even with a soul-cleansing recurrent dream, far outside the theater of retribution and sustained in the smallest space of existence.[12]

When this small space of existence is bracketed for us, the story begins; what it cannot do is move. Diddy "recovers" enough to take that fateful business trip to Buffalo on the train called the Privateer, into a dingy part of America, the part lodging privately in his soul. In the compartment of this otherworldly train, he joins a set of less than hopeful others. The train "sheathed" by the tunnel is forced to stop, and "Then suddenly, the day failed. So did our conversation" (14). As the passengers learn as they sit in darkness that there is a barrier; Hester, in her virgin–temptress role, speaks her first words, "Crash right through" (15).

Diddy may have heard her, but he has been distracted by an attack of panic, and "Unbiddened, the thought of his death settles like a flat stone on his chest. . . . Death, thought Diddy, is like a lithographer's stone" (17) because it is reusable. This stone will continue to press on him, a reminder through cycles of bearing up and giving in, that he has to finish something. Frightened and dizzy, he goes out, or rather "He had left the train." And in that heavily sex-imaged tunnel, which might be the "wrong" tunnel the conductor hints, Diddy finds a workman, slamming an ax against the barrier. With a sense of his opportunity, the workman provokes Diddy, and Diddy, feeling he is not "a zombie like the rest of the passengers" brings a crowbar down on the back of the man's head. "Diddy, the Stupefied has never felt more alive" (24).

Back in "our" compartment "nothing in our situation has changed" (25). In a scene written in the improbable terms of Hester's instant mothering and Diddy's childish petulance, she tells him she can't remember his leaving the compartment, and when he cries that she must believe him, she soothingly reminds him that she did not say she didn't believe him. Diddy tells her that "'I was going to kill myself. That's why I went outside'," and that he wants to make love to her, that he did not take his life because he was thinking about her. They stand together, in their passion, immobile, "a tableau of desire. Graven on stone" (29). Hester and Diddy's lovemaking this first time is less erotic than comforting, "like sleep." After they both come, it is "Time to wake up" (33). Death, sex, the cold tunnel, the imperious motion of the train, and the interjected pleas of the hospital staff are (now) inseparable.

The rest of the story springs from that tense binding. Hester is convinced that Diddy daydreamed the workman. "Outsized and brutish, like an armed angel" so he seems a phantom of the death-watch, but then so does the country Diddy's in. The railroad station in Buffalo, "more indelibly stained and grimier," is about to meet the wrecking ball. The text worries about keeping doomed places clean and in repair: "Especially since nemesis is proving to be somewhat dilatory in paying its anticipated call" (44). In a hotel called the Rushland, Diddy the Guilty pores over the newspaper looking for an account and does not find it until the "Late Final" edition. The trackman, Angelo Incardona, is reported killed by the speeding "Privateer" as the train passed through a tunnel: "circumstances of Mr. Incardona's death do not rule out suicide."[13]

Eros triumphs temporarily, for Diddy discovers that he doesn't want punishment, that he wants to live. Even though the "track curved sharply" (67), he has only to keep on going. Throughout the rest of the book, his is pushed forward or pulled back by the interchange of funeral symbols. For example, while walking across the lobby of his hotel, after sending flowers to Hester, he decides he has a mandate to live from the sight of his business associate's brisk walk towards him. These instant reversals parallel the delicate, panicky sources of his rising and sinking. He is sinking, he admonishes himself, into the "familiar indulgence of women." But this respite too must be extinguished, in its surprising forms. He "married his nurse," and gets to go "on" in making his attempts at picking up and reintegrating the dangling, unfinished part of his unconscious. He has passed through a turnstile, so to speak.

Keeping on going means taking Hester, not cured, home to live with him. She proves stronger and wiser than he, given to such good-sense, nurse-like sayings as "You have to respect my limits. And yours. You mustn't be too eager to change yourself" (227). Despite their lovemaking, in which Diddy finds himself graceful and tireless, thanatos has the orgasm, "a miniature frontal lobotomy" (273). Diddy quits his job, gives up his dog, and their relationship too begins to succumb. Wounded by her insufferable self-possession, afraid of her repressed hatred (her mother blinded her with acid at the age of twelve) yet thrilled by his total possession of her, he death-clutches at her until the emptying is almost over.

In the obsessive sadness of this book, there is one lesson in deep abhorrence, which might be the country's death kit. It's not lodged solely in its platitudes or wastes, in the gore of the body (its earth), or in the lists of items Diddy pores over (its dreary output). It's not an equivalent to the precarious sense of his manhood Diddy feels, so that he would have to kill "in shameful envy of the blind, uncompassionate vitality of men who look like Incardona" (88). America's death kit is assembled from what it sanctions.

> Reminded of the behavior of his own country, currently engaged in the cumbersome, drawn-out murder of a small, defenseless nation—this being only the latest of the country's roll call of historical atrocities, of crimes that baffle the imagination—Diddy's own agonizing during the last four days over the death of merely one person shrank (now) to humiliating size. . . . It's not for an act of violence, resulting in death, that Diddy flogs himself . . . for not having a cause. For lacking a sanctifying public goal. For only killing, not overkilling. (166–67)

To test his capacity for overkilling, Diddy takes Hester to the spot where the Privateer stalled, to find the sanctifying clarity in it—Incardona's death, his death. Diddy and Hester wait at the mouth of the tunnel for the last train to pass through, the Cherry Valley Local, "a slim, puny, rackety train, . . . an emblem of weakness" (280). They too (now) are pastoralizing this revision. They remind Diddy of children in an enchanted forest. "But in the end, Diddy recalls, the girl proves the more level-headed and effective" (281). The tunnel "is like home," as is the darkness he has come to share with Hester. They hear a tapping noise, and Hester wants to go back. " 'Have we found the trackman?' " Hester questions.

" 'Another man,' Diddy not trusting himself to speak further" (284). "To put Diddy's capacity for credence in a less extreme form: he believes two things. That Incardona died and that Incardona lives. Not all that different from, or significantly harder than, believing that he, Diddy, died; and also that he lived" (285). Diddy fights the grinning, dancing-about man incarnate, who's not contempt this time, but lust.

" 'Dalton, don't kill him'," cries Hester, but her cries seemed "to be mixed up with other muddleheaded exclamations and exhortations and assertions such as 'Wake up!' and 'Hey!' and 'Try the oxygen!' " (287). When he does kill him, Diddy wants to gloat. " 'You saw me this time'," he murmurs to the unexpectedly severe Hester, and when she reminds him he can't see, he shouts "I want to be seen!"[14]

To the unconscious Diddy, Hester has shared his truth; she was not asleep in the car this time. Uncertainty and eros now bedded together, Diddy is free to walk naked past the barrier. He's resisted the trackman, the orderly's hands, the stomach pump, the adrenalin; he's won the final, explosive sexuality by defending her. A lightness prevails; love, not violence, may have been his goal all along. Diddy steps over the incompletely dismantled barrier into a funnel of widening walls. "Why not? 'There is another world but it is inside this one' " (292). Saved from guilt or having to discover the meaning of his murderous rages, he enters his death, redeemed by the imagination at last in the service of a capitulated, or fulfilled, nature.

We recoil a little, for the sake of his skin, as he brushes past the rusty coffins in that most interesting place. He is fearless. In the death house, there is much to muse on: order, vanity, pathos, a wonderland of trea-sured, useless things and thoughts. The poor are roped off without caskets, the smaller rooms are specialized for firemen, stuffed priests, children, civil war vets, etc. As he walks on, the house gets more crowded and distinctions obliterate. Scrawled on walls or lettered on cardboard placards, there is an "unremitting pageant of quotations and mottoes" of no "ethical, temperamental, or cultural consistency" as if "randomly chosen people had been invited to contribute their favorite bit of wisdom" and a host of other, sad charms. The accumulation seems to have stopped at Diddy's (and Sontag's) birth. No corpse dates after 1933, and Diddy is thirty-three at the time of the manuscript's completion in 1966. The house has been waiting for him. With him, we are somewhat enjoying ourselves, relieved that the overwork is near done. Even here, he's "looking for Hester": "Love's power sweeping him up from the kingdom of death. 'Death and the Maiden?' " (311). He vomits at that moment, at the sound of another train, a dog barking. He goes to his death much less than a prince: he's "Diddy the Soiled." That is his last epithet for himself; he walks on, "looking for his death. Diddy has made his final chart; drawn up his last map. Diddy has perceived the inventory of the world" (312).

One could say that the inventory of the world is a fairly hubristic idea, and it would give more offense had not this man already given himself seventy-five categories of being. He's "good" ironically no less than six times, but other self descriptions are a litany of horrors, a gambit of life's sodden roles. He is sequentially, Diddy the despicable, the mortified, the stupefied, the jealous, incomplete, guilty, depraved, deluded, disconcerted, ghoul, criminal, despairer, the damned; alternately, bitterly, he's Diddy the companionable, the seducer, the comedian, the pious, gentleman, bold, educated, daring, docile, intrepid, and, curiously, the reluctant Democrat. Dying becomes a parade of placards announcing the next scene; life passing before the eyes (eyes examined themselves for all the metaphoric accumulations)—a review in pantomime of stage types, none of whom are appealing. Diddy's world consists only of his dehumanized nature; we guess that because he merely "inhabits" his life moving around the blocks of perception is all he can do. Diddy asks himself perhaps only one question that could trouble us: "Life = world. Death = being completely inside one's own head. Do these equations refute the puzzle of the two nightmares?"—the "nightmare that there are *two* worlds. The nightmare that there is *one* world. This one" (310). Sontag does not give Diddy any more permission than she gives Hippolyte to operate independently of her dictum about modern art— that thinking and acting are one in consciousness. Only in a last moment of fear does he make a separate assessment: "He may be about to ask himself what he has done. Whether all this is dishonorable isolation, a useless ordeal" (311). Hippolyte's airy retrospective on an extreme life forcibly excavated has been thrown over into an examination of the body's messy recalcitrance. Diddy succeeds where Hippolyte does not; he succeeds in being exhausted, he brings off his story entirely in his own head.

Diddy's walk in the charnel house is the part of the book most imaginatively rendered; here we are invited to a languorous roaming about of the kind and in the manner Hippolyte would admire. Sontag is here paying respect to the experience she says makes her stop at each graveyard she passes.

But neither book is very sentimental about its themes. Both protagonists distinguish themselves by the literalness of their "self-concealing." Each can claim, as Sontag has claimed for her modernist writers, that they are "perpetually in training to defeat themselves."[15] They have been pushed by their own merciless principles of erasure into and through the "guts" of their own existence entirely as a set action, methodically fulfilling a purpose. In other words, the effect Sontag achieves in their stories is to be understood in the terms she lays out for the modernist project: programmatic, inexorable, absolutistic, unwholesome. What happens to them is Sontag's way of offering a quiet dissuasion of the ethos they represent.

These are over-explicit novels, perhaps. Both go about "busily colonizing all strange domains of experience" (*AI* 77), and proceed to [Sontag quoting Cioran] " 'nowhere, when no external condition obliges you to do so'." And both willingly go to pains " 'to extricate oneself from the world—what a labor of abolition!' " (*SRW* 90). They become slightly showy, slightly academic as self-conscious works can be when ensnared by an idea. They are no less internalized works, however, for being moved by Sontag's disputes with her chosen realm of concerns. She relinquishes the role of modernist artist to her characters in their peculiarly death-loving quandaries, so that she can withdraw a little. She does not stand very far back.

Her remarks on Canetti's relationship to his novel *Auto-da-Fé* (1935) disclose what she thinks makes an author choose this faint dissimulation, and, by that way, she hints to the same process, same themes of her own books. "In the guise of a book about a lunatic—that is, as hyperbole—*Auto-da-Fé* purveys familiar cliches about unworldly, easily duped intellectuals. . . . It is impossible not to regard Kien's derangement as variations of his author's most cherished exaggerations" (*USS* 186).

> *Auto-da-Fé* depicts the stages of Kien's madness as three relations of "head" and "world"—Kien secluded with his books as "a head without a world"; adrift in the bestial city, "a world without a head"; driven to suicide by "the world in the head." And this was not language suitable only for the mad bookman; Canetti later used it in his notebooks to describe himself, as when he called his life nothing but a desperate attempt to think about everything "so that it comes together in a head and thus becomes one again," affirming the fantasy he had pilloried in *Auto-da-Fé*. (*USS* 187)

Admittedly, most often Sontag's formulations characterize someone else's aesthetic. She mutes the polemic in her views by description. She keeps herself from being moved into a position where her epigrams might coincide with an argument—an agility she would have the critic practice against interpretation. She is hard to pin down on what to her is a presumption of the times or an idea she endorses. Only when her descriptions are asserted and reasserted can we guess that both attitudes might be true.

Sontag finds Canetti in a role she recognizes because she too has come to use her fiction as the negative complement of her thoughts, "a pillory" that dignifies her preoccupations. Their fiction serves as tools for these intellectuals to flush out in their own clever, tempting, but inverted "exaggerations." Self-negation is Sontag's beast. Morbidity is its mad finale. Her curiosity or her fear leads her to see how much the sensibility informs her views, then she closes the matter off, so that the stories prove axiomatically adverse to propagation.

4

The Burden of the Aesthetic

In her first set of "case studies for an aesthetic" Sontag encircles art as if she were playing the chorus to an archaic form. She stands "a living wall"—to borrow Nietzsche's paraphrase of Schiller—"to guard arts" against the demand for utility and to preserve the arts' ideal domain. Facing the audience, she warns off hermeneutics, looking back to the performance, she nods and sighs over the extremes of modernism and its necessary dilemmas. She gives us a picture of criticism as an ideal boundary against the vested interests of the decoders she dares call philistines. The spectators are served by having the critic tutor them in the revels of art; art can then free itself from the parody it had imposed on itself in reaction to hermeneutical attack. Instead of hiding, it can now become "transparent."

Those artists who become didactic do so, Sontag thinks, by being caught up in the militant language of the avant-garde. They are taken in by the metaphor. Art's natural field is the gratification of intellectual pleasures and the refinement of the senses. Art does not give rise to conceptual knowledge, but "judgement in the state of thralldom" (AI 24). This is serious work enough, and full of its own magic. The enthralled spectator turns from it quickened to life, prepared, if the meaning-mongers could be deposed, to be unconcerned about the reflection of reality or the artist's point of view.

Her title essay, "Against Interpretation," carries the book's flag into the divided and tense territories of criticism. It is regarded as a high moment in her work, a hallmark of the period, as it should be. It is still a solace to students who protest that criticism makes the artist look dead; indeed, that criticism is the "revenge of the intellect on art." She takes up the questions of aesthetic meaning in a sweep of the textbook chapters in neat, quick numbered sections, resonant with thought, in language tempered on the most trustworthy, generalized use of words. With that balance she can then give way to grand opinion-making and the thrill of tastemaking: Thomas Mann is an "overcooperative writer," "uneasy before the naked power of his art" (AI 6); "it is precisely to the extent that Williams' plays and Cocteau's films do suggest these portentous meanings that they are defective, false, contrived, lacking in conviction" (AI 9); "a few of the films of Bergman—though crammed with lame messages about the modern spirit—thereby inviting interpretations—still triumph over the pretentious intentions of their director" (*AI* 11). She uses intuitively the bombastic nastiness of a critic who expects to tutor: interpretation is a "hindrance, a nuisance, a not so subtle philistinism"; it is "reactionary, impertinent, cowardly, stifling"; interpreters are "like leeches," and art has to protect itself from falling "prey" to their "zeal"; to interpret "is to impoverish, to deplete the world"; it is "the compliment mediocrity pays to genius."

To ears trained in the nuances of literary goodfellowship, this is sophomoric, rebel talk, written as if the critical mind itself held no fathomless ambiguities. Later it would remind conservative critics of what was wrong with the 1960s: it could not be chastened, was not willing to dig " 'behind the text, to find sub-text which is the true one" (*AI* 6); it was as shy of analysis as it was defensive about learning from history. On its own behalf, these last twenty years, the academy has proven that the hermeneutical impulse can shoot way past Marx's and Freud's "aggressive and impious theories of interpretations," (*AI* 7) to use evermore declamatory, deconstructive projects for its hermeneutical "mucking about." Seemingly, what Sontag here calls for returned with the eagerness of the suppressed. If she had an antiprogram in mind, she has lost.

Or perhaps not. Read again and not merely remembered, "Against Interpretation" rings with good sense and now appears all the more insightful for what will come when the European structuralist and post-structuralist theories hit hard against the political, moral, and Freudian readings then institutionalized. The aroused march of Sontag's essay is drummed along by her instinct for the essence of a polemic. Even so, what the essay explains is forgiving; it attempts to explain the difference between good and bad interpretation: "The old style of interpretation was insistent, but respectful, it erected another meaning on top of the literal one. The modern style of interpretation excavates, and as it excavates, destroys" (*AI* 6). "Interpretation must itself be evaluated, within a historical view of human consciousness. In some cultural contexts, interpretation is a liberating act. It is a means of revising, of transvaluing, of escaping the dead past" (*AI* 7). "What is needed is a vocabulary—a descriptive, rather than a prescriptive—vocabulary of forms. The best criticism, and it is uncommon, is of this sort that dissolves considerations of consciousness into those of forms" (*AI* 12), to which thought she adds examples of criticism that are passionate and finely wrought.

Sontag's new New Criticism, as inaugurated here, arches over the "transparent" work of art, pursuing ideas in the forms it discovers; the work itself is bracketed off in a language of untouchability. Meaning glints off its surface. The silence of a work that Sontag repeatedly asks be respected, resounds.

It is easier now to see what a thoroughly formalist age the later twentieth century is. Criticism proudly compares itself to art, even boasts that it is more important. Modern art may be as Sontag describes it in "One Culture and the New Sensibility,": "as much an act of criticism as an act of creation," so conscious is it with history of its past. Criticism, in turn, has become as much an act of creation as an act of criticism, so interested in itself and its overcoming of its past. And sometimes, it is true that criticism goes about making its "beautiful theories" (Elizabeth Bruss' term for writers such as Sontag, Gass, Barthes, and Bloom) that are subtle and self-defensive, for reasons similar to why the modernists "put silence into poems" in "flight from interpretation" (*AI* 10).

But secretive formalism is not quite Sontag's aim. She worked those five, extraordinarily productive years (represented in this volume) challenged by a line of thought: "Although I did not set out to devise a 'position' about either the arts or modernity, some kind of general position seemed to take shape and to voice itself with increasing urgency no matter what particular work I wrote about" (*AI* "Notes to the Paperback edition" 5). What is urgent for Sontag to resolve, so that the new sensibility as she calls it and however variously she defines it here may deserve her heart and mind, is the oldest questions about poetic vision and moral readiness. She knows she must overcome the old dichotomy between freedom of the aesthetic apprehension and the strictures of the moral. Few modern critics are as troubled; fewer still force the opportunity (the necessity of writing reviews) in search of an aesthetic at home with her sense of moral action and moral reflection, yet keeping art unapproachable by the usual reflection and mediation theorists.

This volume does hold together an attitude, if not a position, even though it is comprised of occasional pieces, not arranged developmentally. The rhetorical banner of the beginning and the inclusiveness of the last essay are placed as volume-making devices. They tend to shout more than they believe. What one does hear a good deal about is a set of persuasions, such as the "excess" of present culture and its "battering" of the senses, how art "nourishes" despite the fact it so often draws its "authority from unhealthiness." Sontag likes art that is intelligent and honest and at an edge. Frequently, and with some equivocation, she describes a form as "exemplary." Art itself is to be recognized when something has a " 'style,' and being both autonomous and exemplary" (*AI* 36). The finest works of art are to her those that preserve their "sublime neutrality."

She disparages the solace art can bring; pleasure, when she speaks of it is the pleasure of stretching, learning. It is typical of her to seek what this thing "is really about": "what pornography is really about, ultimately, isn't sex but death. . . . It's towards the gratification of death, succeeding and surpassing those of eros, that every truly obscene quest tends" (SRW 60). In her high-toned, principled style, she rejects the slide into accommodating metaphysical thought to American optimism. She finds this tendency endemic in her "own generation" in the "backwash of broken radical political enthusiasms" (AI 250). This backwash (as backwashes frequently do to American critics) brings out the complaint in Sontag that Americans tends to homogenize ideas in the service of some social glue, a kind of intellectual small townism anathema to her spirit. World spirits, like world-encompassing ideas, are not to bend to the trials of daily getting along. She may agree that "religious beliefs may be options, as William James described them, but they are not generalized options" (AI 253). Moral seriousness is not to be confused with religion; liking religion for reasons of comfort or human betterment is just so much "religious fellow-travelling." The intellectuals of her day were missing an opportunity: "most secular Western intellectuals have not really thought through or lived out the atheist option" (AI 254).

As in the realm of the spirit, so too in the realm of the flesh. In the same year (1961) Sontag writes: "the revolutionary implications of sexuality in contemporary society are far from being understood" (AI 257). The ebullience of these kinds of statements, toughened by the rebuke of the current generation, are axiomated in Sontag; they never leave her. In these earlier essays, they are based on a strong sense that the sociological imagination reflexively withdraws from the interior life. It will be in the inner life that the new great expanse of being will be found—at a cost. The inner life and the life of the body, reflection and will—each is conceived as tyrannical.

Sontag does not like incursions and mixing. Boundaries have to be clear; the substance and totalizing of a concept of being have to be appreciated. Her choice will always be reserved for those works and artists and thinkers who expand their vision until the sense of the world is made over. "A work of art," she tells us, "proposes a type of experience designed to manifest the quality of imperiousness"; it seduces "with the complicity of the experiencing subject" (AI 22).

In Sontag's aesthetic good art arises from the force of will to see the vision out as a completed idea. When she rethinks about what is wrong with Resnais's Muriel she writes: "Resnais knows all about beauty. But his films lack tonicity and vigor, directness of address. They are cautious, somehow, overburdened and synthetic. They do not go to the end, either of the idea or of the emotion which inspires them, which all great art must do" (*AI* 241). The genius of an idea, in art or otherwise, lies in its capacity to be driven onward by its inward force. Its creator must draw it forth and direct it towards its ends. This argument brings her close to accepting an aestheticized view of the world, with its implications. ("And the world *is*, ultimately, an aesthetic phenomenon" [*AI* 28]). So while she defends the autonomy of the aesthetic, even here, in these early essays, she does so "uneasily." She keeps sifting among variations of her description of this "emphatic form of experiencing the world" (*AI* 27) which is the aesthetic phenomenon, testing the right place where she can strengthen her claims for the arts as morally sensitizing. She knows that the trials of artists grappling with the tenets of modernism have been the "soul" of the aesthetic. If she can secularize, demystify, depersonalize that struggle, she might have the core of the moral tale she wishes to write. She approaches that task slowly, by a series of repetitions and refinements, connecting and disengaging aspects, slowly, that is, under that "hortatory" pressure of a heuristic project. She wants to discover how to speak about what is to be *known* in art, and how that knowing is special to the way modernist art carries the burden of its own immanence.

On the Plane of the Search

In her closing remarks on Norman O. Brown's *Life Against Death*, Sontag draws our attention to the grand place of immanence, generally, in the arming of doctrine. This particular essay is a fine example of her gift to quiet a book at once difficult and excitable by giving it a philosophical niche. Not "all eschatological theories are theories of history," she points out.

> There is another kind of eschatology, which might be called the eschatology of immanence (as opposed to the more familiar eschatology of transcendence). It is this hope that Nietzsche . . . expressed in his theory of "eternal return" and "will to power." However, for Nietzsche, the promise of fulfilled immanence was available only to the few. . . . Brown rejects the logic of public domination which Nietzsche accepted. . . . The highest praise one can give Brown's book is that, apart from its all-important attempt to penetrate and further the insights of Freud, it is the first major attempt to formulate an eschatology of immanence in the seventy years since Nietzsche (*AI* 262).

Her own eschatology of immanence awaits the outcome of her struggle with Nietzsche. To Nietzsche's concept that "music is the world's will," Sontag pronounces that "Art is the objectifying of the will in a thing or performance, and the provoking or arousing of the will" (*AI* 31). Morality is a "form of acting," and art, "by enlivening our sensibility and consciousness," "nourishes our capacity for moral choice" (*AI* 25). "What a work of art does is to make us see or comprehend something singular, not judge or generalize. The act of comprehension accompanied by voluptuousness is the only valid end, and the sole sufficient justification, of a work of art" (*AI* 29). She stays as close as she can in this volume to the "impersonal (and trans-personal)," "new classicism" in art which sees art "as a new kind of instrument, an instrument for modifying consciousness and organizing new modes of sensibility" (*AI* 296). But behind that reasonableness of her address vies a desire to arrow formulations at the ideals buried in the self, a fearful place that *might* learn the wrong lessons should intelligence be quickened towards its acute states.

In the service of reason, then, most of the essays in *Against Interpretation* are built around the strength of the form in question. True to her statements on interpretation, she does not muse on the artist's psychology, purpose, perspective; we hear little of the artist's creative sources; she little values the audience's appetite for self-recognition or coziness of any kind. She is not interested in what later impresses postmodern critics: repetition, pastiche, reversals of hierarchical orders of interpersonal roles, neo-mythologizing. The continual comment upon the history of its forms, which is modern art for her, must be about the extension of the form as an assault, not for the mutual amusement of artist and audience. She severs the line of expression from the artist. Audiences may be used, as they are in the Happenings, as "scapegoats." In no sense does she want us to understand that the voluptuousness of art is an embrace.

Given Sontag's prescriptions for criticism, the word scapegoat is harsh. She is reaching through the "painterly style" of these events (which is not their true form, she warns) into where Surrealist wit turns into Surrealist terror. Happenings stir up the hidden content of dreams, and, armed with these, they then skip the limits that allow the audience to enjoy them as pieces. The living wall of criticism—that distancing that the critic presides over—disappears. The audience becomes the innocence upon which vengeance is played, another element to be made expendable, as all elements of the experience must be expendable.

Finally, of course, Happenings can be viewed without self-annihilation. It is easy enough to shake off art's impressions, and Sontag, to her credit, always seeks out the way in which art enforces its power. The violence embedded in modern art must be made to dance its macabre dance before our eyes. She pushes the form to reveal its content—the purposes it can serve—in this case the "aggression" of Surrealism's art of "radical juxtaposition."

Yet, what one hears in Sontag's essays, despite all this talk about art's afflicted and harassing nature, is a moderating tone. Sontag "good husbands" (her words for Camus' disappointingly mild character) the bad side of art. She speaks in rounded tones about "some (but not all) insanity, some (but not all) unhealthiness, some (but not all) denials of life are truth-giving, sanity-producing, health-creating and life-enhancing" (AI 51). She does not "mean to decry a fashion, but to underscore the motive behind the contemporary taste for the extreme in art and thought"; that is, "the morbid, the hysterical, the sense of the unhealthy, the enormous indulgence in suffering—. . . [which is] what we value today" (AI 50). We desire to preserve mystery in the world is her answer. But that answer functions not unlike the cap placed on religious experience by her own generation. She too is given to containing (once she has pointed it out), more pleasantly rearranging, the troubling inner life of modern art. This effort can be felt in what is smoothly elided in her discussion of false division between form and content in "On Style."

"Art performs a 'moral' task because the qualities which are intrinsic to the aesthetic experience (disinterestedness, contemplativeness, attentiveness, the awakening of feelings) and the aesthetic object (grace, intelligence, expressiveness, energy, sensuousness) are also fundamental constituents of a moral response to life" (AI 25). This is a generous, lucid concept; unfortunately, it obscures many problems. It does not help her to specify the ethics of holding a camera, for example, or viewing a film in relation to its intentions (Riefenstahl); or separating the regrettable from the exemplary (Artaud). It does not help her explore her own sympathy for the heroic completeness of tragedy—to the totality of death. Her position here in the essay "On Style" is too general. She will need to know which sensibility is enlivened, so that when faced with a choice, the individual can throw off the contemplativeness of aesthetic morality in order to act for the good.

Here, for instance, her allegiance to the beautiful encourages her to make the famous assessment she later recants:

> To call Leni Riefenstahl's *Triumph of the Will* and *The Olympiad* masterpieces is not to gloss over Nazi propaganda with aesthetic lenience. The Nazi propaganda is here. But something else is there, too, which we reject at our loss. Because they project the complex movements of intelligence and grace and sensuousness, these two films of Riefenstahl (unique among Nazi artists) transcend the categories of propaganda or even reportage. . . . Through Riefenstahl's genius as a film-maker, the "content" has—let us even assume, against her intentions—come to play a formal role (AI 25-6).

Sontag will have to come back to the point that the intelligence, grace, and sensuousness in these films serve propaganda *in* their formal roles. But this thought requires principles not recoverable from Sontag's early Nietzschean perspective, not to be found in that region where "the exuberant fertility of universal will" feeds us eternally.[1]

Elsewhere in *Against Interpretation*, we see Sontag applying an antidote to the seductive, youthful Nietzsche. Even in "On Style" she adds the little allowances that it is the historic which lends our awareness of style, that intelligence in art can be addressed by its statement. These are minor notes, however, made for the sake of argument, qualified as soon as they appear. Her better effort touches a warmth missing in Nietzsche. To his imperious will, imperious beauty, imperious sense of life, she adds sensibilities. She finds she can like, when she wants to, the absurd, "sly" fun and definitive unimportance of Camp. It has an egalitarian spirit—it loves unabashed fantasy, the kitsch as dream, style as the delightful reach of the common away from itself. It does not trample on high art, rather it frees the lowly from snobbish, theoretical lockout. It knows distinctions, it just incorporates more. It is, as a sensibility, "wholly aesthetic," a dandified, comic sense of life unspoiled by the elitism of its forebears.

Art is successful when intelligence rises out of and suppresses the brilliance of the work's conception; in Camp, the unsuccessful artform, this essay teaches, all the extravagance of effort stays put, on the naive, innocent, instant character of the effect sought. That effect has to be, in some way, wonderful, a parade, an unabashed flaunting of small gifts, the sentimental flourish of the death of Little Nell, a simple actress such as Garbo, pretending to her depth, both incapable of being otherwise—the joy of complete self-acceptance when all the world is in quotation marks. The effect has to be, moreover, indelible. Great Camp happens from those performances that no one else can do because the actors or auteur are intent on being good, at their limits, in their oddball natures, steadfastly missing a larger reach but genuine in every respect in their own. Self-consciousness in any part, as Sontag tells us, and the Camp spirit dies. The studied attempt to play the Camp personality, to make Camp, when good is comedy, another thing. The Camp sensibility does not mock: "It only seems like malice, cynicism. It wants to enjoy."

In the hierarchy of sensibilities, Sontag makes it number three. The first, high culture, is "basically moralistic"; the second, "that of extreme states of feeling"—the avant-garde—"gains power by a tension between moral and aesthetic passion. The third, Camp, is wholly aesthetic" (*AI* 287). From Sontag's own keen perception that Pop Art is not Camp, we could slip in a fourth sensibility: above Camp and below the avant-garde lies Pop creating its own tension. Presumably, there could be more.

What happens in her last essay in this collection is that she lets the idea of sensibility recover from division and take charge of a whole age. The "new sensibility" sweeps past literary culture to mimic the sensory extension of modern technology. It explores what science has already given, in—if we think on it further—a somewhat disappointing, belated fashion. Nevertheless, the new scope of modern life, its speed, materials, discoveries, so thrills artists they need not be chided for forgetting humanist fears. The province of narrative culture is superseded, and with it, seemingly, the very purpose of the distinctions she makes in the essay on Camp.

In the new sensibility there are no judgments, no morality, no avant-garde, really, since there is no tension. The new sensibility advocates immersion in perception, taste, movement before thought reduces their phenomenal resilience, and it pushes past the senses "to that which is only with difficulty intelligible, and is invisible" (AI 301). It joins science seriously. Even the neo-realists, we could suppose from this scheme, join the science of photography uncritically. Ten years after "One Culture and the New Sensibility," Sontag will pick apart the aesthetic generated by a technology—photography—but here she remains sanguine. Something of the magic of art is here invoked, the "aura" of modernism is recreated. She would almost like to restore art to the ideal of servicing truth, when art needed no justification, when the artist worked under no false hubris.

What Sontag is working for in this essay is a way to name, not a sensibility, but a Weltanschauung. The Weltanschauung of a culture that may not know itself tasks that critic to hyperboles of inclusiveness. By contrast, Sontag's law of immanence presses her to take the claims of modernism's rhetoric of autonomy to its depths. The autonomy she lends art begs the artist to consummate a marriage and disappear, to experiment without purpose, to be violated as much as violate. This autonomy of the aesthetic in freeing art from a restrictive sense of purpose lays it open to a deadly arrogance. Instead of criticism driving art into irony and exaggeration, the wide open field (art, artist, audience) lets everyone be splayed. Yet ultimately, for Sontag the danger of art lies not in exhaustion, but in aestheticization. Art makes up the world. It no longer competes with reflective knowledge, it tempts us to believe that style, or form, wills the world into being.

And in that way lies madness, and madness beckons in the seductive myths of modern art, the madness of solipsism and the torment of carrying on the age's "spiritual project" (SRW 3). In these first essays, doubts about that project are fended off by what Sontag believes the critic must do. The critic must describe the uses to which form can be put. The "concern with insanity in art today," freed from psychological explanation, lends the artist a form "more heroic, more rich in fantasy, more philosophical" (*AI* 169).

Compared to the reinvention of madness in the middle 1960s as the most fertile, honest, intrepid of experiences, Sontag's invocation is quiet, with the further safety of aesthetics to support her. The totalizing imagination (which she later characterizes as belonging to "the artist, erotomane, the left revolutionary, and the madman" [*SRW* 69]) in her is held in check, as it is not, for instance, in Deleuze and Guattari. Her practice is difficult, however. For the rules that govern the way of her own sensibility stem from the extremes of modern art and ideas. She is not merely documenting the times. She selects along a narrow band of its most cerebral and cold, or impassioned and tortured. Then she submits it to her dichotomizing intelligence, the technique of making distinctions, which heightens (or lets fall) the work from planes of abstractions. Her style is much like what she says about Bresson. His is a "spiritual style" chaste, reflective, which uses naked devices of distancing (she believes) "as a source of great emotional power." "The detachment and retarding of the emotions, through the consciousness of form," Sontag insists, "makes them far stronger in the end" (*AI* 181).

The age is nihilistic, the senses need reviving, disciplined by the knowledge of its forms. No thrashing art, no irrationalist provocations, no art of revenge rituals, no art that turns the world upside down, no art that incites, is really to her taste. The ill she splashed on Baldwin and Baraka reveals how she is not prepared to be assaulted, except by the pain of Europe, in the mood of its chosen formal vehicles. Masques (of black and white) of victim and virtue need a greater social stage, such as Vietnam.

She is most comfortable in debates around the oldest forms, which we bury, she says, only as acts of "self-entombment." Tragedy, she argues with Lionel Abel, lives, not in the mourning for lost values, for it never lived in values. Tragedy is a way to acknowledge the world's "implacability." "Tragedy is a vision of nihilism, a heroic or ennobling vision of nihilism" (*AI* 136). Comedy succeeds in a "precarious ascendancy of comic detachment over the morally ugly and terrifying" (*AI* 150). It is the more timely vehicle, "the hope for intelligence in the theater," (because it requires "intellectual simplification"); one of her favorite examples of good comedy is Daniel Talbot and Emile de Antonio's editing of the TV kinescopes of the 1954 Army-McCarthy hearings. If that choice reflects a rather distilled interest in comedy, she is being sincerely ironic within the tradition of what we laugh at in Happenings.

I don't think this [impulse to laugh] is because we are embarrassed or made nervous by violent and absurd actions. I think we laugh because what goes on in the Happenings is, in the deepest sense, funny. There is something that moves one to laughter . . . in the most terrible of modern catastrophes and atrocities. There is something comic in the modern experience as such, a demonic, not a divine comedy, precisely to the extent that modern experience is characterized by meaningless mechanized situations of disrelations. (AI 274)

The metaplay (the third of the three forms: tragedy, comedy, metaplay) does not moralize or teach. The true metadramatist seeks the "studied neutrality—the mutual cancellation of all values" (AI 139) by fusing "posthumous spirit of tragedy" with the most ancient principles of comedy: "counterfeit, deceit, role-playing, manipulation, self-dramatization" (AI 135). The metaplay weds the soul of McCarthy to the implacable world.

When our joys ring so hollow, and our cries against the world sound ludicrous, then, indeed, silence appears as a gesture of elegant fulsomeness—all our conflicts therein held are held in check by the modernist void. In the aesthetic of silence, Sontag seeks out the broadest condition of modernist art. In a way, she answers Abel. The aesthetic of silence does not dismiss (or strip the face off) the traditional divisions among the modes. The "prestige" of all languages has fallen. And in the fall "one must recognize something like the perennial discontent with language that has been formulated in each of the major civilizations of the Orient and the Occident, whenever thought reaches a certain, high, *excruciating* order of complexity and spiritual seriousness" (SRW 21).

The "Aesthetics of Silence"

Before she can make that restoration, there are all too many myths to be demystified. The age is prone "from the Story of O to Mao" to the "incorrigible survival of the religious impulse." One of "the primary tasks of future thought" is to "try to make a fresh way of talking at the most serious, ardent, and enthusiastic level, heading off the religious encapsulation" (SRW 69). What could be more egregious than the myth of art's absoluteness, that makes art "enemy of the artist, for it denies him the realization—the transcendence—he desires" (SRW 5).

This later myth about art:

> installs within the activity of art many of the paradoxes involved in attaining absolute states of being described by the great religious mystics. As the activity of the mystic must end in a *via negativa*, a theology of God's absence, a craving for the cloud of unknowing

beyond knowledge and for the silence beyond speech, so art must
tend toward anti-art, the elimination of the "subject" (the "object,"
and the "image"), the substitution of chance for intention, and the
pursuit of silence. (*SRW* 4–5)

In the 1967 essay "The Aesthetics of Silence" Sontag sets about
exposing modernism's annihilistic, "self-engorging" quest for purity of
vehicle and motive. She forces its paradoxical involutions into the
open as one thing, as a silence, which in turn should be understood as
multiple strategies, multiple styles. The tendency of the 1960s to up
the sound of the approaching end, its peculiar reapprehension of an
apocalyptic, to her is another case of the "loud style" of silence, "fre-
netic and overgeneralizing," which "must suffer the indignity of all
apocalyptic thinking: namely to prophesy the end, to see the day come,
to outlive it" (*SRW* 32).

Significantly, as her structuring censure, conducted mostly with a
philosophical evenness, falls over its essences, silence does not withdraw. Inspection, a homage, opens the secrets of silence until they seem
equal to the very spiritual project Sontag acknowledged is its aim.
Perhaps the language of spirituality, whenever invoked, defies the
speaker's admonitions; perhaps silence's quiet reintegrates mysteries,
retangles thoughts. In Sontag's hands, silence reproved becomes silence
overwrought.

What she would have argued earlier, for instance, as the age's sensibility, she deepens into thoughts about its spirituality. She starts off,
"Every era has to reinvent the project of 'spirituality' for itself" (*SRW*
3). This spirituality is a special plan—no diminutive sensibility to be
shattered or outgrown. It is those "ideas of deportment aimed at resolv-
ing the painful structural contradictions in the human situation, at the
completion of human consciousness, at transcendence. In the modern
era, one of the most active metaphors for the spiritual project is 'art' "
(*SRW* 3).

The fall from transcendence to metaphor reveals the plot of the essay,
or rather conceals Sontag's quandary over pinning the right merit on
this art. She can make the artist's ambition delirious: in art which
"aims to become a 'total experience,' soliciting total attention, the
strategies of impoverishment and reduction indicate the most exalted
position art can adopt. Underneath what looks like a strenuous modesty
. . . is to be discerned an energetic secular blasphemy: the wish to attain
the unfettered, unselective, total consciousness of 'God' " (*SRW* 14).

She can make art's liberatory pretexts flatten out to nullity. As a
strategy, silence was to transform art, "art itself being the herald of an
anticipated radical transformation of human values. But the success of

this strategy must mean its abandonment" (SRW 18). This art is bare, literal, and before such "fully conscious works," "one feels something like the mixture of anxiety, detachment, pruriency, and relief that a physically sound person feels when he glimpses an amputee." Artists, swayed by these ideals, long for the total object. "But exactly what is a totality and what constitutes completeness in art (or anything else)?" Sontag questions. "The problem is, in principle, unresolvable. . . . The necessity of these parts in this order is never given; it is conferred" (SRW 30). Once so understood, once we give up this "refusal to admit this essential contingency" we would not need to give closure to a work by way of interpretation, nor suffer the sense that the artwork is "inadequate to its 'subject' " (SRW 31).

Be advised, she writes, that the silence of these works speaks not to the ineffability of beauty (beauty is a "not very interesting," "essentially vacant concept" [SRW 31]); rather, the "aura of the unspeakable" is "always connected with systematic transgressions of a formal sort" (SRW 31). In that formal address, the aesthetic of silence acts as "meta-ethical tact, a standard of decorum. . . . the unity of certain preference about what can and cannot be said (or presented). At the same time that it may make a tacit proposal for upsetting previously consecrated rulings on what can be said (or represented), it issues its own set of limits" (SRW 32).

Whether loud, "sensuous, ecstatic, fragile," collapsing into the void of negative silence where it risks spiritual nausea, madness; or soft, "classic reticence stepped up to the nth degree," "in ironic openness rather than didactic seriousness," the aesthetics of silence functions as a boundary notion, falling to the line between the unstable antithesis of plenum and void. There, in its contradictions, it changes into myth. The myths of silence and emptiness are about "as nourishing and viable as might be devised in an 'unwholesome' time—which is, of necessity, a time in which 'unwholesome' psychic states furnish the energies for most superior work in the arts. Yet one cannot deny the pathos of the myths" (SRW 11).

Sontag often assumes an air of resignation:

> Art is so far along the labyrinthine pathways of the project of transcendence that one can hardly conceive of it turning back, short of the most drastic and punitive "cultural revolution." Yet at the same time, art is foundering in the debilitating tide of what once seemed the crowning achievement of European thought: secular historical consciousness. . . . To compensate for this ignominious enslavement to history, the artist exalts himself with the dream of a wholly ahistorical, and therefore unalienated, art. (SRW 14–15)

But art that is silent can only stare at history; what it wishes is for a cultural "clean slate." This cannot be realized: "Either it is taken to the point of utter self-negation (as art) or else it is practiced in a form that is heroically, ingeniously inconsistent" (*SRW* 11–12).

Nor can irony rescue it permanently: "But if irony has more positive sources than Nietzsche acknowledged, there still remains a question as to how far the resources of irony can be stretched. It seems unlikely that the possibilities of continually undermining one's assumptions can go on unfolding indefinitely into the future, without being eventually checked by despair or by a laugh that leaves one without any breath at all" (*SRW* 34).

What she writes here is a tale riddled with self-disclosure and self-investigation in the guise of critique encompassing all "serious" art. She is reconnoitering in this essay a barren realm she forbids, in a sense, anyone from leaving. Art's nearly ineluctable predicament closes exits, to the stylistically inventive as well as the exhausted. All sensibilities shrivel next to the transcending ideal. Silence, for all its crushing irresolutions, defines what is art for those "committed to the idea that the power of art is located in its power to negate." For them, "the ultimate weapon in the artist's inconsistent war with his audience is to verge closer and closer to silence" (*SRW* 8). And from there, as she says, they can only stare.

We need to catch the effort at appeasement in this exceptionally fine, deceptively neutral mapping of an aesthetic. The times are pressing her to find a radical will—when comedy, Camp, irony, eclecticism widen the gulf between will and aesthetic pleasure. Only the tragic, or in her muffled word, the serious, champions an effort grand enough to be the Nietzschean metaphysical equivalent to the political, that is, to be a contender to the political, imaginatively. But to do so, means that this serious art must come to a true negating principle. It cannot fall back, like Greek tragedy, into the prophylaxis of Nietzschean disburdenment.

In the fullness of her critique, attempting no less than the corrective to the age's aesthetic dilemmas, perhaps it was appropriate that she not mention that it was her own hermetic art she seeks to adjure. Perhaps she had not fully recognized it as such. She stands so charged, for she will name it herself. Her own art is a "dramaturgy of silence."

The Two Films: *Duet for Cannibals* and *Brother Carl*

Released by the exuberance of completing a work that, unabashedly, has found its subject, that has "unmasked itself as pain," Sontag can say quite simply of her second film, *Brother Carl:*

The characters that become Martin and Carl are people who have
lived for decades inside my head—emblems of the dramaturgy of
silence (or voluntary mutism) that has been a recurrent theme in my
life and my novels as well as my films. Silence haunts *The Benefactor*
not only as an option stated in the plot but, more important, in
the off-centered loquacity of the narrator (which gives an oppressive
weight to all that he does not tell). Voluntary mutism is what tempts
Diddy throughout the long meditation on dying which is the pilgrim's
progress toward death, Hester's blindness is another, transposed form
of silence. In *Duet for Cannibals* the catalytic member of the quartet,
Francesca, refuses to speak. And the Francesca figure reappears in
Brother Carl doubled: as the almost mute Carl and as the autistic
child. (*BC* x)

We can look back at that first film (*Duet* . . .) since Sontag here
synthesizes them for us, and recall that hammering in the opening shot
as the last drum roll. The film opens with a poster being nailed to the
wall. Supposedly the sound drives home the point that Bauer, the man
in the poster—a crude version of the international political mindbender,
the intellectual apparatchik of the revolution, self-important, with a
past—will cannibalize his young workers, almost systematically. Indeed, the camera moves with spare jolting shifts from one scene to the
next as the young man, Tomas, hired to edit Bauer's papers, gets trapped
into being the item whetting the sexual appetites of Bauer and his wife
Francesca. Neither eros or appetite, however, are given "expression"
in this stiff, staring film. They are represented, as Sontag explains,
emblematically.

Francesca plays a wide-eyed victim of Bauer's bullying—impassive,
then seductive, and then a maitresse of the erotic closet. She tricks
Tomas into believing Bauer intends to kill her while Bauer plots to
push Tomas at his wife in order to rage in jealousy. In one scene she
locks herself in the car. Frightened she will do herself harm, Bauer
arouses Tomas from his sleep. When she accelerates hard for the closed
garage, Bauer leaps between and she stops in time. She calmly opens
the door for Bauer and sprays shaving foam across the inside of the
windshield as he pants over her. In another scene, when more cutting
suggests the exploitation of "thematic resources," i. e., the juxtaposition of what would take place in the character's mind's eye (see Sontag's
discussion of this technique in her essay on *Persona*), Francesca and
Tomas make love while Bauer goes, with feigned reluctance, into the
bedroom armoire. She locks him in, but he can get out as Tomas learns
after being disturbed by Bauer's rhythmic knocking. Bauer simply walks
through the bedroom having now dressed for the outdoors.

As these entanglements multiply, Bauer's voice on the tapes, which

Tomas has been transcribing, begins to talk to Tomas in real time, as Tomas does in turn. Who is recorded and who is recording, who knows and who suspects, twist into the confusion that is soon extended to Tomas' girlfriend, Ingrid, the second partner in the duet. She bravely offers herself as a servant, hoping to get Tomas to quit. But her resolve sinks into the pleasures of submission, as she yields to the carefully orchestrated seduction into being their child, Bauer's lover, and Francesca's alter ego.

Silence stultifies, deliberately warping the pacing and camera work of the film. When the characters speak, their language is stripped of communicability. They speak in artifices, directed by something extenuated and ugly. Most scenes are "motivated" by a game steps ahead of Tomas and Ingrid, so that the mechanical puppetry of the older couple is countered by an off-balanced style of the younger. The impact of being duped and swallowed is pitched equally at the audience. It is given no knowingness to savor, no hints to reflect upon the intentions of the characters, no forewarning. The suggestion is that there is no purpose behind the plot, above or below its symbolic level. The mounting sequences of entrapment feel invented only by some generalized practice on the part of Bauer and Francesca, not planned, inspired rather by the death wishes they keep restaging for one another. The possibility or impossibility of their seemingly perfect timing becomes a pointless question, as does the danger Bauer may or may not be in, the paranoia he may or may not experience, her illness, his, her madness, his or their desire to kill, their "deaths." The tableaux of their emotions are panned much as the camera pans a large landscape on the wall before resting on the smokey images of a pornographic movie being screened while Ingrid pumps on top of Bauer. Tomas, entering, sits by Francesca, who turns his head to watch—that is, pain blank as a landscape, sexuality crudely displayed, jealousy as taunt—all in two dimensions.

In a quickly managed finale, Francesca pretends to be murdered; Bauer shoots himself; Francesca and Tomas joyfully burn Bauer's papers; Ingrid comes for Tomas, they run away, united, as the last shot catches Francesca and Bauer standing in the window.

Ingrid and Tomas have been spewed forth, intact. Unlike Bergman's *Persona*, where the loss of Alma to Gertrude's illness keeps drawing on our sympathy and our puzzlement, the duet of these couples finishes off like an antique dance—interesting for its spectacle and formal patterning, striking in its sincerity about ritualized cruelty, a lesson in set pieces of what might be intended. When Bauer shoots himself in front of Francesca's corpse, and Francesca sits up, Tomas, a bleak figure (in words virtually the duplicate in sense and spirit to many other of her fictional moments), asks: "Is it really so hard to die? So complicated?" Francesca answers: "Yes it is . . . Unless it's very easy." Tomas: "But you were helping him." Script instructions: "He looks as if he has just understood something. He points the gun at his chest." Francesca: (Off) "Wait" (DC 124).

Each scene is cut from the one before with a new suspicion, from Tomas or Ingrid's point of view, trying to lead the audience in its few surmises: to believe something worth interrogating has happened. The still of Bauer and Francesca in the last shot reminds the viewer that the game can test all the participant's talents for deciphering, if they have the will for it.

Since the film is set up to resist meaning, and the feast is a private one, seemingly no allegory of our time is being proposed. Yet it is impossible to have used this material in 1965 without still another taunting of expectations. The young revolutionaries, restless, student-ish, needing a toehold for the next step might see the importance of working with a Bauer. Bauer to Tomas:

> Don't you want to do something useful? Something more than being a perpetual student, running around to demonstrations or, like your girlfriend, sitting in an office, peddling posters and pamphlets exhort-ing people to support noble aims they have no idea how to carry out? I'm giving you the chance to *do* something, by helping me. (DC 79)

Tomas, our hero, replies, "It's out of the question." Thereupon, to prove to Bauer that Bauer does not understand him, Tomas reaches for his gun. With what cynicism is this scene drawn! The anguished exile, his inner devolution matching the outward fading of power, is interpo-lated as being alive only to the plots to overthrow him, and manages his excitement accordingly. Tomas, never enthusiastic, nonetheless, is given no chance to measure what he is learning. He must prove his "manhood" against this monster in purely personal terms. Would the killing of the icons of the old, failed revolutions bear no more dignity?

The jacket to the Noonday edition of the screenplay calls this film a "bone-dry serio-comedy" meant, at least in places, to be funny. The abrupt shift in moods is sometimes funny, the explicitness of its devices sometimes reaches inane proportions, and is funny. Occasionally, a scene clowns, such as when Ingrid, asleep between Bauer and Francesca, gets pounced upon by them in unison. But humor does not rescue this film or make any point at all. And only from the evidence of Sontag's other stories can one surmise that her goal was not to trivialize the young activists. Her greater interest lies in her recurrent themes, the will against powerful authority, the will to resist transforming into the wish to die, the silence that falls over the heavy burden of death. This earlier film needed a villain to hide her theme's relationship to her. The second film, closer to an intensely painful experience, could let go into the "pathos" of the myths of silence.

In this second film, *Brother Carl*, she chooses to make an *ex voto* painting (clue: one is prominent on the wall in an early scene). By crisscrossing the illness of one set of her characters with the strength of the other, the film begs for a mystical transference. This is an utterly sincere film (it has given up all tricks). The viewer is asked to sacred ground, not in the presence of God and the drama of lost and resurrected faith of religious miracle plays, but in the presence of goodness, the "caring" that each of the characters seeks to elicit and seeks to offer, in order to rescue and be rescued.

Their story folds out upon itself as a triptych on an altar, the central passion occupied by the suicide of Lena, a strong, talented woman, who calmly walks into the sea, unable to reawaken her ex-husband's (Martin's) love for her. On one side stands an autistic little girl against the image of Magritte's "The Red Model." On the far side, the ex-dancer, broken and made helpless by his director friend (Martin), lies catatonic beside the sea at the feet of the standing autistic child, who can now speak. Her mother (Karen) and father are rushing towards her, reunited around the miracle they have been granted by grace. In the background, symbols of the twinning cavort: twin actors in lyotards mock battle under Lena's direction, twin dancers under Martin's, an enlarged photograph of fetal twins grow into real, obstreperous ones, signaling Lena's and Karen's intertwined positions. Behind Carl's story his decrepit parents, gross and stupid, accuse. Not even Carl can now tell them apart. Overall the tones of this black-and-white film, about duplication and exchange, are muted grays with stark images. Its language is odd, raw, abstract. When the characters speak they speak in the voice of Sontag's autobiographical pieces. It is a calling out, over the silence of injury and pain. Understood as anything less, the bathos of the material strains tolerance.

Carl, the ex-dancer is the film's "holy fool": he pantomimes what the others will do or are trying to do. We cannot sneer. His feeble gestures and knowingness are wrenching in their contrast to the speech of the other characters, often again, in Sontag's idea of imaginary psychology, full of threats and taunts. Carl silhouetted: he looks so fragile, so thin, one imagines his heart pounding too closely to the surface of his chest, competing with his voice. His silence results from the struggle—made audible by the rhythmic "pounding" identified with him and Anna, the child. On the outside of the triptych, before the

credits, their pairing is foretold. Anna has climbed into a kitchen cabi-
net; Carl in the next scene, smiling down at Anna, joins her in one of
his favorite tombs, a recessed area in the walls of an abandoned fort.
Heavy doors close upon him.

Anna's only interests in the course of the films are any sounds not
human, until Carl lays his body on top of hers, grows rigid with catato-
nia, and she speaks. He has given up to her the last of his capacity
to communicate, silently or otherwise—he dies to expression. "He's
heavy," Anna says, her only words, summarizing the longer passage in
which Lena' suicide had been "heavy" for Karen, and implicating the
"heavy" conversations of the film, the only ones Carl likes.

This heaviness from the burden of another's death also condenses
the silence around the solemn, spare questions in Sontag's piece "Trip
to China." "A trip that might ease a private grief?" asks the narrator.
"He died so far away. By visiting my father's death, I make him heavier.
I will bury him myself" (*I,E* 19). (It can be found also in "Debriefing"
when again she writes of her friend, Susan Taubes' suicide: "How I
groaned under the burden of our friendship. But your death is heavier"
[*I,E* 52].) The film and that piece share many details, written under
simpler impulses, close in time to the purest moments of Sontag's
aesthetic of silence. In the screenplay, Karen, standing beside a bright
window of the hotel, abruptly pulls the heavy curtains close and intones
these lines: "To act without hope. / To speak without an echo. / Not
to dream of saving anyone. Not to long to be saved" (*BC* 46). They were
cut from the film—too artificial for Karen, but an almost perfect echo
of Sontag's many other fictional voices.

The paradoxes of the aesthetic of silence can paralyze, Sontag had
written: Carl's spiritual disease glues him to the moment. He gets
stuck, Martin says, as Martin leads Carl back from the water; he forgets
the cause of the emotion. The others are trying to become unfrozen
too—close-ups emphasize the severe middle-life faces of the characters,
embittered. What can be done short of a cultural revolution, argued
Sontag in her essay, what short of a miracle?

"From the beginning, when I first imagined *Brother Carl*," she writes,
"the center was the miracle."

> The only interesting action in life is a miracle or the failure to perform
> a miracle, and miracles are the only subject of profound interest left
> for art. I say this as someone who has tried to perform a kind of
> miracle (that effort being the deepest personal source of *Brother Carl*)
> or, more modestly, to help a miracle come to pass. When I started to
> write the script, I was in the throes of that effort. The week after the
> end of the shooting, in Rome, I learned I had failed. That failure has
> not destroyed my belief in miracles. (*BC* xv–xvi)

Interestingly, paralyzed love does not appear in Sontag's catalogue of the aesthetics of silence. The silence of Bergman's *Cries and Whispers* and Woody Allen's *Autumn Sonata* are not easily adaptable to her theory either. Both of Sontag's films bend too much to be "Swedish," as Allen's film does. The strain of that kind of homage may have invited the spleen she vented in "A Letter from Sweden." These are groaning silences, silences so without parody or irony they need miracles to lift them out of our temptation to laugh. And whether the miracle is performed or not, the miracle is "the only subject of profound interest" left for these films: they are so much moved into the recesses of pain.

There is another way to consider this point about the last, profound subject of art. Miracle plays are the purest form of allegory. A message is being delivered here about charity, goodness, martyrdom (Carl's), where disbelief is impossible. The tug between monstrous unfeeling-ness and the awakening of feeling, or between tormented child and tormented adult starts up old machinery gratefully accepted in a society where alienation is valorized. If we no longer care for our alienation, we wait for a miracle. Or if, after the aesthetics of silence, the pit yawns for our fall, we want wings. Miracles, then, are the purer theme of allegory, not heroism. With miracles, the codes and emblems of this world gain mystery under the rule of grace. In the secular allegory, the plot has to drum up glory for the hero. In miracle plays, unwarranted good fortune descends. The unexpectedness unnerves (cynical or guilty) modern consciousness, already seeing its art "floundering in the tide of what once seemed the crowning achievement of European thought: secular historical consciousness" (*SRW* 14).

It is part of the trajectory of modernism that Sontag creates melodra-matic, miracle-based scripts in her early ventures into the world of sentiment. Hippolyte's "off-centerness" and Diddy's dead-end cannot get at the burden of the aesthetic. Miracles break down the walls of aesthetic closure, and miracles keep stylization (the other impulse of the aesthetic) contained. In modernist literature one "negates" self-negation by miracles—of kindness, health, and speech.

Arguably, one way around the harsh rule of self-negation is by plural-izing, adding sensibilities or imaginations (now commonly identified as the postmodern temptation), like the pornographic imagination, or the imagination of disaster. Still a third way might be by taking trips. Yet a fourth way might be to free oneself from being under the influence of another's death, or (more a message for others, presumably) the possession by a group, or from under the sway of a gross and malignant charmer, or a sect leader of convincing magical powers—all subjects of the short stories "Old Complaints Revisited," "Doctor Jekyll," and "Debriefing."

These ways out prove no way out, of course; they were never intended to be. The figures in the above stories are not given exits from their dilemmas. The language spoken here is silence, the rational, cool aspect of silence if that ironic, and paradoxical, meaning can be sustained. And it usually is, as an expressive range deliberately muted in loyalty to Sontag's dictum that rhetorical demonstrativeness wards off intelligence.

Only occasionally her rhetoric gives over to its heart, its near inert heart. For out of the heart of the aesthetic of silence pulses another substance—sometimes choking in its sluggishness, as in the films *Promised Lands* and *Unguided Tour*. In these the camera attempts to write epitaphs for the dead of an ancient land, Israel, in the desert of rusting tanks, and for a love dying among the worn monuments of Italian art. The explicitness of her prose, one of silence's "strategies" of literalness and inventory, in the camera becomes leaden, being already too much a tool of the pointing at and the pointing out. She wants her conceptual ideas "heavy"; her aesthetics of silence, carefully dedicated to the logics of the method, tells us about the "meta-absolutes" of the mystical tradition in the reassuring way of a compendium. In the "dramaturgy of silence," in the stories told from the heart of the matter, there is no such restraint. Her aesthetics of silence wishes to move facts: "Krishnamurti claims that we must give up psychological, as distinct from factual memory. Otherwise we keep filling up the new with the old, closing off experience by hooking each experience into the last" (*SRW* 23). The dramaturgy interprets this as a charge to "destroy continuity" "by going to the *end* of each emotion or thought" (*SRW* 23).

This end, the end which pulls on this artist in contradictory impulses ("a barely controlled abhorrence of the void" [*SRW* 27]) feels like "unfinished pain." The aesthetic of silence believes in an overseer; silence "supervenes." "And after the end, what supervenes (for a while) is silence" (*SRW* 23). The dramaturgy of silence feels the presence of the completeness, the stillness of "unremittable, unnegotiable . . . unassimilable" (*I,E* 19) death.

An overriding principle controls these separate strains in Sontag's art. Because she is also an aesthetician, framing her concerns between Plato and Nietzsche and setting up as her object the passionate, but secularized (and moral) study of modernism, her works "think" upon the larger scheme. But what of Artaud so frequently referred to in her essays for his "exemplary madness"? Artaud, screaming, out of control, a puritan of violence, and a seeker in ways that had by then (1973) become part of a movement, a troubling part, not at all what Sontag means by an aesthetic. What of his exemplariness? As she collects and edits the major edition of his work to appear in the United States, she reconsiders.

Approaching Artaud

Defining modernism as self-negation (the necessary "myth") is not Sontag's invention, of course. That thought has accrued since the first manifestoes, as art pitted against art, ultimately the artist against art. There were also lives thrown against life, in some lives an unaccountable derangement of the contemplativeness of art from experience. For such lives the end was not silence, or if these people could no longer speak, it was not that they had reached that point by an ascetic jettisoning or in some ironic double-cross. Their end was to pull back into the light what was suppressed, maddening, terrible as it may be. Their theories about art were built out of substances, the paths of their lives towards an encounter; the inversion of values they attempted were daring and not abstract. They tested themselves at levels darker and more totalizing than a mere vying with godlike absolutes: they were "enraged by all limits, even those that save" (USS 55).

For Sontag, the person of Artaud, exhumed, is dismembered, agonized, capable of only fits and starts of utterances. She acknowledges his work as "shamanistic," but shamanistic in the sense of "shock therapy" and shock therapy only. For her, his career "starkly sums up these revaluations. Both in his work and in his life, Artaud failed" (USS 17).

He belongs to the company of Nietzsche, Sade, Reich, "who are rewarding to quote and read bits of" but whose work must "vanish" behind our use of it. He had a program:

> of heroic regression similar to that formulated by every great *anti*-political moralist of our time. . . . A radicalism that is purely 'cultural' is either illusory or, finally, conservative in its implications. Artaud's plan for subverting and revitalizing culture, his longing for a new type of human personality illustrate the limits of all thinking about revolution which is anti-political. (USS 46–47)

Though her introduction must contain Artaud, out of obligation to the times and the strength of her political commitments, this essay, so active in its disengagement, does not "starkly sum up its revaluations" at all. Instead, as Sontag claims Sartre does with Genet, it "immoderately, obsessed, stridently" repeats itself—a tribute to the most modernist of all, a man who bequeathed not works of art, "but a singular presence, an aesthetics of thought, a theology of culture, and a phenom-enology of suffering" (*USS* 17).

This has become the moment to take up her struggle with the self-annulling and irrationalist core of the modernist aesthetic, once again. For some fifteen years she committed herself to bringing her particular understanding of this sensibility to terms, and part of the effort had been directed towards curing its transformational delusions. What better subject, what more pressing concerns than the so-called romantic mod-ernism in the streets over which an Artaud might preside. What she needs to do once more is offer a modernism which remains nongenera-tive, nonrepresentative, nonoptional for anything other than the aes-thetic apperception.

The "malaise of the 'author' " has not now "become outmoded or inappropriate," she begins her essay, "as is sometimes suggested," add-ing in parentheses: "People tend to become cynical about even the most appalling crisis if it seems to be dragging on, failing to come to term" (*USS* 14). Modernism once stunned audiences by "closing the gap be-tween art and life" or between art and consciousness. To this dangerous immediacy the artist brought his or her courage and duplicity. The audience was treated to skirmishes, ironic fencing, loping circumven-tions when not bruised in a frontal assault. Artaud jumped into the gap by making the "brilliant" intelligence of the body equal to conscious-ness, cursing and espousing both in their defilement. He imagined the perfect theater as a cruel pantomime, cosmic yet "intimately physiolog-ical," a "paroxysmic art" of debased impulses, a portrait and an invita-tion, via ritual, to its truths.

Sontag approaches Artaud with the four modes of thought that have been her mainstay. First, his moralism: Artaud is a moralizing artist, but he inverted the normal route. "What Artaud proposes is a theater that Savonarola or Cromwell might well have approved of" (*USS* 34); his moralism "takes a distinctly anti-Platonic turn: the naked truth is a truth wholly material" (*USS* 35).

Second: the question of art's reflection of reality. Artaud implies that the difference between reality and representation "can be vaulted . . . if the spectacle is sufficiently, that is excessively—violent" (*USS* 37). She grants him the credit of seeking to overcome the mind-body split, not in the "superficial distinction, cherished by the Surrealists, between the rational and the irrational" (*USS* 38), rather in theater as a metaphor for the "self-correcting, spontaneous, carnal, intelligent life of the mind" (*USS* 39). He fails (his influence on the theater, "a constituent part of the authority of these ideas being precisely his inability to put them into practice" [*USS* 48]), and he stops writing, losing touch with the "promise of an ideal art form" (*USS* 50). He is silenced by the inevitable exhaustion of the "impulse to use art as a medium of spiritual transformation" (USS 50).

Third, his life reveals the truth of a project that attempts to transcend the "limits of the mind"; its "practitioners collapse into what society calls madness or into silence or into suicide" (USS 62). With "the wall between art and life still down . . . everything being assimilated into art, the movement swung the other way; and Artaud moved without mediation into his life—a dangerous, careening object, the vessel of a raging hunger for total transformation which could never find its appropriate nourishment" (USS 51).

Fourth, he followed the Gnostic way, tempting the demons to complete their possession of him, testing his magical powers in an "inhuman, desperate" fight for freedom. Gnosticism holds that "this world" must be broken away from without acknowledging "the importance of the mediating levels of the various social spheres and institutions" (USS 52). Gnosticism leads the spirit through the life of the damned into no life to be "accommodated" here.

It would have been better if Artaud had followed the "wholesome" André Breton. If there had not been that difference of temperament between them, Artaud might have abandoned his "heroic regression" and adopted Breton's "hope of reconciling the demands of individual freedom with the need to expand and balance the personality through generous, corporate emotions" (USS 55). He might have, like Breton and Paul Goodman, formulated a view "doggedly sensitive to everything repressive and mean while remaining loyal to the limits that protect human growth and pleasure" (USS 55).

Though this might be "a form of conservative, humanistic thinking"—a term she once threw at Lukács and his followers—it now seems to her to be one choice we should make. The other life, the one led by these "willed classics," is for piecemeal inspiration only:

> Most of the once exotic themes of Artaud's work have within the last decade become loudly topical: the wisdom (or lack of it) to be found in drugs, Oriental religions, magic, the life of the North American Indians, body language, the insanity trip; the revolt against "literature," and the belligerent prestige of non-verbal arts; the appreciation of schizophrenia; the use of art as violence against the audience; the necessity for obscenity. Artaud in the nineteen twenties had just about every taste (except enthusiasms for comic books, science fiction, and Marxism) that was to become prominent in the American counterculture of the nineteen sixties, and what he was reading in that decade—the *Tibetan Book of the Dead*, books on mystificism, psychiatry, anthropology, tarot, astrology, Yoga, acupuncture—is like

a prophetic anthology of the literature that has recently surfaced as popular reading material among the advanced young. (*USS* 69)

Thus reading Artaud requires "moral tact." Sontag means even to protect us from "interesting" readings, for such readings "scarcely convey (perhaps even conceal) the real nature of the work itself, which may be, among other things, extremely boring, or morally monstrous or terribly painful to read" (*USS* 69). Artaud's "exemplariness" is returned to Parnassus, Sontag's Parnassus, a magic mountain of trembling undercurrents and distraught giants, more safely cerebralized and kept in dread. In editing Artaud for this generation, she is not only resurrecting and preserving his work, she is also keeping untouchable a modernism she cannot bear being made topical, and one which she fears becoming integral. It cannot be a path, only a form of flagellation. Her moralism, and during this period her politics, insist upon it.

On Photography

Even though Artaud's work cannot be appropriated, his "shadows of life assembling themselves" can be a way to describe how the photograph gives us a picture of the world—with this twist: photography supposedly verifies reality while Artaud's theater is recognizably a planned fracturing. These assembling shadows are now, in number and comprehensiveness, amassing such an assured assault on consciousness, that, for one thing, one has to put aside talk about self-negation. The defeat of consciousness here is not caused by a hyperreflection on history. Consciousness loses to the world shaped by the tool in the photographer's grasp. The rule of self-negation may yet be pending for photographers. For the viewer, that rule is somewhat beside the point. Or, let us say, it is an attitude so ineffectual it sounds like this: let me hurry not to take photographs or look at them so that society cannot trick me by its appearance. Where does one rest the eyes? The enemy here is the logic of consumption, not the desire of transcendence through art. What started off as a delectable pastime, looking at pictures, soon grew to a steady diet, then a compulsion, then a world viewed. Photography replaces the world in the most devious method of any aesthetic—through the eye.

On Photography demonstrates what it means to look at photographs with moral tact. How do images appear, Sontag asks in her first essay, "In Plato's Cave"? For this is a time of cheap reproduction when the wall is plastered not just with shadows but with bits and pieces of tangible "reality"—these images we hold in our hands. Taken together, she warns, they build an "arsenal." More than a grammar of seeing

(Barthes' idea) they constitute an "ethics" of seeing, a negative ethics which "raises the ante of novelty" while depressing our sense of distinctiveness. Using a camera is "an act of nonintervention"; photography's ubiquity, an aggression. Photographs link all sorts of fragments together with no particular ideology in mind, or rather with a concealed ideology—the world is the same, equally interesting and equally assimilable.

Sontag makes so many observations in this book that synopsis is difficult. She is best when like a finicky cat she sniffs, walks away from, comes back in whatever mood, in anger, disbelief, or by temptation. She is best, in other words, as she herself notes, when she is both aloof and resolved on airing her fascination. Though she composed these essays over five years, they come closest to her ideal of being secreted. Since she has dispensed with some of modernism's most trying premises—the artist's self-sacrifice, for example—she has no odd heroics to worry about. Photography is modern by being without effort a Surrealist project.

In the third essay, "Melancholy Objects," she begins: "Photography has the unappealing reputation of being the most realistic, therefore facile, of the mimetic arts. In fact, it is one art that has managed to carry out the grandiose, century-old threats of a Surrealist takeover of the modern sensibility, while most of the pedigreed candidates have dropped out of the race" (OP 51).[2]

Crowning photography as Surrealism's victory represents something of a dilemma for Sontag. If photography's reconstruction of a convincing, completely aestheticized world comes to exemplify modernism, what is left of modernism's power to be critical, intelligent, angry, difficult? Photographs select, possess, "take" pictures of this world in an underhanded affirmation. They refuse experience as much as they "certify" it—"by limiting experience to the search for the photogenic, by converting experience into an image, a souvenir" (OP 9). "The ethical content of photographs is fragile" (OP 21). Time "eventually positions most photographs, even the most amateurish, at the level of art" (OP 21). But most importantly photography, unlike the other modernist arts, affronts ethics and the spirit of negation most directly by making the world feel "more available than it really is" (OP 24).

More available and, of course, more beautiful. Finally photography's insidiousness comes about for moralists ("the Marxists and would-be Marxists," who are, according to Sontag, the best writers on photography) "by the way photography inexorably beautifies" (OP 107). We can fault the medium, partially, for their inexorability: glossy surfaces and shapes emergent from reality are already touched with beauty. Nor are photographers as free as painters to mix harsh colors and to create terrible forms, as a way to beg us to consider what the painter is destroying. A photograph is either "lenient or cruel," never negating, rarely uglified. "But its cruelty only produces another kind of beauty, according to the surrealist preference which rules photographic taste" (*OP* 104). Photographers may be imperious or satiric or sympathetic, somehow cruelty pleases them: they "catch" destruction.

Photographers are caught in that Surrealist tolerance, that damning combination of "formalist approach and Camp taste" as predatory collectors, or as haunting beauty-makers, to their splendor and our unease. The photographs that W. Eugene Smith took in the late 1960s in the Japanese fishing village of Minamata, most of whose inhabitants are crippled and slowly dying of mercury poisoning,

> move us because they document a suffering which arouses our indignation, and distance us because they are superb photographs of Agony, conforming to surrealist standards of beauty. Smith's photograph of a dying youth writhing on his mother's lap is a Pieta for the world of plague victims which Artaud invokes as the true subject of modern dramaturgy. Indeed, the whole series of photographs are possible images for Artaud's *Theater of Cruelty*. (*OP* 105)

Photographs fail to make theater, needless to say; their "main effect is to convert the world into a department store" (*OP* 110). We buy them and put them on our cave walls where they "have in effect de-Platonized our understanding of reality, making it less and less plausible to reflect upon our experience according to the distinction between images and things, copies and originals" (*OP* 179).

Sontag is not hiding here behind an elitist complaint: it is not photography's commonness (though its ubiquity, yes) that bothers her. She objects because she cannot find photography's negating principle. Like easy nihilism, photography offends because it has it all: the person of the artist is already deleted (photographs are appreciated anonymously). Their morality waits upon the place they are "inserted." As art they have no morality at all—with captions, they are temporarily useful. They are convincing as objects on the strength of mere mechanics. They always make statements on the pathos of life.

Photographs trouble Sontag to the extent they are infectious. They have given us a modern sensibility we did not choose and cannot really argue with. The best we can do, Sontag tells us at the end of her book, is apply a "conservative remedy." "If there can be a better way for the real world to include the one of images, it will require an ecology not only of real things but of images as well" (*OP* 180).

The Elegist of a Posthumous Culture

With the morality of photography at issue, Sontag does an about-face on the defending wall she once erected around the arts. Behind her still is the difficult, singular masterpiece to protect (as she argues for Syberberg's *Hitler, A Film from Germany*), before her a modernism marching in the hands of every camera-carrying cultural tourist. In the early 1960s she saw art denuded by interpretation and rushing to obscurity in order to gain back its independence. Now in the mid 1970s, modernist art, not directly because of its commercialization or aesthetic poverty but because of its beauty and openness, seems to her ready to overwhelm us. What photography has done is push us further into the culture of looking than those writers of silence probably meant for us to go. We only have to recall Sontag's characterization of modernism in *Against Interpretation*—as the feeling of an era whose "greatest artistic pleasure is self-laceration, an era suffocated by the sense of eternal return, an era which experiences innovation as an act of terror" (*AI* 138)—or her words on the unavoidable myth of silence in *Styles of Radical Will*—where serious art is "a deliverance, an exercise in asceticism"—to recognize her frustration with this takeover of the modern sensibility. Silence's stare at history has become a cultural fest of looking, more out of nostalgia than defiance or embittered irony. So to defend whatever is left of those acts of discontent, Sontag rears up against this new habit of seeing. Her word "ecology" merely acknowledges the immensity of the situation.

What she misses, in her own seriousness, is Benjamin's expansive conception of "The Work of Art in the Age of Mechanical Reproduction": his conception of the liberating nature of habit. Benjamin believes that between the two ways of viewing visual art, by contemplation or distraction, the first is purely optical and absorbs the viewer, as a person contemplating a painting is absorbed in the work. But films, Dadaist collages, architecture [and by extension, photomagazines] have a tactile component which we absorb while we muse in a state of distraction. "Tactile appropriation is accomplished not so much by attention as by habit," Benjamin writes, in order to argue that "the tasks which face the human apparatus of perception at the turning points of history cannot be solved by optical means, that is, by contemplation alone. They are mastered gradually by habit. . . . More, the ability to master certain tasks in a state of distraction proves their solution has become a matter of habit."[3]

The wealth of new images has given us not just a new interest in the human, in time, in history, in nature, but also an impulse for these things—even granting Sontag's idea—for nostalgia that lives within details, not abstractions. We have been absorbing details so long we have an extraordinary capacity for them. Under our hurried pace, filled consciousness, mass obscurity, runs a resistant force of habit for details fed by photographs and perhaps now ready to prepare us for new tasks.

One task, for example, might be the humanization of the world not in the rhetoric of transcendence or nationalism or in the aestheticized politics of Fascism, but with the sense of difference and sameness the shuffling and sorting of images have made intuitive.

Certainly we are "absent-minded examiners." Our view of the totality fades. Our critiques lose their radical pointedness. The cult aura of the rituals of criticism suffers—we have accumulated and consumed too much. Yet our numbness in the *face* of so many crimes internalizes a great hurt we then attach to an individual's pain. Photographs call for the little boy with his hands up walking to the gas chamber to be snatched away, for the face of the dust bowl farmer to endure to the rains, for the napalmed child to walk out smiling from the hospitals (as a recent photograph has her do). Photographs (as the other popular arts, films and serial novels do, only more so, because their subjects are more likely real) beg sequences openly the way contemplative arts do not. In contemplative arts we are most satisfied by how they come to be finished, or at what point the artist stops. Not photographs—their next moment is as important as the one we have.

What Benjamin suggests is that photography's very cheapness rescues us. We can finger a photograph and toss it away while photography's accumulative aestheticizing of life into witty, banal, interchangeable experiences supports a habit for seeing everything—even what we cannot have and what would be hidden from us. This impulse might carry us further into manufacturing of false needs and protective cynicism; however, it has also formed a demand for documentation and reappropriation which might yet find the solution to new tasks.

Photographs amount to a collector's comedy when the touch of the real world is painful. Sontag may distrust the art of pain, but somewhere, stated or concealed, she believes it is more worthy. To know art, she believes, is to come to bear the burden of the world, and as an artist to take on the burden of art as an act of will.

Unfortunately, modernist forms rarely muster the necessary carrying strength. Sontag usually writes out of disappointment. The "truly great work" which "extends the reach of art but also complicates and burdens the enterprise of art with new, self-conscious standards" (*USS* 137) is not only rare, Sontag admonishes in 1979, it is received by lapsed taste. "The modernism that reckoned achievement by the Romantics' grandiose aims for art (as wisdom/as salvation/as cultural subversion or revolution) has been overtaken by an impudent version of itself which has enabled modernist tastes to be diffused on an undreamed-of scale" (*USS* 138). A masterpiece is "immense, solemn, and restricting," while art is now the name of a huge variety of satisfactions—of the unlimited proliferation, and devaluation, of satisfaction itself" (*USS* 138).

Sontag writes these words as an introduction to Syberberg's film. They say at *The New York Review of Books* that she insisted, with manuscript in hand, that this review go into the very next issue. Her excitement alone is worth inspecting for it reveals a telling attitude: *Hitler, A Film from Germany* harkens back to a time before modernism was "stripped of its heroic stature, of its claims as an adversary sensibility" (*USS* 138). Indeed, a masterpiece in today's consumer society appears as "a retrograde feat, a naive form of accomplishment," and perhaps recognizing it as such, Syberberg plays off that naivete with puppets, amateurish camera work and child stars. Finally, he succeeds because he skirts the Surrealists on a major point; unlike them he does not "surrender to chance, to the arbitrary, the fascination with the opaque, the meaningless, the mute" (*USS* 147). Everything in his film, "means, everything speaks" (*USS* 147). Syberberg is an "elegist" (*USS* 164) of a posthumous culture, a Symbolist artist of "all a mind," whose meditation on history remains "in a deeper sense invisible" (*USS* 158).

Sontag's essay on Syberberg swoops down on all the old issues with the gratification of at last coming upon a work of modernism that is "true, not just interesting, a necessity, not just an experiment." The film *Hitler*'s conceit, Sontag tells us, is that Hitler was a filmmaker—thus it images the penultimate aestheticizing. What makes this film great is that it destroys this aestheticizing with a play directed at, in its difficulty and length, the megalomaniacal dimension of Fascist consciousness itself.

If we fear Syberberg's reconstruction of Nazism in "the state of disbelief" because it may encourage the presumption Hitler was not a fact (as Fredric Jameson worries, slightly) or that Syberberg faces Wagnerianism with too much *"tendresse"* (another Jameson worry) we have a defense at our disposal. We are not in danger of forgetting the false otherness of art if we remember that art is an image competing with images. In Plato's cave, the art we throw on the screen or pin to the wall bursts apart the last preconception, or nudges it or confirms it. When life has stolen into the cave to gall us into rationalizing, compartmentalizing, creating ideologies, mere art competes for attention. It does not tell what has happened or what is true. Art nourishes us by sensitizing us to what is at the base of our intuition. The modern masterpiece knows what kind of consciousness it thwarts and steadfastly competes with it. In other words, great art needs a great subject so that it can (for want of a better word) negate it.

As long as we do not expect art to revolutionize life, we won't be misled into hoping that an artist's life exemplifies a revolutionary act. It is this ethos of exemplariness that calls forth from Sontag her greatest efforts. She wants to give up this pathetic fallacy of modernism's aesthetic, yet she cannot bring herself to think less of the heroism of its burden. It will be interesting to see if Sontag will continue to hold out against the accumulating force of the postmodern rhetoric with her critique of the aesthetic she believes has not failed to live posthumously.

5

Thought Commemorated

The modern consciousness is "predatory," thinking "devours" itself, and the thinker "plays the roles of both protagonist and antagonist. He is both suffering Prometheus and the remorseless eagle" (SRW 81), Sontag writes in 1967 on Cioran, in an essay called "Thinking Against Oneself." These are words compounded over years from her first insights into the dire and overreaching conditions of the modernist ethos. They are a flight to the mount of agony she has watched so many climb, perhaps having in mind Cioran all along. He does remorselessly savage an idea; the color and drive of his language lances what he writes about and makes it bleed in mauve. Sontag had mentioned him in her earliest essays, before she published her novels, as a tradition in himself, comparable to Nietzsche. And over that period of the 1960s, someone like him accrues until he becomes the emblem of Western consciousness, as he does here in this essay.

When other critics were containing the emotive thrills of writing by structures of language, Sontag contributed her image of the Promethean sublime, the thinker taking vengeance on herself for her godlike thoughts. This was the price, this was the heroism of having worked through or lived out the "serious consequences of atheism for reflective thought and personal morality" (AI 255).

Gradually, into the altogether softer 1970s, Sontag begins to search for a kind of thought more attached to and integrative of the life world. For instance, she gives us an example of her feelings in her eulogy for Paul Goodman. In her tiny room in Paris, she muses on Paul Goodman's "citizenliness"—his courage, his diligence, his willingness to serve, and includes him in "one of that mass company of writers, living and dead, who established for me the value of being a writer" (USS 9). She was at that time "trying to live for a year without books," in that room to "try better to hear my own voice and discover what I really think and feel" (USS 10). She is touched by Goodman's death, and considers how, "without Paul's hectoring, without Paul's patient meandering explanations of everything, with the grace of Paul's example," "we all have to go on in our fumbling attempts to help each other and to say what is true and to release what poetry we have and to respect each other's madness" (USS 10).

Those lines strongly reflect Goodman's own style. Their open rhythms and gentleness can be heard in the writings of the young men and women he deeply influenced; they do not seem like Sontag's at all, though I take them to be sincere. The sign of Saturn has fallen over her mood. Yet, more shaded as it is, it will not blot out her view of the "ethical task of the modern writer" "to be not a creator but a destroyer— a destroyer of shallow inwardness, the consoling notion of the universally human, dilettantish creativity, and empty phrases" (USS 131). Instead Saturn only throws the avidity, the inexorableness of her writers into a slightly different dimension: from sensibility into temperament. In Under the Sign of Saturn, her writers are challenged by and lose to their own, internal, "invincible enemies"—power and death for Canetti; puritanical violence, Artaud; sadness, either absorbing or denied, for Benjamin and Barthes.[1]

Sontag carries over to her criticism an allegorical vision similar to the one in her fiction. These writers do battle with the arrogance and the empty optimism of Western thought. Their minds are "passion." Even the cool Lévi-Strauss, appearing in the earlier Against Interpretation, consciously "exploits" his own intellectual alienation.

So from the first, although they were then more briskly attacked, these intellectuals were made to tread a path to an unreachable, unmerited fulfillment. Some seek to contradict themselves in the tropics, or by a manhood they cast as unobtainable, or by an asceticism unto death. Sartre, sensing his inadequacy relative to the poet Genet, dares to best him and fails. These earlier pieces were shrewd with the kind of eye with which the younger generation looks at the older—a little too knowingly, restlessly, looking for closures within to insert new beginnings. They tend to riddle the writer under consideration with quick shots. But increasingly, Sontag reveals a need to keep company with her subjects, identifying or letting slip what is also close to being true about her own work. When Sontag comes to writing her portrait of Cioran, this most perplexing of "drawn and quartered" characters, she comes upon the one who writes as if he is actually trying to stay, as he says, on the far side of the trouble of being born. He wants to straddle (like her novels' protagonists) the barrier between life and the radical contingency of living at all. " 'The great writers of aphorisms read as if they had all known each other well'," she quotes Canetti. Then she goes on to say: "Aphoristic thinking is informal, unsociable, adversarial, proudly selfish" (USS 191).

The figures that roam the latter essays are given more open terrain. The tropics for Lévi-Strauss, for instance, are not very large because they represent his divestment of himself. But Canetti, Barthes, Benjamin are set loose in a place where the sense of history and ideas are "spatialized."

She believes she shares with Benjamin the melancholy of that sense—because in such a place ideas are "ruins" and life is "commemorated" not lived.

This quietist approach, most evident in *Under the Sign of Saturn*, has won her some disparagement as having an "ideology of personal indulgence," that is, an asocial, *belles lettres* investment in writers who had expected, as Artaud had, to turn over cultural life with their thought.[2] In part that assessment of her must stand, against that provoking neutrality she maintains. She points to, sometimes loudly proclaims, but then dissipates her critique of the conservatism of these writers. What she is doing is holding them off, keeping them in the land she has assigned them where we can watch them intrigued, but not moved.

In her defense, it should be remembered that Sontag's formalism is always motivated by the "great task." "The great task," she writes in *Against Interpretation*, "which remains to critical theory is to examine in detail the formal function of subject matter" (*AI* 20). As the intellectual shapes an idea, she would have it, so too does he or she create a tool, and that tool can bring about a kind of technical revolution in thinking. Always, for Sontag, there lies the potential for a qualitative gain, at least in the universe of thinking. Each of her essays, therefore, is a search for this new technique, this new style of radical willing.

So she labors with this resolve: to demonstrate the style of her subject's thinking after the "debacle" of modern philosophy, that is, after the rise of historical consciousness ("the gesture whereby man indefatigably patronizes himself" [*SRW* 74]) when philosophy also became subject "to the attritions of change" wrought by "the drastically more competent and efficient human will bent on controlling, manipulating, and modifying 'nature' " (SRW 77). Existence, in this post-state of the demise of philosophy's "commerce in metaphysicals," "is no more than the precarious attainment of relevance in an intensely mobile flux of past, present, and future. . . . Meaning drowns in a stream of becoming: the senseless and overdetermined rhythm of advent and supersession. The becoming of man is the history of the exhaustion of his possibilities" (*SRW* 75). In retrenchment after Hegel's system failed in "outflanking the demon of historical consciousness," philosophy has divided into ideologies ("aggressively anti-philosophical systems of thought") and into a "new style of philosophizing: personal (even autobiographical), aphoristic, lyrical, anti-systematic" (*SRW* 78). It is this second style of philosophizing that prompts Sontag's meditations; more recently it is the personal (even autobiographical) towards which she yearns.

I cannot go further without remarking that the styles of the decades themselves—the 60s, 70s, 80s—understandably influenced these styles of thinkings, both in the writers and in Sontag's way of characterizing them. " 'If style is the power to move freely in the length and breadth of linguistic feeling without falling unto banality','" Sontag quotes Benjamin, " 'it is attained chiefly by the cardiac strength of great thoughts' " (USS 130). What compressed the style of the later 1960s, for example, was the thought that one must be living through another turn of the screw of the twentieth century experience of being an "era of permanent apocalypse" (SRW 75). For Americans especially, though the 1960s were a world-wide phenomenon, it was imperative to find a style with which to defend oneself against the state waging a dreadful war, institutions corrupted by racism, sexism, imperialism, or even a style with which to defend oneself against consumerism. This tended to make one read with a most unmodernist urge to purpose. Paul Goodman's style of "drawing the line" had great dignity, as Sontag expresses here. While his arguments for wholeness, liberation, community were far from what she took to be her themes, nevertheless, those essays written through the last years of the 1960s and into the mid 1970s were deferential and investigative about the larger constituents of self—the commercialized uses of beauty and aging, the ubiquity of photographs, the rhetorical constructions of illness, the aims of the feminist movement and the aims of new nations. Unlike Goodman's kind of work, however, they are all constrained as projects of analysis rather than demonstrations of their own style of being. The mid-1960s' effort towards a style of radical will dies (in Sontag and so many others) and is reborn in the critical spirit—the historiographic, ethnographic, theoretic inquiry set to the new modes of questioning inspired by the years before.

In the later 1970s, this turn felt like a defeat to some, while for others it seemed a period of reinforcement. The great idea from which style drew its strength in these years was the invasive and perfidious command of the representational power of all medium, all institutions. Scholarship would amass the evidence, and the theorists by intellectual trapeze-flying, wonderful flips and leaps would keep one above the seduction of the monoliths.

Oddly, the result of all this effort is that criticism has taken on a mannered air. With Sontag, this change has meant letting judgments about style shift into plotting how personal feeling directs thought. The threnody that played quietly throughout the whole century—"the sense of standing in the ruins of thought and on the verge of ruins of history and man itself" (SRW 75)—magnified into a strange, melancholic nostalgia. The lone figure in the lonely landscape drifts back into focus, while outside the frame the culture has relaxed and come to celebrate the ingenuity among the ruins.

In the 1950s, Sontag begins on this trail of "thoughts in ruin" by concerning herself with the weak movement toward religious redemption in modern rhetoric and the echatological mentality through her studies with such people as Kenneth Burke. Within a few years, she is undermining more edifices in her assessment of the therapeutic community and the culture of therapy while working with Philip Rieff. After, she asks for a more tolerant reading of, but cannot commit herself to or overcome her disappointment in the cultural Marxists: Goldmann, Lukács, Sartre, Lévi-Strauss, Adorno.

During this time (that "sharply defined period" in her life, 1962–65) she saves part of her energies to contend with the "taste for extremity" in contemporary cultural life which drew so many, herself included, to the "unhealthy" Simone Weil and Artaud. As I have explained earlier, she is drawing on the sources of her "morbidity" in order to feed her art, and this opens her to the same strain in the late European character. But she is also invested in the more playful, sensationalizing, democratizing mass culture of films, photographs, and Camp. She has Barthes and Benjamin to help her in these discoveries, yet intuitively, perhaps inevitably, what she finds in these men is a fateful sadness in their pleasures, their delicacies, their solitudes.

Thus, while eloquent, discerning, her essays on these intellectuals register more loss than gain. Whether by extremity or homelessness, their guilt or their pathos mitigate their power. Perhaps Sontag senses formalism's limitations without a willingness to readdress the tenets of the great task. Reading Sontag on these critics, one gets the impression that as intimate as she is with their mode of thinking, she jumps too quickly over their content. We watch them struggle, but their true partners, their ideas, are left behind under the rule of being authentic in the modern world. The writer's energy, spent in self-purification, pulls against Sontag's ethical hopes, her secular toughness. The side of her that has plumbed the depths of the aesthetic feeling, however, leaves the more lasting impression. The reader is encouraged to savor these works, highly self-conscious (to prove good faith) and aestheticized (Benjamin writes in "freeze-frame baroque"), as emblems of a lost soul.

Pavese, for instance, emerges under Sontag's mode as a lost soul, so do Weil, Camus, Lévi-Strauss, and even Sartre. The result is haunting—to make a pun—and it is meant to be. Sontag describes well and selects carefully; she praises only those authors capable of engendering this effect. Lukács, for example, slips in her regard not only for his questionable literary tastes, but also for his insistence on the totality of some objective world. We could say that for Sontag he shows too little regard for the fantastic and the abandoned. By temperament, he's too eager to make rules, by design, too obedient. She objects because Lukács does not play on the fields of the new: he refuses to like the ideology of modernism.

From this view of the critical life, Sontag is naturally focused on those writers who sustain passion in this cluttered, "frozen" place where history is, according to Benjamin, "a death's-head." It is easy to succumb here; the best of these writers are difficult and they never capitulate to certainty.

Unfortunately, Sontag leaves the impression that these writers test their condition of difficulty and critical openness by feeling their own pulse. Their will survives upon a conviction that needs constant self-reflection. It is her image of these people so very much alone that suggests they have no choice but to look to themselves. The modernist in Sontag turns curiously elegiac despite the reputation she won for these essays as the champion of the new. Her writers join "that melancholy parade of European intellectuals in revolt against the intellect" (SRW 83) with little freedom. Once caught up, they can recover nothing, not the "world" nor even the "Eastern abnegation of the mind."

> "The only free mind," Cioran remarks, is "the one that, pure of all intimacy with being or objects, plies its own vacuity." . . . Yet, throughout, this mental disembowelment retains its "Faustian" or "Western" passionateness. Cioran will allow no possibility that any-one born into this culture can attain—as a way out of the trap—an "Eastern" abnegation of mind. (SRW 80)

Sontag repeats that one can resist or evade degenerating contradictions—like "thinking against oneself," "disburdenment," "mental disembowelment"—only so long. Then one has to give them up or play them out on oneself.

She is drawn on because melancholy presides over her seriousness. She joins up with that parade of intellectuals in revolt against the intellect as a kindred soul. There she keeps more in step with Benjamin. Benjamin's superior breadth, his conscience (politically left, tormented for the world), his taste (complex, modern), his view (the solitary figure alone among the ruins), his defeat (suicide in 1940) resonates archetypi-cally for Sontag. His name and his way of criticism appear in all three collections of essays: he as much as Cioran shaped Sontag's gathering position on modernism. Ignoring his critique, she adopts his description of the modernist as allegorist.

" 'The only pleasure,' " she quotes Benjamin, " 'the melancholic

permits himself, and it is a powerful one, is allegory' " (USS 124).
For Sontag, the baroque allegory that Benjamin wrote about with
such depth was a solace to him because it was his way of looking
at the world. It is a view that sees history as a barren relic, a record
of delusion and suffering. Morbidity lies at the center of this vision—
the death of the self, the death of culture, the death of history. For
alienation, Sontag quotes Benjamin as saying, has turned history into
a "corpse" which the allegorist "sees from within." Out of history's
dead symbols the allegorist makes a "privileged mode out of our own
life in time, a clumsy deciphering of meaning from moment to
moment." Experience is felt only in retrospect, or, to repeat Benjamin's phrase, "commemorated." The fuller version reads: "In commemoration there finds expression the increasing alienation of human
beings, who take inventory of their past as lifeless merchandise. . . .
Relics come from the corpse, commemoration from the dead occur-
rences of the past which are euphemistically known as experience."

This passage recalls Diddy's thought that he has made an "inventory
of his life" since it appears to him as merchandise, and of Hippolyte
who abandons the outside world to colonize the inner. They are like
the baroque playwrights Benjamin writes of here: they take over the
melancholy stance of their heroes and assign meaning to objects after
"the life has flowed out of" them.

But one wants to know whether the intellectual is dependent upon
the same allegorizing mode as the artist. In Sontag's portraits one
senses that they are so dependent. The fragmenting of thought, the
disconnecting of interpretative systems, the loss of feelings—the
plethora of modernist complaints—pits the intellectual against his
or her own hypertrophing self-reflection. From then on they are
abandoned to their allegorical self-reconstructions, honorably, bril-
liantly, desolately.

" 'Allegories are in the realm of thought, what ruins are in the realm
of things' " (USS 120), Sontag quotes Benjamin. Benjamin is Sontag's
exemplary connoisseur of thoughts in ruin as Cioran is their forger. She
lets the others fall in their own way into complementary pathos. Of
Camus she writes, "Camus' life and work are not so much about morality as they are about the pathos of moral positions. . . . This pathos is
Camus' modernity" (AI 57). Typically, the pathos stems from a paradox:
"Camus is . . . the heroic figure . . . in permanent spiritual revolution.
. . . who advocated that paradox: civilized nihilism, absolute revolt that
acknowledges limits—and converted the paradox into a recipe for good
citizenship" (AI 55–6).

With Lévi-Strauss Sontag finds the reverse set of motives: the
paradox of being "a critic at home" and a "conformist elsewhere"

(*AI* 74). For Sontag, Lévi-Strauss's "homelessness" is the "struggle of the most serious thought of our time." The "nausea of intellectual vertigo" is "cured" by "exacerbation," by seeking the "other" in a kind of "applied Hegelianism." "Europe seeks itself in the exotic—in Asia, in the Middle East, among the preliterate peoples, in mythic America. . . . The 'other' is experienced as a harsh purification of the 'self' " (*AI* 69).

Whether this effort is necessary, whether it is the trap of a self grown so imperious it cannot incorporate otherness and expand, are questions ignored here. Lévi-Strauss turned the anthropologist into a "total occupation" involving "spiritual commitment" (*AI* 70) where "he acts out a heroic, diligent, and complex modern pessimism" (*AI* 81). The anthropologist's purpose: "Essentially he is engaged in saving his own soul, by a curious and ambitious act of intellectual catharsis" (*AI* 79). His style: "a mixture of pathos and coldness" (*AI* 79).

In such an ambitious, catharsis-seeking intellectual there is a virtue. The intellectual spares the world more meaning, spares the subjugated and oppressed of the world more proselytizing. Her heroes, for the good of all, throw their ideas into a cauldron from which they drink, vomit, and purge themselves (Sontag's images). Or to use Benjamin's images, they wander among the desecrated landscape of ideas where morality stands upon one premise—the premise of permanent loss and despair. In the sad tropics, archaic peoples already know the modern world thus. The anthropologist, as exemplary intellectual hero, has to take care not to perpetuate an error: that there is a discourse which is unmolesting or that there is a purpose not already condemned by history.[3] By suggesting that Lévi-Strauss wants only to save himself, Sontag turns him into another model of "moral tact." In the company of the "other," he acknowledges the West's abominable behavior and the complicity of the Western thought he serves. His cool rendering of pathos tastefully affirms his host's situation; his retreat into himself relieves his host's anxiety that meaning will be unwillingly wrenched from their lives.

She does not make this applied Hegelianism seem the way she believes one ought to act. It remains, like all other modernist efforts, trapped in a prism. Lévi-Strauss's mode is, as is Sarraute's, Robbe-Grillet's, Michel Butor's, "*l'esprit géometrique*" the mode of "infinite precision," "narrow dehydrated subject matter and cool microscopic styles" (*AI* 79).

Being inside this geometry, the self that appears to be negated is actually sheltered, cocooned. The writer does not risk being wrong, just lost and uninteresting. How then does the anthropologist stay a hero to himself? Having overcome "the horror of the primitive (which is)

... never far from the anthropologist's consciousness" (*AI* 75), what then remains to be conquered?

A hero needs a vision and an enemy, and Sontag finds both for Lévi-Strauss. The enemy is the temptation to historicize, and the vision is a utopia predicated upon a retreat from history. Sontag hesitates again before this quest of her hero, as she had with Simone Weil and will with Artaud. Again she guides her essay to a close with an ambiguous analysis.

> Any serious critique of Lévi-Strauss, however, must deal with the fact that, ultimately, his extreme formalism is a moral choice, and (more surprisingly) a vision of social perfection. Radically antihistoricist, he refuses to differentiate between "primitive" and "historical" societies. ... There are only what he revealingly calls "hot" and "cold" societies. The hot societies are the modern ones, driven by the demons of historical progress. The cold societies are the primitive ones, static, crystalline, harmonious. Utopia, for Lévi-Strauss, would be the lowering of the historical temperature ... in which man would finally be freed from the obligation to progress. (*AI* 80)

In offering this critique of Lévi-Strauss's "surprising" moral choice and his "revealing" descriptions, Sontag lets the anthropologist hero grow passive, caught by inevitability. A lonely crier, "the mourner of the cold world of the primitive ... its custodian as well," she leaves him on the stage "lamenting among the shadows" (*AI* 81).

The intellectual catharsis Sontag speaks of in the beginning of the essay, the purging, becomes veritable tears. The anthropologist weeps for the sad tropics and in mourning becomes the custodian of another life. She has shrunken the man; her judgements are withering: "thus the man who submits himself to the exotic to confirm his own inner alienation as an urban intellectual ends by aiming to vanquish his subject by translating it into a purely formal code" (*AI* 77). She intends, it seems, to lend no quarter to this effacement of the subject in the guise of the objectivity of diagrams and scales.

An opposite difficulty arises relative to the representations of reality, as it does with Sartre, when the writer has a "compulsion to assign meaning." Sontag already called Sartre the antithesis of Lévi-Strauss. "With his philosophical and political dogmatisms, his inexhaustible ingenuity and complexity, Sartre always has the manners (which are more often the bad manners) of the enthusiast" (*AI* 79). In this essay, "Sartre's Saint Genet," she gives another distinction:

> Corresponding to the primitive rite of anthropophagy, the eating of human beings, is the philosophical rite of cosmophagy, the eating of

the world. The hallmark of the philosophical tradition to which Sartre
is heir starts with consciousness as the sole given. Sartre's solution
to the anguish of consciousness confronted by the brute reality of
things is cosmophagy, the devouring of the world by consciousness.
(AI 98)

Sartre goes too far in this book. "*Saint Genet* is not one of the truly
great, mad books; it is too long and too academic in vocabulary for that.
What made the book grow and grow is that Sartre, the philosopher,
could not help (however reverentially) upstaging Genet, the poet" (AI
94). In this, of course, "his enterprise is fundamentally impossible. He
cannot catch the real Genet; he is always slipping back into the categories of Foundling, Thief, Homosexual, Free Lucid Individual, Writer.
Somewhere Sartre knows this and it torments him" (AI 94).

Sartre is confronted, "with something of the autonomy of the aesthetic," and he concludes, that Genet's works are a "saving ritual, a
ceremony of consciousness. . . . [that is] essentially onanistic" (AI 98).
And this conclusion Sontag finds "apt."

> According to European philosophy since Descartes, world-creating
> has been the principal activity of consciousness. Now a disciple of
> Descartes has interpreted world-creating as a form of world procreat-
> ing, as masturbation. . . . Jerking off the universe is perhaps what all
> philosophy, all abstract thought is about: an intense, and not very
> sociable pleasure, which has to be repeated again and again. It is
> rather good description, anyway, of Sartre's own phenomenology of
> consciousness. And, certainly, it is a perfectly fair description of what
> Genet is about. (AI 98–99)

Sartre may be wonderful, full of ideas, but he cannot escape under
the false impulse to find meaning, to devour the world and jerk off on
his own perceptions. He is not properly resigned to what Sontag calls
"the impasse of the speculative mind." Encompassing, procreating
ideas in the sense of reaching out to the past in order to lay seeds for
the future are for her a disregarded intellectual style. Anyone writing
in this vein ignores the Nietzschean revolution and risks bad manners,
like Sartre's masturbatory excesses. Cioran's writing, for instance, is
the model of "spiritual good taste":

> Whether the vocation of the philosopher is any less compromised can
> hardly be proved. (Reason is dying, Cioran says in "Style and Risk,"
> in both philosophy and art.) But at least philosophy, I imagine Cioran
> feels, maintains somewhat higher standards of decorum. Untempted
> by the same kind of fame or emotional rewards that can descend on

the poet, the philosopher can perhaps better comprehend and respect the modesty of the inexpressible. (*SRW* 91)

Cioran avoids not only the poet's "accumulation of confusions, an inflation of horrors, of *frissons* that *date*," his delicacy extends to the rejection of history. Sontag quotes him: " 'History is merely an inessential mode of being, the most effective form of our infidelity to ourselves, a metaphysical refusal' " (*SRW* 91).

With their minds at an impasse, with their view that history "creates insurmountable conditions of inauthenticity" (*SRW* 90), Sontag's writers trudge in great circles around history and meaning, as the route of African herds is said to exclude water holes in the midst of a drought. Each writer uses up his or her stored resources of knowledge without even expecting, finally, to take in new sustenance. Sontag keeps looking for their sad gestures of self-recognition, and hopes, as she admires them, that they dislike their condition. For characteristically, at the end of this essay, Sontag pulls away from this image. Cioran's aim is "diagnosis" not relief, so in that he cannot be entirely faulted for not being convinced by Nietzsche's "heroic effort to surmount nihilism."

On the other hand, Sontag needs relief. "The time of new collective visions may be over: by now both the brightest and the gloomiest, the most foolish and the wisest, have been set down. But the need for individual counsel has never seemed more acute. *Sauve qui peut*" (*SRW* 75). All this retiring nihilism, she suggests, by comparing John Cage to Cioran, can be aborted. We may not need to be left only to the worn and difficult and never-to-be-completed argument against thinking. Cage offers a vision that is spiritually and intellectually simple, perhaps, but also uplifting in an optimistic, anarcho-democratic way. Cage has the last line: "'All that is necessary,' says Cage with his own devastating irony, 'is the empty space of time'" (*SRW* 95).

This offering of Cage as the antidote to Cioran jarred her critics into some of their most contemptuous remarks about her judgment.[4] Whether they could tolerate the comparison of a philosopher and a musician, or not, it is more certain that they were outraged by how the stakes are setup in this essay. Historicizing consciousness has given us, Sontag writes "the most energetic, dense, subtle, sheerly interesting, and *true*" speculation "in the entire lifetime of man. And yet the equally incontestable result of all this genius is our sense of standing in the ruins of thought and on the verge of the ruins of history and of man himself. (Cogito ergo boom)" (*SRW* 75).

"*Suave qui peut*," indeed. Had Sontag expressed these thoughts in any of a hundred less alarming ways, maybe she would have mollified her critics. The ideas are not new. But mollifying has never been her style. That her language oversteps her purpose is another thing. To me it is a rhetoric of collision those more conservative, irony-protected critics would not have heard. Her language comes from the impact of reading and thinking about those "indignant or stoical diagnosticians of defeat" in a climate nearly the opposite. Cage's modernism of possibility was part of an energy nearly run riot with having learned that Western thought could be set aflame with Eastern, and that Eastern could bring creative nerve to the modernism of "nothing." " 'Every now and then it is possible . . . to have absolutely nothing: the possibility of nothing,' " Sontag quotes Cage in her epigraph. Cage, a distilled enthusiast, a great figure in that climate, seemed to her a less problematic example of how the conceptual tools of philosophy might be "rectified: through the passion of thinker" (SRW 79). Whether Cage has escaped the "frissons that date," she was not in 1967 free to say. She may have decided that he would so escape because of the decorum of his "nothingness."[5]

Nevertheless, her critics do have their point in one matter at least. One can feel how much Sontag tries to press her faith in the new sensibility, as if she were herself trying to escape from the influence of Cioran, his "pathos" as a representation of the grandiosity of Europe. He is another irresistibly "gifted elegist" of the "passing of 'Europe'— of European suffering, of European intellectual courage, of European vigor, of European overcomplexity" (SRW 86). The passion Cioran evinces is another instance of that "sacrifice of the intellect," along with health or even sanity, that is for all her heroes indicative of that "aptitude for martyrdom" that she cannot belittle away. For though this martyrdom is only a stance, "merely a certain coquetry of the void" (SRW 82) yet, it voices "the painful, genuinely paradoxical experience that the free intellect can have of itself when it commits itself to writing" (SRW 83). This stance reminds Sontag of all that troubling absolutism of Christian Gnostic-mysticism, of the kind she has been trying to worm out of the heart of modernism. Mystics, she lets Cioran tell us, " 'invent their adversaries'." Unfortunately, Cioran gets "nailed to the cross of an atheist-spirituality" (SRW 87) for his frank desire to find the immortal in his experiences. Had he not climbed thus, Sontag hints, he would have maintained that tact that allows him to rest between the "avowed contempt for philosophy" and the blessedly empty realm, devoid of metaphysics, history, or collective visions.

When the spiritually impassioned get nailed to the cross of their own nihilism, as they inevitably do, the believers like Sontag turn away little dismayed. Since they are not tied to old concepts of truth, modernists have the possibility of rising into a taunting, mercurial nothingness. Cage, "whether from spiritual strength or from spiritual insensitivity is a secondary issue" (*SRW* 94), provides another way by an easy mixture of accepting and jettisoning the past and present. Over the tight words of Cioran's "inherited anguish," Cage's stress on the free virtually levitates. Cage is America's answer to the problem of historicizing— you forget it, and thus let go of those interior dialectics of seeking otherness and self-negations.

The history that plagues Cioran on the other hand lies in the rubble at his feet. And this history drifted in on the smoke from the ovens. In the literary realm, it lifts off the page in front of him from the duplicity and collusion of writers who were among the best. It comes too from bitterness over the state which Eastern European communism made and his exile from it—a consideration about Cioran Sontag feels she underappreciated at the time. At the time of this essay (1969), Sontag wrote as if she too would like to forget that the modernists and their hubris of form were caught under the searchlight of a history and under the boot of power that impressed questions on them that they could not answer.

In the 1960s context, in a barbarism to which American privileges were specifically attached, "forgetting" no longer looked innocent. It is one thing to ask if the present self conforms to a history in order to maintain guilt, as Sontag asks of Cioran, and another to posit that willful nonconformity creates a sphere of autonomy. The creative play of thought began to look much like avoidance while doubts nagged, and time moved quickly toward a reckoning. To maintain Cage's errorless present, Americans had to keep ahead of pressing issues of the just past present—issues of regret, approval, horror, fault, value, action. The errorless present keeps shrinking to the breadth of a wish.

Modern conceptions of thinking separate over autonomy, but from a different standpoint, the standpoint of what Benjamin calls commentary and critique. Though thinking can approach art's syncretic method, in no sense can it be innocent relative to the value of experience. Art can be surreal, intuitive, naive, or constitutive of reality: thought somewhere needs to comment (if not critique). Moreover, for the writer for whom the present does hold the possibility of redemption, as it does for Benjamin, rather than just the springboard for the new (Cage), thought has to acknowledge the past's debts. In his "Theses on the Philosophy of History," Benjamin writes:

> There is a secret agreement between past generations and the present one. Our coming was expected on earth. Like every generation that preceded us, we have been endowed with a weak Messianic power, a power to which the past has a claim. That claim cannot be settled cheaply. Historical materialists are aware of that.[6]

This charge for the present, in other words, in contradistinction to Cage, is not born free to determine itself but comes weighted with past's expectations to happiness, the past's warnings and failures, the past's enemies. For Benjamin, living in the present has meant, since the seventeenth century, living in a state of emergency. To articulate history "means to seize hold of a memory as it flashes up at a moment of danger." He continues,

> Historical materialism wishes to retain that image of the past which unexpectedly appears to man singled out by history at the moment of danger. The danger affects both the content of the tradition and its receivers. The same threat hangs over both: that of becoming a tool of the ruling classes. In every era the attempt must be made anew to wrest tradition away from a conformism that is about to overpower it. The Messiah comes not only as redeemer, he comes as the subduer of Antichrist. Only that historian will have the gift of fanning the spark of hope in the past who is firmly convinced that even the dead will not be safe from the enemy if he wins. And this enemy has not ceased to be victorious.[7]

For Benjamin there can be no errorless present, neither can a true grasp of historical experience serve to patronize us. Intellectual history, where ideas are seen in their attachment to time, if we follow Benjamin, also would have to be "cut through" and "forced 'up' against the grain" by materialism. We would not be endlessly cannibalizing thought, engorging ourselves on our intellectual forebears while we despair of originality. We would not wish for an easy freedom from the past, even as a toy of an idea, nor fear a tiring overcomplexity. History would act as a rear-defense by exposing the enemy and reminding us of our aims. The past's intellectuals, the good ones, shock the nerves out of conformity: their ideas could be repeated by the way in which truth sets off the alarms.

In Sontag's reading of Benjamin, we see Benjamin the melancholic, not Benjamin who discovered a new use for history (materialism) and a way to praise revolutionary pessimism (surrealism).[8] Taking a comment from his memoirs, that he was born under Saturn, Sontag elaborates his life from a "theory of melancholy" (USS 111). "Dissimulating, and secretive," with an "unforgiving relationship to self," the saturnine personality, slow, blundering, stubborn—"from the longing to be superior in one's own terms" (USS 114)—views everything from a distance. Sontag forces Benjamin to be both a character and a playwright of the baroque dramas, the Trauerspiels, for whom " 'chronological movement is grasped and analyzed in a spatial image' " (USS 117). In this labyrinthine map of his life, Benjamin falls under the "melancholic pathology"; he projects his "inner torpor outward," convinced of the "immutability of misfortune." His only "deep transactions take place with things" (*USS* 119). With the Surrealists, Benjamin collects ruins or fragments because "a world whose past has become (by definition) obsolete, and whose present churns out instant antiques invites custodians, decoders, and collectors" (*USS* 120).

One more time Sontag writes an allegory of the intellectual to save him/her for a seriousness against this trivializing, mortifying world. The melancholy may be Benjamin's constitution, but it grows under her view into a state of apprehension, in both meanings of the word. She leaps over the work into the writer at work, his predilections and tastes, his ironic self-descriptions; she fixes her eye on the haze above the language.

Benjamin becomes to her that tragic figure, the lone intellectual who senses he is the last of a kind. When Benjamin writes of Karl Kraus that he stands not on the edge of the new, but on the "threshold of the Last Judgment," Sontag says Benjamin is thinking of himself.

> At the Last Judgment, the Last Intellectual—the Saturnine hero of modern culture, with his ruins, his defiant visions, his reveries, his unquenchable gloom, his downcast eyes—will explain that he took many "positions" and defended the life of the mind to the end, as righteously and inhumanly [sic] as he could. (*USS* 133–4)

Sincerely and respectfully, Sontag avoids the content of Benjamin's "positions." To her, his "vacillations" let him mark a place. That would be his inclination as a Saturnine type, and thus fitting if not ingenious. Communist, mystic, surrealist, aesthete, he was open to all of them, because (and here Sontag comes closer to the truth) "one position corrects another" (*USS* 133).

Sontag makes Benjamin a man of temperament because to her an earnestness relative to history is a trap set for the naive. Equally, the fear of being provoked by history and used up in the continuum reveals the fear of mortality. In her essay on Canetti—another "genuine hero, in the guise of the martyr" whose "real task" is to set the largest, most edifying standards of despair"—she writes: "His protest against seeing historically is directed not just against that most plausible of reductionisms. It is also a protest against death" (*USS* 200).

The strictures Sontag places on the sense of history call for a distinction: historical-mindedness is a sensibility, while historical consciousness, the older idea, holds within it an immanent drive. With or without a language of redemption, this consciousness finds the necessary in our actions and puts it to the critique of a *telos*. To historical consciousness, we step forward, whether we pay a higher price for each step, whether our accomplishments result in a greater barbarism. For the future, what is significant comes before us as a decision. In the modern allegorical realm, there are no individual significances; no specific content compels or impedes our development. In this realm, we shift around, selecting our affinities, as Sontag thinks Benjamin shares one with the Baroque.

Sontag's reading of the life of the intellectual speaks of the central problem in interpreting the modernist artists or thinkers which she took up from the first of her essays. Have they liberated themselves, in fact, from necessity and faith with the past, i. e. have they proven their case for autonomy on the basis of their great achievement? Has it become "equally true (and perhaps more important to say now) that all content may be considered a device of form" (*AI* 92)? Undoubtedly the modernists' achievement has been great; undoubtedly Sontag is right to insist that only devotion to that achievement can be the basis of good criticism. But of the success of their enterprise, relative to any other value outside of subjectivity? "Philosophy is conceived as the personal task of the thinker," she writes. "Thought becomes confessional, exorcistic: an inventory of the most personal exacerbations of thinking" (*SRW* 79).

If we could guess Sontag's motive for conceptualizing philosophy thus, putting aside the difficult matter of her tone (for the interpretation of her tone is a tug of war the reader has to make against the epigrammatic resilience of her writing), we might guess that she is still offering a rebuttal to Lukács. He denounces modernism for its "doctrine of the external incognito." These masques of the impersonal, Lukács feels, hide a diminished self and concomitantly a diminished reality. Moreover, he remembers men like Heidegger and Gottfried Benn who covered their deeds under fascism with the cloak of this mysterious self. To be "a man without qualities" means for Lukács to hide from the impact of one's practices.[9]

Sontag's men and women are in anguish; even when they are outwardly restrained by the *l'esprit géometrique*, while she has a rebuttal to Lukács' central complaint that the library modernists deny history, she has not found herself free from his sense that they then are subsumed by allegory. This is likely the thought that started Benjamin on his search for modernity in the German baroque. Allegory speaks only to those who know its codes, and then it speaks for the sake of being as grand, and as Benjamin once suggests, as corrupt and ruthless as its age.

It is in this allegorical mode, a particularly brittle form that Sontag, in defending the severe, the difficult, the solitary figures of these essays and their "faithless leaps," has wandered. She may not realize that she makes the error of that vantage point, the error Benjamin believes is endemic (and evil) in modernist allegory, the ultimate transferability of all content. One writer begins to look like another. They differ in temperament and subject, but not in a kind of negative perspective. What Sontag has not succeeded in doing is to find a way for these writers to get out of the layers of images, the pile-up of abstractions that is the allegorical experience. With Lévi-Strauss she was at least willing to consider that one motivation for traveling intellectually was to find that "other" place for the writer to disburden himself. By the later 1970s, she rather would give us the picture of intellectuals carrying their burden everywhere with a stubborn unwillingness to dispose of it.

In other words, they grow increasingly character-bound and more and more like a type. Of Canetti:

> Portraits drawn from the inside, with or without the poignant inflections of exile, have made familiar the model of itinerant intellectual. He (for the type is male, of course) is a Jew, or like a Jew; polycultural, restless, misogynistic; a collector; dedicated to self-transcendence, despising the instincts, weighed down by books and buoyed up by the euphoria of knowledge. His real task is not to exercise his talent for explanation but, by being witness to the age, to set the largest, most edifying standards of despair. As a reclusive eccentric, he is one of the great achievements in life and letters of the twentieth century's imagination, a genuine hero, in the guise of a martyr. (SRW 185)

All thinking, goes the rule, is autobiographical, and it is the exemplary persona that teaches us a new strategy. Benjamin's discussion of allegory in the baroque, intended as a preliminary study of what is modern, becomes for Sontag a universal high practice. It is appropriate that we perform our heroic acts of will among the ruins; we cannot see past the dramaturgy of our thinking.

Demanding as she is upon herself, insistent as she is cornering and deciphering the ethos of modernism for its intrinsic paradoxes, as knowing as she is about its "martyrs," as unyielding as she is to the temptations of postmodernism's happier eclecticisms, too much gets slighted in these essays. She is given to remarking lately that:

> See, I've always thought of the essays and the fiction as dealing with very different themes, and I've been irritated by carrying what I thought to be a double burden of two very different kinds of activities. It's only recently, because it's been forced to my attention, that I realized the extent to which the essays and the fiction share the same themes, make the same kind of assertions or nonassertions. It's almost frightening to me to discover how unified they are.[10]

The trouble is that the model for fiction—the dramaturgy of thinking—does not coincide well with intellectual work and turning intellectuals into artists, no matter how inventive and refined, sets off the wrong pattern of associations. The emphasis shifts to sensibility: the work becomes reshaped for what it reveals about the writer; the writer is given a mission separate from what he or she has to say. We watch them perform against odds; one of the greatest odds being our American incredulity.

Conclusion

In these last pages I would like to turn to those essays that address the more openly political and social issues. Few though they are, they have exposed her to a cross-fire considerably worse than she received for seemingly breaking the pact American critics had made with highbrow culture. She broke code with American anticommunism in the 1960s, and later in the 80s with anti-anticommunism. The replies have been stinging.

She was being corrective, in her distinction-drawing, argumentative way, for example, when she wrote about Cuba in 1969[1] that there was a disparity between the Cuban's ambitions for their revolution—a refocusing of energy, a moralizing of work—and the liberating hedonism Americans wanted for themselves. American radical youth, she warns, are apt to over-respond to Cuban spontaneity and eroticism, missing the Cuban's definition of their own underdevelopment. Americans need to recognize that their fear of puritanical repression in Cuba is a projection of the struggle Americans were waging, one, in fact, they ought to revise. American youth "appear to underestimate how radical values and psychic states can also be co-opted," perhaps because they have been tutored by "not very political types" such as "Marcuse (a radical Freudian first, a tame neo-Marxist second), Brown, Mailer, Laing" and such "openly apolitical, or even reactionary types like Alan Watts, Leary and McLuhan. . . ." Furthermore, their "task of creating a radical life-style puts a serious obstacle before their development as effective and intelligent political militants" (6). Her comments go like this:

> The new American radicalism is, I think, undeniably more intelligent and more sensitive and more creative than the so-called Old Left. But it is also, as part of these same virtues, more provincial, more excruciatingly American. If the main struggle at this moment is to establish an alternative or adversary culture, it is entirely American that that struggle flourishes around the goal of freedom (not, for instance, justice). And even more specifically American is what is understood as the content of freedom—the guarantee of freedom to the individual.
>
> American radical thought verges on a kind of Adam Smith doctrine according to which, even in matters of revolution, the pursuit of

private advantage inexorably leads to public benefit. Americans are notoriously optimistic people, but I think we shall have to wait a long time for our *Laissez-faire* revolution. (7)

To the extent that one recognizes this portrait (most likely in others), Cubans' efforts do stand out in larger profile, as long as one is content to allow Sontag to describe how the "moral and cultural and historical phenomenon" of underdevelopment is spoken about in Cuba. Her explanation is, in fact, loose and, for one thing, damning to Cuba's Yoruba inheritance: "This is the underdevelopment which is the heritage of a rather complex set of causes—certain aspects of the culture brought by the Spaniards, the still strong African strand in Cuban culture, and the demoralizing and corrupting influence of American colonialism. . . . It is out of these not very promising elements that Cuba's human resources were formed" (14). Neither does she mention that she had written admiringly of Brown, or that Marcuse too lashed the counterculture for hedonism and was the primary theorist of cooptation. On the other hand, how "atrocious" (Hilton Kramer's word) her defense of Cuba sounds now depends on the assessment of Castro's subsequent twenty year rule. Sontag had her show of regret by appearing in a brief interview in the anti-Castro film *Improper Conduct*.[2] She spoke stiffly, remotely, of the persecution of homosexuals as the product of Cuba's militarization. Gay men remind the regime "that power is not the only goal of adult life." The Left has been relatively silent on the military ideals of communist thought because of its history in not dealing with "questions bearing on the moral and political aspect of sex." "The discovery that homosexuals were being persecuted in Cuba shows, I think, how much the Left needs to evolve. It's not just a serious case of injustice that must be exposed, but something that compels people to take note of a lapse in attitude of the so-called Left that goes back a long way."

She used the same device of consciousness meeting its corrective in her essay "Trip to Hanoi" 1968. Then, too, she framed her observations under the guidance of a persona whose over-sophistication (in that case, a need for intellectual gratification) parried and lost to the collective will. Apparently, for a while, Sontag believed that to understand the revolutionary aims of underdeveloped countries one had to part company with the luxurious self and its excessive demands for stimulation.

She might have used a model less self-reflexive and less axiomatically reductive of both consciousness and revolutions. That mirror she uses in her writing and her manner of speaking "ultimately" work against political observation. However, if these two revolutions blur under Sontag's attention to cultural attitudes, she takes advantage of more current awareness, missing, for example, in Mary McCarthy's essays on Vietnam collected in *The Seventeenth Degree* 1974. The pleasure in reading McCarthy comes from her unmatched satiric jabs, her old-hand style of journalism, from her point-by-point answering of criticism (as her one-on-one with Diana Trilling). Moreover, she assumes the right of comparison: she sees in Hanoi much that reminds her of communism in Eastern Europe. The older understanding of revolution, the idea of being part of an historical development gives her a much greater range into which she can cast her observations. Most importantly, McCarthy wrote those essays as separate tracts, pedagogic tools for the antiwar movement. Sontag states that she had gone to Hanoi not intending to write at all. She is, as Alf Lourve calls her, a "reluctant historian."[3]

What she refuses to lay down before the North Vietnamese is the permission to use her in the *delegacija* system without a confrontation of who she is.[4] Her attitude reflects what the 1960s took much time in developing ideologically, the sensitivity to subjectivity and to otherness. But heard in every corner, grumblings and sounds of shock greeted this essay. In the midst of so much trouble, who needed to hear about the awkwardness suffered by intellectuals, her critics fumed.

An old argument against left consciousness surfaced—Sontag was indulging in pastoralism, or so it was bandied about, Third World romanticism. This is the substance of Leo Marx's critique, "Susan Sontag's 'New Left Pastoral': Notes on Revolutionary Pastoralism" 1972.[5] Unfortunately, Marx is thoroughly entangled in his own metaphorical net. There is quite a difference between a romance of otherness and an acknowledgement of it, of seeking the primitive and of being thrust into a land nearly dying from the suffering inflicted by one's own country. The falsehoods of officialdom are what Sontag does care about and what she cannot lift. When she cannot, she assumes her counterparts are sincere. Fatigue, shock and the North Vietnamese refusal to adopt irony brought her to that new point. She has never shown any particular love for the landscape nor any particular amusement in the pastoral.

McCarthy is able to take all the incongruities in stride, as part of the historical stage about which her Old Left training had prepared her to be rational, cynical, and explicit. She says, however, very little about the Vietnamese. Sontag, in this essay, is watching the constituents of the moral self flounder, and thinking again of what it may also be made up of. Of course her individualism has not been conquered, rather it has been added to, some small part Vietnamese, for some small period of time. The presumption (of thinking she may have understood) and the indulgence (of wanting to understand) annoyed everyone. Yet, the writing on Vietnam from those years is rotten with arrogance of the other order: "our war," "our crisis." Sontag's essay is a tonic.

The second half of the 1960s, especially, compelled one to stretch. For Sontag this means a dialogue between what she understands as the basis of moral readiness (still, for her, the aesthetic sense), against the demands of a national project (Hanoi, Cuba), and, with increasing confidence, the issue of national character and reform—in her "A Letter from Sweden." This last is quirky and exasperated and wonderfully detailed, paralleling the "spectacularly honest" Swedes and their heavy character armor and their flight from urbanity with their false social- ism. It, too, is a dated essay because of the way it approaches social change—through the revolutions of the self. And it is honest or dishon- est, depending on how one grasps the "personal as political" debates of those times, because she was then doing films indebted to a Swedish aesthetic she was trying to cast off. The essay knocks the Swede inside her, though it is completely addressed to the public manners and con- temporary politics of the actual country. She is here engaged, as it was once called, on all fronts.

The contrast between this political self arguing its way into politics and the kind of narrators dominant in her fiction and films could not be more telling. Stilled or thwarted, most of them move about in con- fines so small they might be statues, speaking, if at all, to an absent listener and trying to disconnect themselves from masterminds of obei- sance. She herself has been sometimes cast as a figure of haughty diffidence, a ponderer on things uncomfortably glittering and swift— the modes of modernist expression. She drops, as it were, into modern- ism's deepest contentions, most unwilling to see them paraded as an advance to be attached to anyone else's progress.

She's an odd character to be called to the podium. But she wore this mantle of *noblesse oblige* very early. One should not forget how young she was. She was only seventeen when Philip Rieff married her, struck by her carriage and beauty from the first day she walked into his class and by her seriousness which she has kept. By her early twenties she had already been taken into an inner circle at Harvard, a group including, for example, Jacob Taubes who may in fact have set out to know every- thing. To such people, almost all experiences are opportunities to hone an argument. Sometimes they grow fascinated by their ability to carve up others, as the two older protagonists do in *Duet for Cannibals*. Perhaps it is all too easy to surmise that for reasons of being won over by their sense of empowerment and burden, for reasons of having been selected and hurt by the entanglement, Sontag has had to spend time demystifying and "disburdening" herself from their influence. She has also had to prove herself worthy of their faith in her, and in a style of her own. That has meant striving for a sense of public discourse they did not have. She became a more famous person, trading downward in intellectual prestige for a higher place in the public's eye, that is, the better part of the bookish public's eye. If now it is excessively worried that the independent writer for the independent public has disappeared, Sontag is remembered as that kind person of letters who has not a generalist's tolerance at all.

In the political life, it was the way she was selected or selected herself that grates on the social scientists and historians of the period. She was that figure of the engaged writer, whose name and words were meant to lend symbolic force, usually moral force to a position. The oddity for such writers as Sontag who made this choice, and who make it now, is that the force of their position does not come from having been themselves victims of a regime, censored, jailed, or tortured. It comes from the perception that writers think more nobly. Who among the workers in the field of thought are willing to grant that?

And indeed, the acrimony she has gained for her so-called political "conversions" comes from trivializers who are certain her politics are "rapturous," her thoughts "instant." They mostly can be dismissed. They are out to get her, and their accusations are dulled by belligerence. For others, the matter is somewhat more principled. It is the whole class of writers who went to Vietnam and Cuba in such roles that must be countermanded. Sontag, and those many others like her (Grace Paley being a favorite target), represent an unknown element, one that cannot be easily inscribed in the factors signifying real politics—voting patterns, state structures, alliances, war strategies—not in material factors, certainly, not even well into the production of ideologies, not even, as intended, in the battles around media effectiveness. They float somewhere freer, in cerebralized space, a scream against the unconscionable, or a more quiet plying of other waters not explored by practitioners of real politics.

Sontag, in language quite restrained, thought about Vietnam's, Cuba's, China's, Sweden's, "moral, cultural, historical," self-sense, which she paired with hers and ours. Writers such as Sontag do not do political analysis. To judge their statements as such, the so-called positions they take as such, misses their project. Most likely they see themselves throwing stones into the cogs and pistons of the mighty engines of the *raison d'etre*.

What I am suggesting is that the two perspectives (real politics—the politics of conscience) rarely say much that is helpful about the other. Paul Hollander's critique of Sontag in his book *Political Pilgrims: Travels of Western Intellectuals to the Soviet Union, China, and Cuba, 1928-1978* is a case in point. One has to assume what he assumes, the nightmare of communism, and then let him collect his flock of gullibles as he stresses the proclivities of intellectuals to be disenchanted with the West because of the power they never achieved. He selects opportunistically, psychologizes motives, and admits he cannot understand the disaffection for the West his intellectuals or youths evince. He does not mention any of their post-War reasons: the bomb, the brutality of racism, the history of American hegemony in Latin America, its expansion into Asia and Africa, its funding of anti-nationalist wars and its training of terrorists, backgrounded by the growing might of its military machine and its grip on the country's future. They were soon to learn about the state's surveillance and repressive measures in response to their protests—all this belying the morally superior, guardian of democracy rhetoric that fired the fear-mongering, two-superpowers thesis of the 1950s. Hollander pretends to scratch his head over these middle-class, pampered youth and their alleged anti-intellectualism, and rains indignation over the writers they supposedly (paradoxically?) looked to. Sontag never "sided with youth" in her spokesperson role; she tries to anticipate and refute her audience's most likely expectations.

More recently, Sontag shocked a number of people again at a rally in New York for Polish Solidarity (1982) by saying that communism is "the most successful variant" of fascism. Her comments were taken as her relinquishing the vestiges of her left sympathies. Her critics, all offended, reminded her of the details she swept away, the history, even her own history of first hand observation. She replied that she too can like some communists, like the Italians, because they "talk like social democrats; so do—am—I. My argument is about countries in which a Communist—that is, a Leninist—party has taken power and rules. The fact that *every one* of these countries is a tyranny that oppresses workers and corrupts intellectual life and free inquiry seems not to have led [my critics] . . . to draw any conclusions about Communism as a system. It has me."[6]

She said that night at Town Hall that the "utter villainy of the Communist system" was "a hard lesson to learn. And I am struck by how long it has taken us to learn it. I say we—and of course I include myself."[7] She remembered, she said, in 1953 "reading a chapter of Czeslaw Milosz's *The Captive Mind* and putting it aside as an "instrument of cold war propaganda, giving aid and comfort to McCarthyism." But in 1980, "on the eve of my first visit to Poland, I took down my old copy . . . , reread it (for the first time) and thought, and thought only: But it's all true. And in Poland, I was to learn that Milosz had, if anything, underestimated the disgrace of the Communist regime installed by force in his country." "We" had closed our ears then, she went on, because we "had identified the enemy as fascism. We heard the demonic language of fascism. We believed in, or at least, applied a double standard to, the angelic language of Communism" (230).

> We were so sure who our enemies were (among them, the professional anti-Communists), so sure who were the virtuous and who the benighted. But I am struck by the fact that, despite the rightness of any of our views and aspirations, in particular our sense of the madness of nuclear war between the super-powers and our hopes for reforms of the many injustices of our own system, we were not responding to a large truth. And we were countenancing a great deal of untruth. (231)

Poland's martial government's turning off the phones, forbidding the sale of gasoline, rucksacks, and writing paper, "offered fascism a whole arsenal of new techniques." There can be only one conclusion: "Communism is fascism—successful fascism, if you will" (231).

Her critics answered that her *mea culpa* attitude was an old liberal stance inapplicable to them; that she had forgotten the New Left's severe attack on Leninism in the intervening years, that her generalizations about tyranny and fascism clouded the picture beyond recognition; a few recalled, as Marshall Berman did, Sontag's tendency to exaggeration. He thought fascism had nothing to do with the dialectic between democracy and communism. He writes:

> I find it hard to believe that Sontag doesn't know it already ... But those of us who know her work know that, again and again, over the years, she has said things that she must have known were off the wall. Thus, in "Against Interpretation" (1964), the act of interpretation "poisons our sensibilities" and "is the revenge of intellect upon the world ... " In "What's Happening in America" (1966), "The white race is the cancer of human history ... " In an oeuvre full of this sort of dramatic violence, statements like "Communism is fascism with a human face" are all too comfortably at home. Something seems to drive her, not merely to say explosive things that are absurd—we all do that sometimes—but, often, to say explosive things because they are absurd.[8]

Sontag did not respond to Berman's charges, nor to the other notables like Chomsky, Foucault, and Gary Wills, who were rounded up and given a special issue of the *Soho News* (a New York weekly). She was suing it for printing her speech without permission. That action caused still others to worry about her sense of political responsibility toward the freedom of the press. Her speech was, after all, public, they complained; has she placed herself in the center of a court, one asked, so that the staff of the *Soho News*, to show sufficient penitence, may "have to journey to Canossa to wait, barefooted in the courtyard, until they are received? If ever?"[9]

Some of this flurry, of course, has the tone of a media-sponsored cocktail party. The images of dismay tend toward the picturesque, and the quotable snipes come from careful posturing. Still, Sontag was serious and she was answered roundly. It is interesting to note how many commented on her bravery; those who sweat under the public spotlight, some murmured, deserve respect. But Sontag wanted to be sure they did not mistake her: "I was never a Communist (and therefore am not now a 'repentant' ex-Communist of the god-who-failed variety). . . . I hardly thought Milosz was lying. Nevertheless, detesting the reactionary uses to which anti-Communism is put— . . . I bracketed what Milosz and the other emigrés were saying. That is the phenomenon I was addressing."[10]

Sontag may have bracketed Milosz's book; here she is still bracketing by way of the epigram, the "something" which drives her to say things because they are hinged by antithesis. The epigrammatical mode is a slash-and-burn technique.

That kind of polarity-talk is what disturbed many in her audience. What she had to say came too close to defending, implicitly, American superpowerism. The restraint she exercised during the McCarthy period she abandoned as the United States poured more misery into Central America. Again, she missed her audience in a self-serving way. Many there were veterans of the New Left's years of consciousness raising against all instances of Leninism, from "deformed" communist states to "deformed" practices between individuals. She forgot, in other words, the New Left's own coming into being.

It is possible that Sontag had been half-consciously responding to Bertram Gross' book *Friendly Fascism: The New Face of Power in America* (Boston: South End Press 1980). He, however, at least begins with the acknowledgement that "fascism" is an "all-purpose nasty word" (11). In another vein of speculation about Sontag's speeches, one also wonders why most realizations come to Sontag on the eve of her trips. My guess is that it comes from that pause before the fear of having to give up the truth won by introspection.

Sontag may be sorry that writers are now "denied the hectic consolations of being part of a movement." She does think it is important that now "there are just individuals doing their work. . . . The people whose work is very good are usually people who are very single-minded, who are quite separate. Kafka said once you could never be too alone to write, and in the end the life of a writer *is* very solitary."[11]

In giving up one set of illusions, I am afraid Sontag returns to another. This theme of the solitary writer has become a "piety without content" for the modernists. Separateness and intelligence have fused in modernist rhetoric into the image of the pure. Since purity draws on deeper sources than virtue, because it is both elemental and transcendent, because the word has so long been associated with light, the real value of the writer's purity is lost in a substance already over-bright (brilliant perhaps). We see the unrewarded writer in the study rebuking the hypocrisy of the salon, the trivializing of the public, and the texts appear more precious for answering no call. The classic ideal of the self-contained work has been adopted by modernists as a literal subject, and by later modernists like Sontag as an emblem of ennobling persistence.

Sontag begins her career arguing for the autonomy of the aesthetic, although "uneasily," troubled by the way the artist's eye can remake the world, how it can aestheticize perception. She was bold enough, however, to try to blend those ideas of art, morality, and the will discussed in *Against Interpretation* into her title of her next collection, *Styles of Radical Will*. She told the *New York Times* interviewer in 1980: "A decade-long residence in the 60's, with its inexorable conversion of moral and political radicalism into 'style,' has convinced me of the perils of overgeneralizing the aesthetic view of the world."[12] She had just worked out what those perils might be, in part, in her book on a very different topic: photography (1977). Overall, the 1970s were a chance for a slower sifting through ambivalence and doubts (about the importance of the uninterpreted artist, uninterpretable art) and a closer reconnoitering of self. Her chief concerns, her habits of thinking, went another round. In the "painstaking explicitness" interviewers draw from her, she tries to encapsulate her transformations. In 1975 she told *Salmagundi*:

> As it turns out, "the aesthetic view of the world" is extremely hospitable to many of the uncivilized ideas and dissociated yearnings that were made explicit in fascism, and which also have great currency in our consumer culture. Yet it is clear—China has made it clear—that the moralism of serious communist countries not only wipes out the autonomy of the aesthetic, but makes it impossible to produce art in the modern sense at all. A six-week trip to China in 1973 convinced me—if I needed convincing—that the autonomy of the aesthetic is something to be protected, and cherished, as indispensable nourishment to intelligence.[13]

And she then continues with the phrase she would repeat to the *New York Times*, "a decade-long residence in the 1960's, with its inexorable conversion of moral and political radicalism . . . [etc.]." The rhetorical roll of the phrase may have struck Sontag as just right, in the manner of a Steinian insistence, as a way of *not* telling that she has *not* stopped thinking about styles of being. Rather, she has shifted the values between radical and autonomous again, and now autonomous has its turn.

I do not mean to belittle this shifting about for values. Thinking people do this, public thinkers are forced to do it publically. What I wish to point to is Sontag's qualification, "impossible to do art (in the modern sense) at all." It is self-evident that the most admired works in the history of western art were commissioned, that the "autonomous artwork" was a product of a small and late movement, supported by the growth over several hundred years of an art market that included collectors of significant taste, and that we have come to rely on that network of taste makers and collectors to a very high degree. She is part of that network, and she must strain very hard to imagine (as she tries in the Vietnam essay) what *is* the aesthetic sense without this autonomous artworld.

This "autonomous" artworld is the historical and material precondition of being western aesthetically, which has also meant for nearly a century being *trop moderne,* that is, overwhelmed by the awareness that the present exists as a period in time that has eradicated all previous feelings for time. In the supposedly abandoned past, art and thought were vehicles to the beyond, whether that beyond was the timeless realm of pure idea, ennobled sentiment, a golden age of ethical beings, a conduit to a redemptive god, or (more recently, more modestly) a forging of a nation. The condition of modernism is a way of living with the loss of these purposes—by irony, paradox, obscurity, or, with the unique emphasis Sontag gives the word, by pathos. And while writers of all ages have known the crippling effects of perplexity, irony, or loss of faith, the later modernists gave a heightened and pervasive character to their sense of blockage; post-modernists, it can be said, to having survived blockage. No clear line of demarcation separates the late and the post-modernists, but there was a strong and swift evolution in America in the late 1960s that caught many critics' attention. I have not dwelled on these differences because Sontag's thought falls with the late modernists, inheriting a time when, as George Steiner believes, "For all its wit and incandescence, the American scene was one of the epilogues to modernism."[14] It has been Sontag's practice to try to write her way out of the rules of closure and overcommentary an epilogue requires.

When Trilling once asked if there was a politics to the contemporary (in my term "late modernist") spirit of the "perverse and morbid" in literature, Sontag set about looking for an answer, a politics itself being a kind of answer. Her uncertainty about that spirit made her take up a cudgel with which to beat her brains, and to beat (tendentiously) at those meanings the intellectual effort of the last 150 years (since Hegel) have labored upon us. In Sontag's description, the past swallows up the inventiveness of the present; no one stands up well next to it nor can anything spring from it. After the wars, that is, in the post-war modernity, art and thinking presumably rested in the mourning and rubble, trying for some zero degree of pure factuality, entirely overshadowed by the war-heated, world-transforming power of technology. The spirit of negation enlisted by these later modernists went in search of principles with which to defeat themselves. They kept finding them in the house of multiple self-reflections or in the definitions of their actions that admitted no exits. In summarizing this time, Sontag said that art yearned for silence, by accumulating absurdities until it could no longer be understood, or by eliminating all references until it was empty.

When Sontag couches her discussion of art and writers in such phrases as "committed to the idea that the power of art is located in its power to negate" (SRW 8), she is writing in the textual strategies of that epilogue. Negation was that tenet of modernism which poised creation at the moment of destruction of older artistic forms. By the 1960s, time had allowed a review of the fate of the artistic-political avant-gardes; their programs were replaced with empty promise, with a kind of fetishization of the negative. Sontag writes warily, in that suspended critical voice that has become so identified with her, seemingly looking for the meaning of this power to negate, suspicious of its totalizing capacity, finding nothing like it, as a moral or visionary concept, with which to replace it. She's not ready to relinquish it, and she does not seem through with trying to demystify it.

Hence her concentration on the word "disburdenment," on the heroism of disburdenment, on what I call Sontag's allegory of disburdenment. When Nietzsche used the term he saw the tragic hero shouldering the cradle of disaster, the Dionysian wholeness, so that we might be disburdened of our terrible longing. In many of Sontag's portraits of the "exemplary heroes" of modernism, she shows us their suffering in these Nietzschean terms; in her political essays she asks us to give up something.

Benjamin grasped the allegorist's intention thus: "The intention which underlies allegory," he writes, "is so opposed to that which is concerned with the discovery of truth that it reveals more clearly than anything else the identity of the pure curiosity which is aimed at mere knowledge with the proud isolation of man."(43) The hero of the modernist allegory is the solitary figure, the bride and her bachelors, the *machine célibataire* of Duchamp. The practice of modernism is a view of our times in which positions melt away into the precisely worded inscrutable with a toughness which does not transform the problems of being in the world.

It is a self-perpetuating practice designed to gain mere knowledge, that is, mere knowledge of a self insulated from all that is burlesqued in life. It's a practice that dwells in death, appreciates irony and confoundedness, admires the unconscious, can even enjoy frivolity, but throws almost all that's left of its faith towards the expressive power of form. What it rejects most of all is the excess, the cruelty, the bloody and bittersweet *promesse de bonheur* of nature.

How could there be a better test of what it means to brave nature than when stricken with a fatal disease? Nature at its most ruinous, most secret and autonomous exacts its own exemplary heroics from the modernist. More so than in art, more than in thought, the proud, isolated self discovers that it belongs to nature, to be picked up and thrown away in nature's course. When Sontag refuses to "interpret" disease, she means to triumph with her method—not over disease, that matter has been relegated to science and luck. She means to triumph over that part of the self about to fall into the experience of nature and there to find its purpose.

Her first book was a case of the physician curing herself, and so it was appreciated by those close to the illness. But, into what a politicized context her practice has recently fallen! In the midst of the terrible suffering of AIDS, cultural critics mobilized. This is a time when many thoughtful people are forewarned and forearmed by deconstructionist ideas, and they have put their critiques in the service of the fight against AIDS; what they quarrel over is the status of the meanings they find.

Sontag simplifies. Disease has no meaning. "Nothing is more punitive than to give a disease a meaning," she writes in *Illness as Metaphor*, "—that meaning being inevitably a moralistic one" (*IM* 58). Somewhere in our understanding of disease, we will ply it for some agency that did right or wrong, and all too often that agency becomes the sufferers themselves. To their pain, we add guilt, guilt by loose association as much as by assumed wrong action. Her two slim books are a study of these associations, by which she hopes to break the "fantasy of inescapable fatality" and to try to effect a "wholesome dedramatization" of two diseases for which there are now no cures: cancer (*Illness as Metaphor*) and AIDS (*AIDS as Metaphor*).

Her argument rests on the "preposterous transformations" tuberculosis continued to go through in literature even after its bacterial agent was found in 1881. Typically the sufferer was a waif, or someone spiritually ephemeral who died a "symptomless, unfrightened, beatific" death (*IM* 16). TB "dissolved the gross body, etherealized the personality, expanded consciousness" (*IM* 19–20). TB could "aestheticize death." "Thoreau, who had TB, wrote in 1852: 'Death and disease are often beautiful, like . . . the hectic glow of consumption' " (*IM* 21). To the contrary, "in fact, dying from tuberculosis was often hard and extremely painful." "The fiction about soft and easy deaths . . . is part of the mythology of most diseases that are not considered shameful or demeaning" (*AM* 38).

Once there was found an effective treatment (streptomycin in 1944) the fantasies stopped. This, of course, is tantamount to saying that once there were no more consumptive people the representations stopped. What strikes Sontag, however, is the seeming power of the cure to intervene in the popular imagination of the disease. Persons with tuberculosis or syphilis no longer claim anything much from the imagination, not in literature or broadsides or in public outcry. Before the age of the antibiotic, they did.

By contrasting cancer to TB in the first book and epidemic to plagues in the AIDS book, Sontag can then move up and down the associative ladder, from the wish fulfillments of the individual to medical theories to proofs against the culture. Her method heightens distinctions for the sake of seeing artifices, and nothing more. After reading her book, we don't know how better to understand these diseases, only what theory is most suspect because of the way it fills in a picture.

She opposes, for example, the "edifying, refined disease" TB, which dematerializes the body, to the repugnant cancer which turns the body into hard, alien substances. Tubercular persons were thought to have suffered from thwarted passions, often idealized ones, while cancer came as the "wages of repression." TB was the disease of the melancholic, a sign of sensitivity, creativity. Treatment was conducted as a gentle "coaxing" back to health in removes to landscapes high in romantic appeal. Cancer became the sign of "life's losers"—the result of depressions and anxieties over failed ambitions, money troubles, grief. Treatment was brutal.

Both diseases mirror the age's complaints: TB was likened to early capitalistic accumulation in which the profligate tubercular had spent recklessly, burning with the wrong emotions. Cancer was a disease for the era of "unregulated, abnormal, incoherent" growth.

The overall point of Sontag's books is that metaphors of illness themselves know no bounds. Once these cluster of values were firmly struck to the name of the disease, then the name itself entered the discourse of the "body politic." "Cancer" was a staple of totalitarian polemicists.

"But it could be argued that cancer metaphors are in themselves implicitly genocidal," she writes. At the very least, "the cancer metaphor is particularly crass. It is invariably an encouragement to simplify what is complex and an invitation to self-righteousness, if not fanaticism" (*IM* 84). Presumably, we are being given an indirect confession and apology for that famous remark about the white race as the cancer of human history (*SRW* 203).

Cancer is a very old disease even though it seems to feed on every invention of the chemical industry of the past forty years. With contemporary fears of a poisoned world, cancer is that which would kill us, with or without nuclear war.

AIDS (possibly a new disease) "has banalized cancer"; its principal metaphor is "plague," that is, a collective calamity and a judgment on the community. Even for the least socially swayed researchers, the "expanded notion" of the disease "creates a new class of lifetime pariahs, the future ill" (*IM* 34). Thus conceived, AIDS "reinstates something like the premodern condition" of illness as described in Donne's *Devotion*, in which "'every thing that disorders a faculty and the function of that is a sicknesse,' which starts when we 'are preafflicted' and ends in abandonment or 'Excommunication'" (*AM* 35).

After pointing to or at least footnoting the least plausible, deepest racist, homophobic, CIA-paranoid or moral-bankruptcy theories of the disease, Sontag adds this mild remark. "What is surprising," she writes, "is not that the AIDS epidemic has been exploited in this way but that such cant has been confined to so predictable a sector of bigots; the official discourse about AIDS invariably includes admonitions against bigotry" (*IM* 61).

Needless to say, Sontag's coolness here hardly suffices for those on the front lines battling this bigotry. She seems to them callous or dismissive of their extraordinary organizational and individual courage and effectiveness, not to say their accumulated experience of how alive, how general this bigotry is. Her eye is on the century's tendencies, not them.

> The way in which the illness is such a perfect repository for people's most general fears about the future to some extent renders irrelevant the predictable efforts to pin the disease on a deviant group or a dark continent. . . . AIDS is one of the dystopian harbingers of the global village, that future which is already here and always before us, which no one knows how to refuse. (*AM* 2–3)

What Sontag hopes to do is to throw the "ordinariness" of diseases against the glacial movement, the "slow catastrophe" of the end of the millennium's apocalyptic predictions. She knows that "even an apocalypse can be made to seem part of the ordinary horizon of expectation," and that this constitutes "unparalleled violence" to our "sense of reality, to our humanity." "But," she insists, "it is highly desirable for a specific dreaded illness to come to seem ordinary," as is bound to happen when AIDS becomes treatable. The struggle now is for the "rhetorical ownership of the illness" (AM 94).

In her last point about metaphors she states: "they cannot be distanced just by abstaining from them. They have to be exposed, criticized, belabored, used up" (IM 94). The most dangerous—the medical model of the public weal and the military model of the body as the site of invasion and battle—must be "retired."

There is something lulling about Sontag's admissions here, about the need to use up and retire metaphors. Most of her reviewers felt uneasy. She is not as convincing, they thought, as in her first book, not as definite. Her flaming sword of radical rationalism has turned into an ember of idealism. She is so far removed from the dying she does not even use the word "gay". How could she ignore all the critique against the medicine = science = truths equations, all the books and essays documenting how the issues got defined, how money was spent, how institutions stalled, how shamelessly the press behaved? How difficult it is to find out what is happening in Africa? Isn't she just reviving the two cultures antagonism, in Richard Goldstein's words, between "the 'haves' [who] communicate in technical tropes, while the 'have-nots' use the tough talk of activism and art." Could she possibly be implying that the disease disappears under the inspection of language or becomes more "wholesome" because it is "dedramatized"? Why doesn't she speak of the dialectic between representation and reality?

Others have asked: What has it possibly gained us to discount, even momentarily, the fact that the disease has been fatal to all who contracted the symptom-array? By calming public fears about contagion and transmission, to make it seem that the first wave of deaths may have been to the most susceptible only, isn't she encouraging the government to be less inclined to act? and isn't she satisfying those who find a vicious gratification in their view that the disease has been confined to groups, if not continents, which to them are repulsive? Does she not know how bitter, on one side, the struggle has been to fight the system and make it respond, and how rewarding, on the other, to watch the pity and kindness and sacrifice flourish for the ill?

The tough talkers about activism and art tend to be activists who feel that they, not the neutral, depersonal process of normalization or "ordinariness," are the instruments that hold up the wall against the momentum of apocalyptic and vengeful panic. They are the ones fighting against mandatory testing, quarantining; they are the ones who protest at the gates of churches, the army, the doors of the media against exclusion and prejudice. They are the ones who daily have to confront the repercussions of new epidemiological evidence or even their own statements, to keep up the pressure amid internal dissent, to be sources of the most accurate information, the greatest outreach, to offer the most protection and redress, under agonizing questions of political strategy.

A great deal is left out in Sontag's approach. For gay men, especially—how can words describe their sorrow?—this disease puts their love before them, their communal love, their love practices in deadly terms. Eros meets thanatos not in the realm of the imagination, but in the beloved bodies of their lovers. They have had to respond to the very question of affirming their love, their practices, trying to fend off the separation between what it is to be gay from those practices, defending all sorts of gay lifestyles as gay, not one being more admirable than the other. Few diseases test the strength of the sinews of identity as this one has. All that was debated about having a gay identity, its intrinsic as well as extrinsic features, its cultural and political values, has been spotlighted anew. The country heard a resounding "yes, it is good to be gay." That "yes" was uplifting for all. Sontag may have failed here, failed badly. She writes:

> Fear of AIDS enforces a much more moderate exercise of appetite, and not just among homosexual men. In the United States sexual behavior pre-1981 now seems for the middle class part of a lost age of innocence—innocence in the guise of licentiousness, of course. After two decades of sexual spending, of sexual speculation, or sexual inflation, we are in the early stages of a sexual depression. Looking back on the sexual culture of the 1970s has been compared to looking back on the jazz age from the wrong side of the 1929 crash. (IM 76)

Appetite? Licentiousness, of course? Sexual spending, speculation, inflation, depression? Who is speaking here? The passages that follow this analogy make capitalism blameworthy for the ethic of personal fulfillment: "the ideology of capitalism makes us all into connoisseurs of liberty—of the indefinite expansion of possibility" (AM 77). Most of the critique of capitalism familiar to the Left says just the opposite: capitalism perverts our quest for fulfillment into questions of spending, speculation, inflation, etc. How far has Sontag's conservatism gone that she would slip into making metaphorical condemnations herself? Or did she just lose control of the ironic weight to what she is saying here, so that we are confused by whether she is tracing a history for us or describing a common parlance or telling us what *she* thinks?

The evidence of the rest of the discussion is mixed: she keeps repeating, with carefully controlled disdain, the link between consumerism and "recreational and commercialized" sexuality, between the end-of-the-era exhaustion and the general return to "conventions." But she says nothing of what else moves people to love outside of monogamy or to break with conventions. That silence feels like its own abandonment. Perhaps, under the code of the aesthetic of silence, Sontag may think it best not to say. Silence, the absence of constructed meanings, where experience is most present.

But how does one fight armored with silence? How does one tell others of what it means to be dying of AIDS, in silence? Sontag tries to show this in her short story "The Way We Live Now." The man dying of AIDS is spoken of; he does not speak. It is her project to take this stance.

As a project, it does protect her trustworthiness as long as she holds to it. When she breaks it, still, some reviewers note, she is a "paragon of particularity," compared to other critics on this subject. The contributions to the otherwise fine *October* issue on AIDS (no. 47 Winter 1987) are illustrative here of what happens to arguments in an atmosphere of urgency, pain, and a Foucauldian free-for-all of examples and conclusions. Like Sontag, these writers chase many issues at once; they too want to generalize at each encounter. Yet, they are not just drawing distinctions—the method that gives Sontag's book a logic. They advocate, and in the muddle of their purposes not all their statements can be so well taken. If there is a competition for method among these writers, Sontag's work does not come out the worse, for all the justified attacks against her book.

Finally, they are all, Sontag and her critics, worrying over the same problem: meaning cannot be reinstituted or fended off by outrage, or by scientific fact, or in the absence of moralizing. Our age is hard on meaning, to be sure. Too many opposed scales of measurement are put side by side; we have a very grave sense of history, a very strange sense of flourishing in the midst of enormity. Consider: once there were celestial wheels upon wheels turning the fates of individuals. Once there were myths to make a story out of desires and failures, beginnings, affronts, ending. Then there were mediations—in Raymond William's characterization—intercessors, reconcilors, interpreters, agents-to make history cohere. On the very low end of the mediation scale, we have come to metaphors, from which, seemingly, social constructions just accumulate.

"All thinking is metaphoric" everyone seems to agree too readily; for we may not really believe it. Metaphors are simple analogies where one side stays put in an enigma, while the other goes wandering off in hopes of eliciting sympathetic vibrations. In wandering, it is careless: any clump of associations might be resonant, no matter if our understanding of the original undergoes a "preposterous transformation," to borrow Sontag's words. We have too many methods of understanding (besides metaphors) to know where to put the emphasis; our case is more an embarrassment of riches, encircled by the chief anxiety of whether what we think matters at all.

The present age, writes Sontag, lives by a scenario in which "apocalypse looms and it doesn't occur . . . And still it looms." That observation recalls Northrop Frye's remark, that in the world of the apocalyptic is a world of total metaphor, "in which everything is potentially identical with everything else, as though it were all inside a single body."

So, in the age of apocalypse, an exemplary heroism might indeed be to deny metaphors as the radical negator, or to "retire" them as the more perplexed and ambivalent of modernists might say. Either way, one is disburdened.

If, though, one believes with Bataille "how impossible it is at the present moment for anything human to arise except from the cesspool of the human heart,"[15] disburdenment is not the aim. Apocalypse cannot loom, though unimaginable destruction can. Allegories cannot be satisfying, because punishment is not sought. Instead one wishes to return, world to world.

But Sontag's practice, in its inner aim, is more severe. One returns to a stripped bare consciousness, as a descriptive process. She does not trust the politics of will and spiritual completeness, not if one reads her carefully: they "aestheticize." She does not trust photographs, because they too, with their ubiquity and prettifying, aestheticize. She does not trust the myths of modernist art nor the current metaphors of social constructions. She cannot yield to any theater of action that draws from or tries to imitate nature. She can defend only those works and that kind of consciousness that are perplexed by their subject, patronize themselves, and just as stubbornly, paradoxically, seek to simplify.

"Perhaps," the disaffected member of a secret society tells the reader in the short story "Old Complaints Revisited," "if I rewrote what I've written here, it would be more convincing. If I could be lyrical! Unpredictable! Concise! In love with things as they are! But, alas, this thin overscrupulous voice is mine . . . My problem is identical with my language" (I,E 142).

Sontag's voice is never thin. She does share, however, with all her fictional characters, in all their appearances as "I," a manner of phrasing. To the pleasures of her writing—the beauty of distillation, the ghosts that come alive between juxtapositions, the spirited intrusions captured in epigrams—must be added its self-imposed restrictions. Her language is made up of principles, insistences, statements pulled from the flow of things against all temptation to reproduce the object she is thinking about. This is her philosopher's habit, her instinctual discounting of the tremulous behavior of writers after the abject, *écriture*, the sublime. But what her writing most often holds off is the amorphous tangle of the vivid. Whatever care she takes, overscrupulous and precise, to make sense of an argument, what is allowed to slip away is the unplanned, the mortal, the fecund.

One concern of this book has been the extent to which Sontag's characteristic manner of voice has reflected her understanding of the late modernist aesthetic. I have questioned whether she seeks the end of the modernist sensibility or whether she is not being just "excruciatingly" sensitive to those wanderers among the ruins. And it seems to me that she has presaged the complaint against modernism (now so thoroughly detailed by the postmodernists), but not for the sake of abandoning it. Rather, she is poised at the border between the sensibilities, unable and unwilling to stride, unburdened, forward. Her tone, her style, and her ideas tell about this condition, against what she is more popularly remembered for. Those essays about jettisoning (interpretation, for instance) are more about purifying, and those forays into the lesser lives of culture—Camp, pornography, imaginations of disaster—are in defense of the highest way: the difficult and the extreme.

Sontag has reproduced herself in her work; she has molded herself into her entire project. Her essays and her fiction and her films have poured into one another until they appeared to her as hybridized things. After being famous for some twenty-five years, she has been tempted to think of her work as having achieved a way of knowing, an identifiable intelligence/style, a practice, as a contribution, even as she delineated it, to modernism in its latter days. Unquestionably, she has done, she is doing, just that.

Notes

Introduction

1. This comment was in response to a counter made by Carolyn Forché about Sontag's use of Céline as an example of great writers whose views are unjust. Forché: "I also do not believe that we are necessarily living at the pinnacle of our enlightenment. I should hope not. Much of our writing probably reflects unconscious attitudes on our parts but may in some future time be deplored." Collected by Toronto Arts Group for Human Rights in *The Writer and Human Rights*. (Toronto: Lester & Orpen Dennys, 1983) 29–30.

2. Roger Copeland, "Habits of Consciousness," *Commonweal* 108 (13 Feb., 1981) 85.

3. Alan W. Wald. *The New York Intellectuals: The Rise and Decline of the Anti-Stalinist Left from the 1930s to the 1980s.* (Chapel Hill: The University of North Carolina Press, 1987) 217–18.

4. Philip Rieff, *Freud, The Mind of the Moralist.* (New York: Anchor Books, 1961) 349.

5. Sontag, "Pilgrimage," *The New Yorker, 21 Dec., 87: 38.*

6. Russell Jacoby, *The Last Intellectuals: American Culture in the Age of Academe* (New York: Basic Books, 1987) 10.

7. Ibid. p. 219.

8. Edmund White, *Caracole* (New York: Dutton, 1985) 271.

Biographical Notes

1. David Sontag Rieff, *Going to Miami: Exiles, Tourists and Refugees in the New America* (Boston: Little Brown, 1987). David Rieff collaborated with Sharon Delano on a text to accompany *Texas Boots* (New York: Viking Press, 1981). Collecting western boots has been a hobby of David's and Sontag's.

2. Judith Grossman, *Her Own Terms* (New York: Soho Press, 1988) 221–22.

3. Nancy DuVergne Smith, "Writing it Out: an interview with Susan Sontag," *Realia,* Dec. 1983: 14.

4. Alicia Ostriker, "Anti-Critic," *Commentary,* Vol. 41, No. 5, June, 1966: 84.

5. Stanley Aronowitz, "Sontag Versus Barthes for Barthes' Sake," *The Village Voice Literary Supplement,* Nov. 1982: 13.

6. Sharon Smith, *Women Who Make Movies* (New York: Hopkinson and Blake, 1975): 53.

Key Terms

1. Lionel Trilling, "The Fate of Pleasure," *Beyond Culture* (New York: Harcourt Brace Jovanovich, 1965) 70.

2. Maurice Blanchot, *Death Sentence*, trans. Lydia Davis (Barrytown, New York: Station Hill Press, 1978) 30.

3. Maire Jaanus Kurrik, *Literature and Negation* (New York: Columbia UP, 1979).

4. Lionel Trilling, "The Authentic Unconscious," *Sincerity and Authenticity* (Cambridge: Harvard UP, 1971, 1972) 171. Trilling also quietly responds to Sontag's "Against Interpretation" in "The Heroic, the Beautiful, the Authentic" essay in this collection. She is mentioned in the text, and pointedly, in a footnote in which Trilling shows that his essay "The Fate of Pleasure" came first. By implication Sontag is linked to the likes of Sarraute's "relentlessly censorious tone [which] suggests the moral intensity we now direct upon the questions of authenticity" (101). She, like Gide, Lawrence, Sartre himself, has added to the " 'gabble' "—those conventions, maxims, etc. of "anyone who undertakes to satisfy our modern demand for reminders of our fallen state and for reason why we are to be ashamed of our lives" (105).

5. Walter Benjamin, *The Origin of German Tragic Drama*, trans. John Osborne (London: New Left Books, 1977) 232–33.

6. Cary Nelson, "Soliciting Self-Knowledge: The Rhetoric of Susan Sontag's Criticism," *Critical Inquiry*, Summer, 1980: 726.

7. Jair Rattner, "Sontag diz que há uma superpopulaçao de escritores," *Fohla De S. Paulo*, 28 May, 1988. (A–31). Translated from Portuguese.

The Two Novels: *The Benefactor* and *Death Kit*

1. "You know I've often thought that *Death Kit* could have been called *Why Are We In Vietnam?* because it gets into the kind of senseless brutality and self-destructiveness that is ruining America"—quoted in interview with James Toback, "Whatever You'd Like Susan Sontag To Think, She Doesn't," *Esquire*, July, 1968: p. 60.

2. Richard Howard, "Two Firsts," *Partisan Review*; Vol. 31, No. 3 (Summer, 1964) 458.

3. "As for myself: by deciding to write 'Notes on Camp' instead of 'Notes on Death,' I was choosing to humor that part of my seriousness that was being zapped and loosened up and made more sociable by camp wit rather than to fortify that part of my wit that got regularly choked off by seizures of morbidity." In "Women, The Arts, & The Political Culture: An Interview with Susan Sontag," *Salmagundi*, No. 31–32 (Fall-Winter, 1975–6) 40.

4. All citations in parenthesis in this section are from the Avon paperback edition of *The Benefactor* (New York: Farrar, Straus, & Giroux, 1963), unless otherwise identified.

5. "How to 'name a sensibility' how 'to draw its contours, to recount its history'— that was the problem I started from, and then looked for an example, a model. And it seemed to me more interesting not to pick Sensibility X from among those heaped with ethical or aesthetic laurels, and to evoke instead a sensibility that was exotic and in obvious ways minor, even despised—as the rather quirky notion of a 'sensibility' had itself been slighted, in favor of that tidier fiction, an 'idea.'

Morbidity was my first choice. I stayed with that for a while, attempting to systematize a long-term fascination with mortuary sculpture, architecture, inscriptions and other such wistful lore that eventually found an unsystematic place in *Death Kit* and *Promised Lands." Salmagundi*, 39–40.

6. Quoted in the Toback interview, 60.

7. Recalled by Naomi Greene in her book *Antonin Artaud: Poets Without Words* (New York: Simon & Schuster, 1970) 41.

8. John Wain, "Song of Myself, 1963" a review of *The Benefactor*, in *New Republic*, 21 Sept., 1963: 26.

9. Roger Sale, *"Death Kit," The Hudson Review*, Vol. 20, No. 4. (Winter, 1967–68) 668.

10. Benjamin DeMott, "Diddy or Didn't He," *New York Times Book Review*, 27 Aug., 1967: 2.

11. All citations are from the first edition of *Death Kit* (New York: Farrar, Straus, & Giroux, 1967).

12. In truth, this material was almost too forbidding. Note how most reviewers balked:

Tony Tanner: "Miss Sontag conveys little sense of *process*. She is capable of making all sorts of arresting clarifications . . . but she cannot, or does not, dramatize the engagement, the interpretation of consciousness and otherness which customarily provides the richness and energy of the novel. Her book is a long renunciation—but it is a rumination without a view." "Space Odyssey," a review of *Death Kit*, *Partisan Review*, Vol. 35, No. 3 (Summer, 1968) 449.

Gore Vidal: "Unhindered by a sense of humor, she is able to travel fast in the highest country, unafraid of appearing absurd, invulnerable to irony. . . . Unfortunately, Miss Sontag's intelligence is greater that her talent. . . . Worse, the literary borrowings entirely obscure her own natural talent while the attitudes she strikes confuse and annoy, reminding one of Gide's weary complaints that to him there was nothing more unbearable than those writers who assume a tone and manner not their own." "The Writer as Cannibal," review of *Death Kit*, *Book World*, (10 Sept., 1967) 34.

Benjammin DeMott: "But because of the irreducible imprecision of the novel, the ambiguous continuities between the narrator's consciousness and her character's consciousness, her anger shades off into Diddy's chucky uneasy self-criticism. And the result is an odd gap between posture and voice. . . . the voice of the shaming demon (Die like a dog, Oh modern man!) gives way to another that is weak and wisecracky (This'll kill ya), and the audience isn't wounded but confused. Miss Sontag's spirit and intelligence have braced people before and will do so again; just at this moment she is—not possible to predict such a turn—surprisingly less deadly than dull." "Diddy or Didn't He," *New York Times Book Review* (27 Aug., 1967) 2.

Denis Donoghue: "Miss Sontag is a novelist with a style inadequate to her purposes. She is particularly engrossed, for instance, in the experience of uncertainty. . . . But she does not possess the imagination of uncertainty. . . . Reading *Death Kit* I wondered why Miss Sontag ascribes representative status to her monsters, Diddy and Hester; why, thereafter, she concedes every sophistry of will as if it were a legitimate claim of spirit; and why, she assumes that the only home for the spirit is in dream and fantasy." "Sweepstakes," *New York Review of Books* (28 Sept., 1967) 5–6.

13. The ironies of the multiple doublings of the text sometimes include whimsical

ones. Diddy, for example, watches a company rehearse *Long Day's Journey Into Night*, through a glass, as a pantomime of himself and his brother Paul. Most of the puns in this novel, and there are many, have to serve as hints to a very unfunny context.

14. Denis Donoghue poses Diddy's cry for sight as a "causerie" on McLuhan. "Indeed, *Death Kit* may be read as a fictional gloss upon *The Gutenberg Galaxy*, its theme the pain of living in a visual culture." "Sweepstakes," 6–8.

15. We can follow this train of thinking from her earliest works. For example, of Pavese she writes in 1962: "The modern form of the writer's journal shows a curious solution if we examine some of its principal exemplars: Stendhal, Baudelaire, Gide, Kafka, and now Pavese. The uninhibited display of egotism devolves into the heroic quest for the cancellation of self" (*AI* 43). Comparing Leiris to Mailer in 1964, she adds:

> Leiris records the defeats of his own virility; completely incompetent in the arts of the body, he is perpetually in training to extinguish himself. . . . Perhaps the essential contrast between the optimistic, populist temperament of most American writers and the drastically alienated posture of the best European can be seen here. . . . Mailer shows us how his private travails and weaknesses produce the strength of his public work. . . . But Leiris doesn't see any continuity between his public self, distinguished as it may be, and his private weaknesses. . . . Leiris' motives are more desperate: he wishes to prove, not that he is heroic, but that he is at all. . . . for him, life becomes real only when placed under the threat of suicide. The same is true for the vocation of literature. In a view like Leiris', literature has value only as a means of enhancing virility, or as a means of suicide. (*AI* 651)

The Burden of Aesthetic

1. Friedrich Nietzsche, *The Birth of Tragedy*, trans. W. H. Haussman (New York: Macmillan, 1924) 128.

2. Walter Benjamin, "The Work of Art in the Age of Mechanical Reproduction," collected in *Illuminations*, trans. Harry Zohn (New York: Schocken Books, 1969) 240.

3. See Fredric Jameson, "'In the Destructive Element Immerse': Hans-Jürgen Syberberg and Cultural Revolution," *October*, No. 17 (Summer, 1981).

Thought Commemorated

1. To Roger Copeland's question: "Were you influenced by Burke's ideas about dramaturgy, or his conception of language as symbolic action?" Sontag replies: "I think by temperament I was attracted to dramaturgical kinds of language. I think of the essays in *Under the Sign of Saturn* as stagings of a certain kind, dramatizations." "The Habits of Consciousness," 87.

2. See David Craven's review: "*Under the Sign of Saturn*," *Telos* No. 48 (Summer, 1981) 189–4.

3. Sontag's phrase "anthropologist as hero" rang true enough for the editors of a collection of critical essays on Lévi-Strauss to use it (with acknowledgement) in their title. E. Nelson Hayes and Tanya Hayes, ed. *Claude Lévi-Strauss: The Anthropologist as Hero* (Cambridge: M. I. T. Press, 1970).

4. Reviewers of *Styles of Radical Will* have noted Sontag's ambivalent reading of Cioran and have been either insulted or surprised.

   Vernon Young, "Socialist Camp: Styles of Radical Wistfulness," *Hudson Reviews*, Vol. 22, No. 3 (Summer, 1969) 513–20:

   > . . . Cioran as well must have deceived Miss Sontag into believing that he was securely identifiable with the dilemmas he was posing. To her disappointment, she discovered that he could not be drafted as an advocate for her cause. Unlike her, he suavely insists on recognizing the absurdity of his position. In fact, more than any writer I know today, saving perhaps W. H. Auden, he is almost wholly quotable against Susan Sontag. (516–17)

   Peter Berek, *"Styles of Radical Will," Commonweal* 10 Oct., 1969: 48–49.

   > As a theoretician of art—a "metacritic," to use her own term—Miss Sontag combines the enthusiasm of the huckster with the zeal for novelty of a garment manufacturer. For example, in her new collection . . . she spends most of an essay speaking with measured commendations for the Rumanian philosopher E. M. Cioran for his "goal of infinite adaptability and intellectual agility," but acclaims John Cage as the truer master because he "proposes for our experience a world in which it's never preferable to do other than we are doing or be elsewhere than we are." . . . Miss Sontag is as swift to throw things overboard as she is to go overboard herself (48).

   Lawrence M. Bensky (*"Styles of Radical Will," New York Review of Books*, 13 July, 1969: 5, 45) is kinder. He finds Sontag's thoughts on Cioran an "auto-portrait":

   > Who she is can be glimpsed in the following passage from her essay, "Thinking Against Oneself: Reflections on Cioran," for it provides something of an auto-portrait of Susan Sontag. . . . The key words are clear: "indignant," "stoical," "enigmatic," "complex," "useful." But the one major adjective must be added "moral"—because the eight essays in *Styles of Radical Will* are mainly exercises in moral definition, as far as a moral definition can be accomplished today in the two supremely and terrifyingly insecure areas of modern art and modern political brutality. (5)

5. See John Cage, *Silence* (Middletown, Conn.: Wesleyan University Press, 1961). Sontag may also have read *A Year from Monday* (Middletown, Conn.: Wesleyan University Press, 1967). She was a friend of Cage, even so he comes under her constant reassessment. She tells Copeland in 1981: "I now think the juxtaposition of Cioran with Cage was sophistical" ("Sweepstakes" 85).

6. Walter Benjamin, "Thesis on the Philosophy of History," *Illuminations*, trans. by Harry Zohn (New York: Schocken Books, 1969) 254.

7. *Illuminations* 255.

8. Benjamin writes in "The Image of Proust":

   > There is a dual will to happiness, a dialectics of happiness: a hymnic and an elegiac form. The one is the unheard-of, the height of bliss; the other, the eternal repetition, the eternal restoration of the original, the first happiness. It is this elegiac idea of happiness—it could be called Eleatic—which for Proust transforms existence into a preserve of memory. (*Illuminations* 204)

9. See Georg Lukács, "The Ideology of Modernism," *The Meaning of Contemporary Realism*, trans. by John and Necke Mander (London: Merlin Press, 1963).

10. Quoted in Jonathan Cott's interview, "Susan Sontag: THE ROLLING STONE IN-TERVIEW" (*Rolling Stone*, 4 Oct. 1979) 53.

Conclusion

1. Sontag, "Some Thoughts on the Right Way (for us) to Love the Cuban Revolution," *Ramparts*, Vol. 7, No. 11 (April, 1969) 6–19.

2. *Mauviase Conduite*, dir. Nestor Almendros, Margaret Menegoz, Bachet Schroeder, Les Films du Losange et Antenne 2, 1984.

3. Alf Louvre, "The Reluctant Historians: Sontag, Mailer and American Critics in the 1960s," *Prose Studies* 9 May, 1986: 47–61.

4. See Hans Magnus Enzenberger's description of this system in his essay "Tourists of the Revolution," collected in *Critical Essays*, ed. Reinhold Grimm and Bruce Armstrong (New York: Continuum, 1982).

5. Later collected in Leo Marx, *The Pilot and the Passenger: Essays on Literature, Technology, and Culture in the United States* (New York: Oxford UP, 1988).

6. Sontag, "Reply," *The Nation*, Vol. 234, No. 8 (27 Feb., 1982) 230.

7. Sontag, "Communism and the Left," *The Nation*, Vol. 234, No. 8 (27 Feb., 1982) 230.

8. Marshall Berman, one of several respondents collected in "Susan Sontag's God that Failed," *Soho News* (24 Feb.–2 March, 1982) 11.

9. Nat Hentoff, "The Authorized Susan Sontag v. That 'Dreadful' Soho Rag," *Village Voice* (16 March, 1982) 4.

10. Sontag, *The Nation* 238.

11. Sontag, interview with Michiko Kakutani, "For Susan Sontag the Illusions of the 60s Have Been Dissipated," *The New York Times* (11 Nov., 1980) C-5.

12. Sontag, "For Susan Sontag ..." C-5.

13. Sontag, "Women, The Arts, & Politics of Culture: An Interview with Susan Sontag," *Salmagundi*, No. 31–32 (Fall 1975—Winter, 1976) 32.

14. George Steiner, "The Archives of Eden," *Salmagundi*, No. 50–51 (Fall 1980—Winter, 1981) 85.

15. Georges Bataille, *Visions of Excess: Selected Writings, 1927–1939*, ed. with intro. by Allan Stoekl, trans. by Stoekl, Carl R. Lovitt, Donald M. Leslie, Jr. (Minneapolis, MN: University of Minnesota Press, 1985) 41.

Selected Bibliography

Works by Sontag

Fiction

The Benefactor. New York: Farrar, Straus, Giroux, 1963.

Death Kit. New York: Farrar, Straus, Giroux, 1967.

I, etcetera. New York: Farrar, Straus, Giroux, 1978.

Essays

Against Interpretation. New York: Farrar, Straus, Giroux, 1966.

Trip to Hanoi. New York: Farrar, Straus, Giroux, 1968.

Styles of Radical Will. New York: Farrar, Straus, Giroux, 1969.

On Photography. New York: Farrar, Straus, Giroux, 1977.

Illness as Metaphor. New York: Farrar, Straus, Giroux, 1978.

Under the Sign of Saturn. New York: Farrar, Straus, Giroux, 1980.

A Susan Sontag Reader. Intro. by Elizabeth Hardwick. New York: Farrar, Straus, Giroux, 1982.

AIDS and Its Metaphors. New York: Farrar, Straus, Giroux, 1989.

Films

Duet for Cannibals. Written and directed by Sontag. Prod. Goran Lindgren for Sandrew Film and Theater (AB) Sweden, 1969 (distributed by Evergreen Films, USA). In Swedish, subtitles by Sontag. Black and white, 105 min.

Brother Carl. Written and directed by Sontag. Prod. Goran Lindgren for Sandrew Film and Theater (AB) and Svenska Filminstitutet, 1971 (distributed by New Yorker Films). In Swedish, with English Soundtrack. Black & white, 97 min.

Promised Lands (a documentary on Israel). Written and directed by Sontag, 1974 (distributed by New Yorker Films). Color, 87 min.

Unguided Tour (from the short story). Written and directed by Sontag, 1983. Prod. Giovannella Zannoni for Lunga Gittata Cooperative, RAI rete 3. Color, 72 min.

Filmscripts

Duet for Cannibals: A Screenplay. New York: Farrar, Straus, Giroux, 1970.

Brother Carl: A Filmscript. New York: Farrar, Straus, Giroux, 1974.

Editions

Antonin Artaud. *Selected Writings*. Ed. with intro. by Susan Sontag. Trans. Helen Weaver: notes by Sontag and Don Eric Levine. New York: Farrar, Straus, Giroux, 1976.

Roland Barthes. *A Roland Barthes Reader*. Ed. with intro. by Susan Sontag. New York: Hill & Wang, 1981.

Introductions/Prefaces

Roland Barthes. *Writing Degree Zero and Elements of Semiology*. Preface copyrighted 1968 by Susan Sontag. Boston: Beacon, 1970. "Preface" xi–xxv.

E. M. Cioran. *The Temptation to Exist*. Trans. Richard Howard. Introduction by Susan Sontag, copyright 1968. Chicago: Quadrangle Paperback, 1970. "Introduction," 9–29.

Dugald Stermer. *The Art of Revolution: 96 Posters from Cuba*. Introduction by Susan Sontag. "Posters: advertisements, art, political artifact, commodity," vii–xxiii. New York: McGraw Hill, 1970.

Maria Irene Fornes. *Plays*. Preface by Susan Sontag, copyright 1985. "Preface" 7–10. New York: PAJ, 1986.

Vera Lehndorff, Holger Trulzsch. *Verushka: Transfigurations*. Introduction by Susan Sontag, copyright 1986. "Fragments of an Aesthetic of Melancholy," 6–12. New York: A New York Graphic Society Book, Little, Brown & Company, 1986.

Uncollected Essays/Fiction

"Demons and Dreams: The Slave." *Partisan Review*, 29 (Summer 1962): 460–3.

"Man With a Pain." (short story) *Harpers Magazine*, Vol. 228, No. 1367 (April 1964): 72–75.

"Yugoslav Report." *Partisan Review*, 33 (Winter 1966): 116–23.

"Literature." *Great Ideas Today*, 1966. Chicago: Encyclopedia Britannica. Eds. Robert Maynard Hutchins and M. J. Adler: 146–91.

"Theater—In London: Inadmissable Evidence." *Vogue*, Vol. 146, No. 3 (April 1965): 51–55.

"Transmitting His Master's Voice: *A Psycho-Analytic Dialogue: The Letters of Sigmund Freud and Karl Abraham, 1907–1926*." *Book Week* 3 April 1966: 2–3, 12–13.

"The Avant-Garde and Contemporary Literature." *Wilson Library Bulletin*, Vol. 40, No. 10 (June 1966) 930–32.

"Some Thoughts on the Right Way (for us) to Love the Cuban Revolution." *Ramparts*, Vol. 7, No. 11 (April 1969): 6–19.

"A Letter from Sweden." *Ramparts*, Vol. 8 (July 1969): 23–38.

"Revolutionary Karma vs. Revolutionary Politics." *Ramparts*, Vol. 9, No. 10 (March 1971): 29.

"The Third World of Women." *Partisan Review*, 40, (Spring 1973): 180–206.

"The Double Standard of Aging." *Saturday Review*, 23 Sept. 1973: 29–38.

"Scenes from *Brother Carl*." *Partisan Review*, 40 (Winter 1973): 37–51.

"Susan Sontag Tells How It Feels to Make a Movie." *Vogue*, Vol. 64, No. 3 (March 1975): 84–5, 118–9.

"Francis Bacon: 'About Being in Pain'." *Vogue*, Vol. 65, No. 3 (March 1975): 136–7.

"Beauty: How Will It Change Next?" *Vogue*, Vol. 65, No. 5 (May 1975): 116–7, 174.

"Looking with Avedon." *Vogue*, Vol. 68, No. 9 (Sept. 1978): 461, 507–8.

"Discussion: 'Archives of Eden'." (Sontag responds to Steiner) *Salmagundi*, No. 50–51 (Fall 1980—Winter 1981): 118.

"Poland and Other Questions: Communism and the Left." *The Nation*, 27 Feb. 1982: 229–31; "Reply" 237–8.

"The Writer and Community," panel discussion on "the Writer's Role," collected in *The Writer and Human Rights*. Ed. Toronto Arts Group for Human Rights. Toronto: Lester and Orphon Dennys, 1983: 26–31, 156, 238.

"Novel into Film: Fassbinder Succeeds Where Erich von Stroheim Was Thwarted." *Vanity Fair*, Vol. 46, No. 7 (Sept. 1983): 86–90.

"The Autobiography of Ardor: In Praise of . . . Poet's Prose." *Vanity Fair*, Vol. 46, No. 8 (Oct. 1983): 90–92.

"Be Bold!" Commencement Address, Wellesley College. *Realia*, Dec. 1983: 15.

"Sontag on Mapplethorpe." *Vanity Fair*, Vol. 47, No. 5 (July 1985): 69–73.

"When Writers Talk Among Themselves." *NYTBR*, 5 Jan. 1986: 1, 22–23.

"Dancer and the Dance." *London Review of Books*, Vol. 9, No. 3 (Feb. 1987): 9–10.

"The Pleasure of the Image." *Art in America*, Nov. 1987: 122–31.

"The Letter Scene." (short story) *The New Yorker*, 18 Aug. 1986: 24–32.

"The Way We Live Now." (short story) *The New Yorker*, 24 Nov. 1986: 42–51.

"Wagner's Fluids." *London Review of Books*, Vol. 9, No. 12 (10 Dec. 1987): 8–9.

"Pilgrimage." (autobiographical essay) *The New Yorker*, 21 Dec. 1987: 38–54.

"This Man, The Country." collected in *For Nelson Mandela*. Ed by Jacques Derrida (New York: Seaver Books, 1987): 47–52.

Interviews (by date)

Toback, James. "Whatever You'd Like Susan Sontag to Think, She Doesn't." *Esquire* (July 1968): 59–61, 114.

Kent, L. "Susan Sontag Speaks Up." *Vogue*, 158 (Aug. 1971): 88.

Bellamy, Joe David. "Susan Sontag." *The New Fiction: Interviews with Innovative American Writers*. Urbana: Univ. of Illinois Press, 1974: 113–29.

Movius, Geoffrey. "Susan Sontag. An Interview with Geoffrey Movius." *New Boston Review*, Vol. 1, No. 1 (June 1975): 12–13.

Boyers, Robert and Maxine Bernstein. "Women, The Arts & The Politics of Culture. An Interview with Susan Sontag." *Salmagundi*, No. 31–32 (Fall 1975—Winter 1976): 29–48.

Rowes, B. "Bio." *People*, 9 (20 March 1978): 74–76.

Kahn, C. "Alone Against Illness: Interview." *Family Health*, 10 Nov. 1978: 50–53.

Cott, Jonathan. "Susan Sontag: The Rolling Stone Interview." *Rolling Stone*, 4 Oct. 1979: 46–53.

Pinard-Legry, J.-L. "Une Américaine à l'école de l'Europe." *La Quinzaine Litteraire*, 306 (1979): 4–6.

Brennan, Paul. "Sontag in Greenwich Village: an interview." *London Magazine*, April/ May 1979: 93–103.

Brandeau, Michael. "Petit Dejeuner chez Susan Sontag: entretien." *L'Express*, No. 1456 (9 June 1979): 28–30.

David, Catherine. "Le Diagnostic de Susan Sontag." *le Nouvel Observateur*, 763 (25 June 1979): 70–72.

Kakutani, Michiko. "For Susan Sontag the Illusions of the '60s Have Been Dissipated." *NYT*, 11 Nov. 1980: C–5.

Beyer, Monika. "A Life Style is Not a Life: An Interview with Susan Sontag." *Polish Perspectives*, 23, No. 9 (1980): 42–46.

Mitgang, Herbert. "Publishing: The Eclectic Susan Sontag." *NYT*, 10 Oct. 1980: C1.

Bockris, Victor. "Dinner with Susan Sontag and Maurice Girodias, New York 1980." *A Report from the Bunker*. New York: Seaver Books, 1981: passim.

Copeland, Roger. "The Habits of Consciousness." *Commonweal*, 13 Feb. 1981: 83–87.

Aguilena, Maria Dolores. "Susan Sontag o la mujer sin qualidades." *Quimera*, 19 (May 1982): 10–17.

Ruas, Charles. "Susan Sontag: Past, Present and Future." *NYTBR*, 24 Oct. 1982: 11, 39.

Smith, Nancy DuVergne. "Writing it Out: an Interview with Susan Sontag." *Realia*, Dec. 1983: 14–15.

Manion/Simon. "An Interview with Susan Sontag." *Canadian Journal of Political and Social Theory*, Vol. 9, No. 1 (Winter 1985): 7–15.

Simon, Sherry. "L'Original et la copie: entrevue." *Spirale*, No. 49 (Feb. 1985): 3.

"Nadine Gordimer and Susan Sontag in Conversation." *Listener*, 23 May 1985: 16–17.

Costa, Marithelma and Adelaida López. "Susan Sontag." Collected in *Las dos caras de la escritura*. Puerto Rico: Editorial sin Nombre, Editorial de la Universidad de Puerto Rico 1988: 180–95.

Berstein, Richard. "Susan Sontag, as Image and as Herself." *NYT*, 26 Jan. 1989: C17.

Selected Criticism on Sontag

General/Replies (by date)

Nelson, Cary. "Reading Criticism." *PMLA* 91 (1976): 801–15.

Graff, Gerald. *Literature Against Itself: Literary Ideas in Modern Society*. Chicago: Univ. of Chicago Press, 1979: passim.

Kher, P. R. "Susan Sontag's Aesthetic. A Moral Point of View." *Osmania Journal of English Studies*, 15 (1980): 55–64.

Nelson, Cary. "Soliciting Self-Knowledge: The Rhetoric of Susan Sontag." *Critical Inquiry*, Summer 1980: 707–29.

Light, Steve. "The Noise of Decomposition: Response to Susan Sontag." *Sub-stance*, 26 (1980): 85–94.

Brooke-Rose, Christine. "Eximplosions." *Genre*, Vol. 14, No. 1 (Spring 1981): 9–21.

Finkelstein, Joanne L. "Sociology and Susan Sontag: Reshaping the Discipline." *Women's Studies International Quarterly*, Vol. 4, No. 2 (1981): 179–90.

Shaw, Peter and Seymour Martin Lipset. "Two After-thoughts on Susan Sontag." *Encounter*, Vol. 58, No. 6 (June–July 1981): 38–42.

Hollander, Paul. *Political Pilgrims: Travels of Western Intellectuals to the Soviet Union, China, and Cuba 1928–1978.* New York: Oxford UP, 1981: passim, and 38–42.

Stone, Jennifer. "A Critique of Susan Sontag's Production of Pirandello's *Come tu mi vuoi* (Teatro Stabile di Tormo, 1980–81)." *Year Book of the Pirandello Society* 1981: 35–47.

"Poland and Other Questions: Communism and the Left." *The Nation*, 27 Feb. 1982: Green, Trilling, Neier, Singer, Kopkind, Hollinger, Pochoda, Hitchens: 232–37. *Soho News*, 24 Feb.–2 March 1982: McCarthy, Chomsky, Foucault, Trilling, Glazer, Wills, Said, Mitford, Lipset, Levy, Wolfe, Berman, Weinstein, Kristeva, Wattenberg, Guattan: 10–13/42–43.

Timmerman, Jacobo. "Moral Symmetry." *The Nation*, 6 March 1982: 261; "Setting the Record Straight." *The Nation*, 13 March 1982: 292.

Lardner, James. "Susan Sontag into the Fray." *The Washington Post*, 16 March 1982: C-1/9.

Kendrick, Walter. "In a Gulf of Her Own." *The Nation*, 23 Oct. 1982: 404.

Grenier, Richard. "Conversions of Susan Sontag." *New Republic*, 186 (14 April 1982): 5–19.

Holdsworth, Elizabeth McCaffrey. "Susan Sontag: Writer-Filmmaker." *Dissertation Abstracts International*, Vol. 42 (April 1982): 4447A–48A. Ohio State University 1981.

Hentoff, Nat. "Celebrity Censorship." *Inquiry*, Vol. 5, No. 10 (June 1982): 8.

Kramer, Hilton. "The Pasionaria of Style." *The Atlantic*, Vol. 50, No. 3 (Sept. 1982): 88–93.

Aronowitz, Stanley. "Sontag versus Barthes for Barthes' Sake." *Village Voice Literary Supplement*, Nov. 1982: 1, 24.

Roudiez, Leon S. "Susan Sontag: Against the Ideological Grain." *World Literature Today*, 57 (Spring 1983): 219–23.

Brooks, Cleanth: "The Primacy of the Reader." *Mississippi Review*, Vol. 6, No. 2 (1983): 289–201.

Simon, John. "The Light that Never Failed." *NYTBR*, 24 Dec. 1984: 1.

Laing, Jeffrey M. "John Hawkes Aesthetic: The William Gass - Susan Sontag Connection." *Notes on Contemporary Literature*, 15 Nov. 1985: 5.

Rich, Frank. "Stage: Milan Kundera's 'Jacques and His Master'." (review of Sontag's direction) American Repertory Theater, Cambridge, MA. (1985). *NYT*, 24 Jan. 1985: C-19.

Kipnis, Laura. "Aesthetics and Foreign Policy." *Social Text*, 15 (Fall 1986): 89–98.

Kramer, Hilton. "Anti-Communism and the Sontag Circle." *New Criterion*, Vol. 5, No. 1 (Sept. 1986): 1–7.

The Benefactor *(a novel)* 1963

Adams, Robert M. "Nacht und Tag." *New York Review of Books*, Vol. 1, No. 4 (17 Oct. 1963): 19.

Bassof, Bruce. "Private Revolution: Sontag's *The Benefactor.*" *enclitic,* Vol. 3, No. 2 (1979): 59–73.

Brown, Marion Marsh. *"The Benefactor:* a review." *Prairie Schooner,* Vol. 38, No. 1 (Spring 1964): 88–89.

Frakes, James R. "Where Dreaming is Believing." *Book Week,* 22 Sept. 1963: 10.

Hicks, Granville. "To Act, Perforce to Dream." *Saturday Review,* 7 Sept. 1963: 17–18.

Howard, Richard. "Two Firsts." *Partisan Review,* 31 (Summer 1964): 456–59.

Sale, Roger. *"The Benefactor:* a review." *Hudson Review,* Vol. 16, No. 4 (Winter 1963–1964): 601–609.

Wain, John, "Song of Myself." *New Republic,* 21 Sept. 1963: 26–30.

Reviews of Against Interpretation *(essays) 1966*

Behar, Jack. "Against the Self." *Hudson Review,* Vol. 19, No. 2 (Summer 1966): 347–52.

Brian, Alan. "The World of Susan Sontag." *Spectator,* 22 Jan. 1965: 97–8.

Brooks, Peter. "Parti Pris." *Partisan Review,* 33 (Summer 1966): 439–43.

De Mott, Benjamin. "Lady on the Scene." *NYTBR,* 23 Jan. 1966: 5, 63.

Ellmann, Mary. "The Sensational Susan Sontag." *Atlantic Monthly,* Vol. 218, No. 3 (Sept. 1966): 59–63.

Green, Martin. "A New Sensibility?" *Cambridge Quarterly,* 2 (Winter 1966–67): 55–65.

Idei, Yasuko. "Susan Sontag's *Against Interpretation* and Her Critical and Political Activities." *Kyushi American Literature,* May 1982: 53–57.

Koch, Stephen. "On Susan Sontag." *TriQuarterly,* No. 7 (Fall 1966): 152–60.

Mazzocco, Robert. "Swingtime." *New York Review of Books,* Vol. 6, No. 10 (9 June 1966): 22–24.

Nairn, Tom. "The New Sensibility." *New Statesman,* 24 March 1967: 408–9.

Ostriker, Alicia. "Anti-Critic." *Commentary,* Vol. 41, No. 6 (June 1966): 83–84.

Rubin, Louis D. Jr. "Susan Sontag and the Camp Followers." *Sewanee Review,* Vol. 82, No. 3 (Summer 1975): 503.

Sypher, Wylie. "That Good Bad Taste in Our Mouths." *Book Week,* 30 Jan. 1966: 340–42.

Reviews of Death Kit *(a novel) 1967*

DeMott, Benjamin. "Diddy or Didn't He." *NYTBR,* 27 Aug. 1967: 1–2, 6.

Donoghue, Denis. "Sweepstakes." *New York Review of Books,* Vol. 9, No. 5 (28 Sept. 1967): 5–8.

Koch, Stephen. "Shaking the Tree of Death." *The Nation,* Vol. 205, No. 10 (2 Oct. 1967): 310–11.

McCaffery, Larry. *"Death Kit. Susan Sontag's Dream Narrative."* *Contemporary Literature,* No. 20 (1979): 484–99.

Nelson, Cary. *"Death Kit."* In *The Incarnate Word: Literature as Verbal Space.* Urbana: Univ. of Illinois Press, 1973: 18–21.

Sale, Roger. *"Death Kit."* *Hudson Review,* Vol. 4, No. 20 (Winter 1967–68): 667–69.

Solotaroff, Theodore. "Interpreting Susan Sontag." In *The Red Hot Vacuum*. New York: Atheneum, 1970: 261–67.

Tanner, Tony. "Space Odyssey." *Partisan Review*, 25, (Summer 1968): 446–51.

Vidal, Gore. *"Death Kit." Book Week*, 10 Sept. 1967: 5, 34.

Reviews of Trip to Hanoi (essay) 1968

Fitzgerald, Francis. "A Nice Place to Visit." *New York Review of Books*, Vol. 12, No. 5 (13 March 1969): 28–31.

Enzenberger, Hans Magnus. "Tourists of the Revolution." In *The Consciousness Industry: Literature, Politics, and Media*. New York: Seabury, 1974.

Louvre, Alf. "The Reluctant Historians: Sontag, Mailer, and American Culture." *Prose Studies*, 9 May 1986: 47–61.

Marx, Leo. "Susan Sontag's 'New Left Pastoralism': Notes on Revolutionary Pastoralism." In *The Pilot and the Passenger: Essays on Literature, Technology, and Culture in the United States*. New York. Oxford UP, 1988: 291–314.

Reviews of Styles of Radical Will (essay) 1969

Bensky, Lawrence M. "Susan Sontag, Indignant, Stoical, Complex, Useful—and Moral." *NYTBR*, 13 July 1969: 5/45.

Berek, Peter. "Susan Sontag's private line to the Absolute." *Commonweal*, Vol. 91, No. 2 (10 Oct. 1969): 48–49.

Capouya, Emile. "The Age of Allegiance." *Saturday Review*, Vol. 52, No. 18 (3 May 1969): 29.

Gilman, Richard. "Susan Sontag and the Question of the New." *New Republic*, Vol. 160, No. 3 (3 May 1969): 23–26. Reprinted in *Confusion of Realm*. New York: Random, 1970.

Houston, Gary. "Susan Sontag." *Michigan Quarterly Review*, Vol. 9, No. 4 (Fall 1970): 272–75.

Phillips, William. "Radical Styles." *Partisan Review*, (Summer 1969): 388–400.

Raban, Jonathan. "The Uncourtly Muse." *New Statesman*, Vol. 78, No. 2022 (12 Dec. 1969): 866–67.

Sklar, Robert. "Consciousness Confrontation." *The Nation*, 2 June 1969: 704–6.

Young, Vernon. "Socialist Camp: A Style of Radical Wishfulness." *Hudson Review*, Vol. 22, No. 3 (Autumn 1969): 513–20.

Reviews of Duet for Cannibals (film) 1969

Ames, Ray. "Three Women Directors." *London Magazine* 9 Feb. 1970: 104–8.

Greenspan, Robert. "Susan Sontag's *Duet for Cannibals* at Festival." *NYT* 25 Sept. 1961: 51.

Kael, Pauline. "Private World." *The New Yorker*, 1 Nov. 1969: 141–42.

Kauffman, Stanley. "Stanley Kauffman on Films." *New Republic*, 15 Nov. 1969: 32.

Tucker, Martin. "Please Don't Eat the Cannibals." *Commonweal*, 5 Dec. 1969: 306–7.

Reviews of Brother Carl *(film) 1974)*

Greenspan, Robert. "*Brother Carl.*" *NYT* 12 Aug. 1972: 18.

Renard, T. "*Brother Carl* (Les gémeaux)." *Cínema* (Paris) 174 (13 March 1973): 151.

Reviews of Promised Lands *(film) 1974*

Christ, Judith. "Now Voyagers." *New York*, 7 (15 July 1974): 65.

Gilliatt, Penelope. "The Current Cinema: Promises." *New Yorker*, July 1974: 58/60–61.

Isaac, D. "Some Questions About the Depiction of Jews in New Films." *NYT*, 123 (8 Sept. 1974): Sec. 2, 13–14.

Kauffman, Stanley. "Stanley Kauffman on Films." *New Republic*, 170 (29 June 1974): 18.

Simon, John. "Film." *Esquire*, 82 (Oct. 1974): 20/24.

Reviews of On Photography *(essays) 1977*

Arnheim, Rudolf. "*On Photography.*" *Journal of Aesthetics and Art Criticism* 36 (Summer 1978): 514–15.

Berger, John. "Photography: God of the Instant." *Seven Days*, 7 April 1978: 28–30.

Copeland, Roger. "Books Considered." *New Republic*, 178 (21 Jan. 1978): 28–30.

Elliott, George P. "High Poetress of High Fashion." *Times Literary Supplement*, 17 March 1978: 304.

Everdon, Neil. "Seeing and Being Seen: A Response to Susan Sontag's Essay on Photography." *Soundings*, Vol. 68, No. 1 (Spring 1985): 72–87.

Gass, William H. "*On Photography.*" *NYTBR*, 18 Dec. 1977: 7, 30.

Houston, Penelope. "Review of *On Photography.*" *Sight and Sound*, Vol. 47, No. 4 (1978): 265.

Lesy, Michael. "An Unacknowledged Autobiography." *Afterimage*, Jan. 1978: 5–6.

Melville, Robert. "Images of the Instant Past." *Encounter*, 51 (Nov. 1978): 69–72.

Zwingle, Erla. "Forgive Us Our Trespasses." *American Photographer*, Vol. 1, No. 3 (Aug. 1978): 84–85.

Reviews of Illness as Metaphor *(essays) 1978*

Brooks, Peter. "Death of/as Metaphor." *Partisan Review*, 46 (Summer 1979): 438–44.

Davies, Russell. "Public Enemy Number One." *New Statesman*, 97 (23 Feb. 1979): 256.

DeMott, Benjamin. "To Outrage and Back." *The Atlantic Monthly*, 242 (Nov. 1978): 96–99.

Dennis, Nigel. "Infirmary Blues." *New York Review of Books*, 25 (20 July 1978): 18, 20.

Jacobson, Dan. "Sickness and Psyche." *Commentary*, 66 (Oct. 1978): 78–82.

Kennedy, Edwin J. "*Illness as Metaphor.*" *New Republic*, 179 (8–15 July 1978): 37–39.

Reviews of I, etcetera *(stories) 1978*

Breslin, John B. "Complexities of Consciousness." *Book World*, 17 Dec. 1978: E-3.

Taylor, Benjamin. "A Centered Voice: Susan Sontag's Short Fiction." *Georgia Review*, Vol. 34, No. 4 (Winter 1980): 907–16.

Tyler, Anne. *"I, etcetera." The New Republic*, 25 Nov. 1978: 29–30.

Wood, Michael. "This is Not the End of the World." *New York Review of Books*, Vol. 25, No. 21 & 22 (25 Jan. 1979): 28–31.

Reviews of Under the Sign of Saturn *(essays) 1980*

Craven David. *"Under the Sign of Saturn." Telos*, No. 48 (Summer 1981): 189–94.

Holthusen, Hans Egon. "Die Abenteuer der kritischen Phantasie: Uber Susan Sontag und ihr neues Buch." *Merkur*, Vol. 36, No. 3 (March 1982): 254–265.

James, Regina. "Illusions of Decisiveness in Susan Sontag." *Salmagundi*, No. 55 (Winter 1982): 226–31.

Kermode, Frank. "Alien Sign." *New York Review of Books*, Vol. 27, No. 17 (6 Nov. 1980): 42–43.

Kendrick, Walter. "Eminent Victorians." *Village Voice*, 15–21 Oct. 1980: 44–46.

Reviews of AIDS as Metaphor *(essays) 1988*

Goldstein, Richard. "Bishop Berkeley's Virus: Two Cultures of AIDS." *Village Voice*, 14 March 1989: 49–51.

Ignatieff, Michael. "Modern Dying." *New Republic*, 26 Dec. 1988: 28–33.

Kolovakos, Gregory. "AIDS Words." *The Nation*, 1 May 1989: 597–601.

Robinson, Paul. "Against Fatalism." *NYBR*, 22 Jan. 1989: 11.

Index